LEN WOODS

UNDERSTANDING
WORLD
RELIGIONS

A BIBLE-BASED REVIEW OF 50 FAITHS

DEDICATION

To Wes H., Jack F., Bobby G., Rod R., Feridoun M.,
Chethan P., Liang Z., and Jeffrey N.

May you never stop seeking the truth.

And may you eventually find it.

And when you do glimpse it, may you discover the grace, the wisdom, and the courage
to embrace it with all your heart and soul and mind and strength.
"Then you will know the truth, and the truth will set you free." (John 8:32 NIV)

Produced by The Livingstone Corporation (www.Livingstonecorp.com). Project staff include: Jake Barton, Mary Horner Collins, Will Reaves, Betsy Schmitt, and Larry Taylor. Compositor, Diane Bay; proofreader, Susan Zimmerman.

Cover images (L to R) - Hindu Priest: Curioso; Cross: jordache; Krishna statue: Shyamalamuralinath; Torah: Dean Evangelista; Mormons' Temple: photo.ua

Published by Barbour Publishing, Inc., P.O. Box 719, Uhrichsville, Ohio 44683
www.barbourbooks.com

Our mission is to publish and distribute inspirational products offering exceptional value and biblical encouragement to the masses.

Member of the
Evangelical Christian
Publishers Association

Printed in the United States of America.

CONTENTS

INTRODUCTION

Everybody believes in something. We hold many beliefs—about politics, the environment, our favorite sports teams. But beyond these types of beliefs—transcending political philosophies, more consequential than trendy cultural debates, and far more significant than personal preferences in art or music or fashion—is the issue of spiritual belief.

Nothing is more crucial than one's conclusions about ultimate reality. At some point, every thoughtful person will wrestle with fundamental questions: How did we humans get here? What is our purpose in this world? Is there an intelligent Designer behind the universe? If so, what is this Deity like? Can the Supreme Being, or Beings, be known in a personal way? If so, how? Can people be redeemed? Do people need spiritual redemption? What about life after this current existence? Is there a heaven? A hell? And perhaps most significantly, how should one's beliefs about spiritual matters affect one's conscious choices in this physical world?

There are, to be sure, other questions worthy of our consideration. What about those religions that exclusively claim to be "the only way" to God? How do we discern which (if any) religious belief systems are legitimate and which are well-meaning but misguided faiths? Logically speaking—if two religions make contradictory claims—can both be true? Or, as we increasingly hear, are all religions equally valid, just different means for reaching the same ends?

Not so long ago, people didn't so much "choose" their religion, as it chose them. Religion was, in large part, a function of one's geography. To be Irish meant to be Catholic. If you were Saudi-born, you practiced Islam. If you grew up in rural north Alabama, odds were you would become a Pentecostal long before you would even know about, much less worship in, an Episcopalian church.

Now, due largely to television, the Internet, and increased proselytizing, religion has gone global. A Hindu teenager living in Bangalore decides to become a Mormon. A businesswoman in suburban Chicago converts to Buddhism. Like a spiritual shopping mall, numerous religious belief systems are "open for business." A few are massive, ancient, and unchanging; many others are small, recent, and very fluid in their theology. Indeed, the religious landscape is cluttered, complex, and ever-changing.

Understanding World Religions looks briefly at fifty diverse "spiritual systems." One can go online (or down to the local library or bookstore) and find scholarly treatises on most of these religions. Some are thick tomes, offering extensive details about the finer points and rich histories of each religion.

I confess I am no academician (though I graduated in journalism and later earned a master's degree in theology). I am a researcher, synthesizer, and reporter. Those looking for a comprehensive resource that offers theological minutiae and extensive commentary should look elsewhere. Those hoping for a book that belittles or bashes unusual religious beliefs will be disappointed. The goal of this guide was to set forth in accurate and simple terms the essential beliefs and practices of fifty diverse faiths. The handbook format means I have attempted to clarify and simplify. A handbook should, by definition, be handy. It must be concise, and, of course, factual.

Readers will notice that each religion in this handbook is compared to and contrasted with Christianity. (See the chart with Basic Christian Beliefs at the end of this introduction.) This approach was chosen for three reasons: 1) I am unashamedly a Christian; Christianity is my reference point; 2) Christianity is, in terms of number of adherents, the world's dominant religion; therefore most readers, even if they do not embrace the Christian faith, will have some familiarity with its teachings; and 3) historic Christianity *is* unique among all the religions of the world, for reasons that—hopefully—will become clear.

The goal, first and foremost, has been accuracy, fairness, and objectivity. In advance, I ask readers to forgive any inaccuracies or any recommended web addresses that may have become obsolete. Please help pinpoint and correct bad or outdated information so that future editions of *Understanding World Religions* can be amended and improved.

FINAL THOUGHTS

What, if anything can we conclude, after reviewing these fifty brief summaries of fifty diverse religions?

First, the human race *is* thoroughly (some skeptics prefer to say "incurably") religious. I always imagined this was the case. Now I know, without question, it is true. What is it about humankind that forces us, if we cannot find a god to worship, to invent one? On the one hand, I am reminded of the droll observation by an unknown person about how, after God made man in His own image, man decided to return the favor. On the other hand, as I read about so many sincere yet opposing beliefs, I am sobered by the ancient statement of King Solomon, "There is a way that seems right to a man, but in the end it leads to death" (Proverbs 14:12).

Second, I am struck by the uniqueness of the Christian faith. The gospel (literally "good news") of Jesus really does stand apart from all the other religions of the world. Perhaps a story will clarify what I mean.

Author Philip Yancey writes of an occasion on which a group of religion scholars convened in England to compare the world's great religions. When the participants began analyzing Christianity, they struggled to isolate any distinctive beliefs. What about the doctrine of God becoming man? No, other spiritual traditions also teach some version of the theological concept of incarnation. What about the notion of resurrection? Again, other religious faiths contain stories of overcoming death. This lively debate continued until scholar and author C. S. Lewis wandered into the room. When the topic at hand—Christianity's unique contribution among world religions—was revealed to him, Lewis replied, "Oh, that's easy. It's grace."

Grace. Grace is why Christianity is unique among the religions of the world. Only the way of Jesus is rooted in and permeated by the amazing notion of divine grace.

Every other religion offers some sort of spiritual merit system. *Do* these things; *don't* do those things. One day you might eventually be saved—or maybe not.

In Christian spirituality, there is zero possibility of earning salvation. No spiritual merit system. No penance to pay. One doesn't have to work in a hopeful attempt to win God's approval. The offer sounds too good to be true: a free, undeserved, unconditional, no-strings-attached gift of forgiveness and new life. To become a Christian means to take the gift. A Christian, simply put, is one who trusts in such grace—and in nothing else. This is how we become new and different people (see 2 Corinthians 5:17). This is where we find the life we've always dreamed of (see Galatians 5:22–23). This is where Christianity differs from all others.

—*Len Woods*

BASIC CHRISTIAN BELIEFS

Belief	Historic Christianity
Sacred Text(s)	The Bible (Old and New Testaments) is God's inspired, authoritative revelation
Nature of God	One God, existing eternally in three persons (Father, Son, and Holy Spirit); loving and holy
Jesus Christ	Eternal Son of God who entered human history to reveal God; died and rose again to rescue people from the effects of sin; coming again as Lord and Judge
Human nature	Physical and spiritual beings, created to know, enjoy, and honor God, but separated from Him by rebellion/sin
About human need	Need forgiveness/reconciliation with God, who is the source of life and love
Salvation	Eternal life is by grace through faith in Jesus Christ
Afterlife	Believers will live forever with God in resurrected, glorified bodies; unbelievers will be denied access to eternity with God

*"Lying does not prevent
one from becoming rich.
Covenant breaking does not
prevent one from reaching old age.
But the day of death will bring retribution."*
—The Odu Onara-Meji Oracle on "lying"

Number of Followers

African Traditional Religion encompasses a broad range of ancient spiritual beliefs and rituals. One source estimates the number of people practicing African Traditional Religion at seventy-two million. This number has fallen slowly but steadily ever since the introduction of the two great missionary religions, Christianity and Islam. Christianity arrived in Africa in the first century. Islam began making inroads on the continent around the time of Muhammad's death (AD 632).

Major Figures/Prophets

No identifiable founders, reformers, or prophets are known. In folk religion, the Supreme Power (or the roster of gods and goddesses) is always the focal point, never human practitioners or propagators.

Short History

African Traditional Religion is the broad label given to the wide range of indigenous spiritual beliefs and practices that have flourished on the African continent for thousands of years. The diverse beliefs and rituals of African Traditional Religion have their origins in ancient, primitive, tribal culture.

The amalgam of beliefs and practices that make up African Traditional Religion are

Belief	African Traditional
Sacred Text(s)	None (oral tradition)
Nature of God	Most believe in a Supreme Power, but also worship other lesser deities and revere ancestors
Jesus Christ	Not recognized in this belief system
Human nature	Flesh and spirit, the latter never perishing
About human need	Need to faithfully follow the laws and customs of the clan, passed down through the generations, taking care to show respect to the Supreme Power through sacrifices and prayers
Salvation	Little, if any, emphasis on personal sin or forgiveness; focus is on the community experiencing blessing
Afterlife	Death is a journey to the spiritual world; one continues to assist the living as a departed spirit

Major Differences from Christianity

A West African fertility goddess idol

believed by adherents to have been directly revealed by the Almighty to the very first Africans. Upon their death, this first generation of people became the first generation of ancestral spirits—messengers of God, mediators between the Creator and human creatures, helpers for their surviving loved ones.

It is an oversimplification, but generally speaking, the Sahara Desert cuts Africa into two subcontinents. North Africa is thoroughly Islamic and has been since AD 700. Sub-Saharan Africa is where African Traditional Religions are still practiced—though Islam continues to spread south, and the Christian faith continues to be embraced by millions.

Slavery resulted in the exporting of African Traditional Religion to the Caribbean and the Americas, and ultimately becoming practiced as the religions known as Umbanda, Lukimi, Macumba, Candomble.

Basic Beliefs and Values

Africa is a vast continent, with an equally broad assortment of cultures and geographies. Because of tribal differences and language barriers, religious beliefs and practices vary considerably. African Traditional Religion is not a missionary faith with printing houses, radio stations, and organized administrative hierarchies. Here are some general descriptive statements:

- Belief in one supreme, transcendent God (almighty, impersonal, aloof)—called by different names in different places.

- Belief in countless lesser gods, quasi-divine beings, and nature spirits.

- Ancestral spirits are an important aspect of African Traditional Religion; loved ones who lived noble lives are believed to be available to offer guidance and loving protection; the living often seek out and speak to the dearly departed.

- The invisible spirit world is all about us—in fact, it permeates every part of life, so there is no separation of the spiritual and physical worlds; no thought of religion being merely "a personal, private matter."

- Prayer is a common practice, thanksgiving being offered in times of abundance; prayers of supplication in times of drought or danger.

- Because sin harms the public good, regular purification rites must be practiced; sacrifices are required (usually the death of a living thing) to secure divine favor and help; sacrifices are also offered as a kind of protection against potential harm.

- Other rites are observed to initiate, to commemorate seasons, to seek healing, to celebrate accomplishments, to signify consecration, and so forth; these rituals provide a kind of social framework in the community.

- Illness is often thought to have a spiritual cause; that is, illness is seen as either punishment from God or as an attack by an evil spirit. Medicine men (or women) are sought out for their help in such cases, and they treat such maladies with herbal potions.

- Beliefs are passed down to the next generation through oral and visual traditions: the telling of stories, reciting poems, riddles, and proverbs, singing hymns, dancing, and art.

View of God

Despite the differences in tribal religious beliefs, there seems to be a fairly common belief in one, ultimate Supreme Being. This eternal, all-powerful Creator is called by various names (for example, *Oludmare* by the Yoruba people of Nigeria; *Katonda* by the Baganda people of Uganda; *Dondari* by the Fulani of West Africa, and so forth).

Beneath the Supreme Power (actually emanating from God) are lesser deities called *orishas*. They rule the elements and forces of nature. For example, the *Mami Wata* is a mermaid-like pantheon of ancient water deities that are viewed as part of the old African priestly religious systems that used to be followed in Africa. These emissaries of God function like the Greek gods. They can be helpful or moody, compassionate or petulant.

View of the Afterlife

Death is passing on to the world of immortals. When people die, they leave the physical realm and enter the spiritual and invisible realm. It is a sweet reunion with those who have gone before, and it affords the opportunity to be of assistance to those one has left behind. Ancestral spirits are mediators and benevolent guides.

Sacred Texts

African Traditional Religion has no holy books or written scriptures, but it does possess many ancient customs, rituals, practical proverbs, and wise sayings that have been (and continue to be) passed down orally. Because of the communal nature of society, the clan (and especially the elderly members) is consulted.

Worldview

With Africa's pervading sense of the sacred (there is no Western compartmentalizing of the "physical" from the "spiritual"), a high regard and reverence for the divine permeates all of life. Most tribes and clans believe deeply in the sanctity of life and the dignity of the individual; the elderly are especially revered. Family ties and solidarity are of utmost importance.

Because every aspect of life is sacred, big events in life are special occasions for celebrating. Practitioners of African Traditional Religion are generally festive peoples. Births (and the naming of newborn children), rites of passage into adulthood, marriage, death—all are occasions involving special rituals, elaborate ceremonies, and lavish meals.

Hospitality is a cardinal virtue. Generosity is a cherished value. The community takes precedence over the individual. Individualism is viewed with disdain.

Worship Services

Practitioners of African Traditional Religion do not erect temples or hold regular worship services. Religious rites take place outdoors in natural settings. The elders of the clan often assume leadership in these ritual observances. Certain geographical features are regarded as sacred—mountains, hills, caves. Other than the rituals observed at special times of life (for example, the birth of a child, a rite of passage into adulthood, a marriage, a funeral, and so forth) formal, regular gatherings are not held.

Important Dates

In African Traditional Religion, there are no set days for worship. Adherents simply gather together communally when they want to perform certain rituals or celebrate special events. Some special events include things such as the first fruits of the harvest or praying for rain. The day or time does not matter; what is important is the ritual itself.

"Asatru is non-authoritarian and decentralized, expressing our love of freedom. While we do have definite tenets, we have little dogma. There is no all-powerful spiritual leader whose word is law, no 'pope' of Asatru to dictate truth. No guru or priest has an exclusive direct line to the gods. The gods live in you!"
—Stephen A. McNallen

Short History

Number of Followers

Asatru is not an organized entity, but rather a loose collection of individuals and scattered, disparate groups who share some general beliefs. It is almost impossible to say how many devotees Asatru has. The number is likely to be only in the thousands. Many followers prefer to be known as "heathens."

The term *Asatru* means "faith in the gods" or "loyalty to the gods" in Old Norse, the language of ancient Scandinavia. It is the native religion of the ancient peoples of Northern Europe, that is, the tribes who lived in what is known today as Germany, Scandinavia, England, France, and the Netherlands. It is sometimes called Germanic Paganism or Germanic Heathenism.

The religion's beliefs are rooted in precedents found in the traditions, customs, myths, folklore, literature, and laws that shaped Nordic and Germanic cultures. The Vikings, for example, were devotees of Asatru.

Asatru, as a dominant, official religion, all but died out between the seventh and tenth centuries with the spread of Christianity throughout Europe. However, the last few decades have witnessed a revival of interest in Asatru as a way of life.

The modern version of Asatru can be traced to an Icelandic sheep farmer named Sveinbjörn Beinteinsson (1924–1993). In 1972–1973, he successfully petitioned the Icelandic government to recognize his group of Asatru followers as an official religious body. At the same time, similar groups were forming in the United States and the United Kingdom. This growth was seen as proof that the Norse god "Odin, the wanderer, [was] once again seeking worshippers" (Rev. Patrick "Jordsvin" Buck).

Major Figures/ Prophets

Asatru has no historical "founder" (such as Joseph Smith for Mormonism), nor does it boast a single revered prophet who made revealed pronouncements of Asatru law or set forth a firm code of belief (such as Muhammad in Islam). The religion has no worldwide headquarters, no central authority, and no recognized hierarchy that makes binding decrees.

Belief	Asatru
Sacred Text(s)	Reliance upon ancient Norse myths and legends; not considered inspired or infallible
Nature of God	Many gods and goddesses
Jesus Christ	Not emphasized or discussed
Human nature	No "original sin"; in fact, we are gods-in-the-making
About human need	Humanity does not need "saving"
Salvation	Striving to live a robust, free, brave, honorable life
Afterlife	Beliefs vary; the precise nature of the afterlife is beyond our understanding

Major Differences from Christianity

Basic Beliefs and Values

Asatru describes itself as the ancient religion of the Northern European peoples and their modern-day descendants. It is, some would argue, reasonably exclusivist and does not promote itself as a universal faith. In fact, some adherents of Asatru (who prefer to be known as "heathens") teach that it is natural for different cultures with distinctive world views to embrace different religious worldviews as well. Other adherents are more tolerant (and perhaps more "evangelistic"), and welcome anyone from any ethnic background or national/geographical heritage.

Asatru is an ancestral religion, and as such, puts great emphasis on genealogy and finding out about one's heritage. It forcibly claims that it does not engage in ancestor worship.

Because of its similarities to Wicca, Celtic Druidism, and so forth, some religious scholars classify Asatru as a "neopagan" religion. However, many devotees to Asatru are quick to distinguish themselves from followers of Wicca and others.

Followers of Asatru do engage in prayer. But they don't think of prayer as begging the gods for favors or bowing the will in submission to the gods. Prayer is a way of communing with and honoring the Norse deities. All of life is "religious" or spiritual. All of life, if lived virtuously and honorably, is viewed as a kind of prayer. Humility and guilt, so common in other religions, are looked upon unfavorably.

The qualities or "Nine Noble Virtues" held in high regard by modern-day practitioners of Asatru are truth, courage, hospitality, honor, perseverance, self-reliance, industry, loyalty to kin and to ancestors, and self-discipline. Dogmatism is shunned in favor of realism. Cowardice and weakness are despised.

According to Asatru beliefs, other religions (especially better known religions) do not have answers to life's big questions. In fact, Asatru believes that the world religions that were founded in the Middle East have a long history of hatred and violence. Asatru is regarded as a better, more natural, more honorable way to live—especially for those who are descended from Northern European ancestry. "Judaism, Islam, and Christianity are alien religions which do not truly speak to our souls. . . . Asatru isn't just what we *believe*, it's what we *are*" (Stephen A. McNallen).

View of God

Theologically, Asatru mixes a sort of New Age pantheism with polytheism. Specifically, adherents believe in an omnipresent divine energy. This spiritual essence surrounds us and permeates our existence, but often remains hidden and just beyond our senses and understanding. Connecting with this divine reality through nature is a treasured experience of awe.

Asatru is also polytheistic, which means adherents believe that the divine essence is revealed through many gods and goddesses. Followers are free to choose which gods and goddesses they wish to honor. The gods are viewed more as approachable friends, models, and mentors, than as masters who require obeisance or who attempt to control people.

The ancient Norse myths and legends are thought to contain truth about the deities, even if they are not literally true as history. Through these ancient stories, one can find answers to life's biggest questions.

A midwinter blot, a ritual offering sacrifices to the gods, in Sweden

The main deities for followers of Asatru are:

View of the Afterlife

The primary concern of Asatru is living well now, in this life. If one does this, the next life will take care of itself. Virtuous people will go on to greater fulfillment, challenge and pleasure, perhaps even rebirth within the family line. Those who have led vice-filled lives will be separated from kin and doomed to a dull existence of gloom.

- *Odin*—the chief god or father of the gods, ruler of Valhalla

- *Frigga*—Odin's wife, the mother of the gods and humanity

- *Thor*—the god of strength and might, and friend of commoners

- *Freya*—the goddess of love and procreation

Just as most Christians do not think their God is really an old bearded figure sitting on a golden chair in heaven, we do not believe Thor (for example) is actually a muscular, man-shaped entity carrying a big hammer. There is a real Thor, but we approach an understanding of him through this particular mental picture (Stephen A. McNallen).

Worldview

We could summarize Asatru with bold statements such as: Be strong! Be courageous! Be self-reliant! Be free! Be decisive! Be happy now!

In every situation, Asatru says the goal is to live freely, reasonably, and with honor. Since followers don't believe that even the gods are all-powerful or all-knowing, they do not feel pressured to live perfect lives. A simple code of behavior for Asatru might be, "Maximize one's virtues; minimize one's vices."

Within Asatru there is no command to proselytize. Intolerance of other beliefs is also officially condemned.

Sacred Texts

There is no holy book or "bible" for Asatru. However, followers do rely upon three "guides." One is the written collection of ancient Norse myths and sacred lore that have been passed down. However, these documents, known as the Eddas, are not regarded as infallible or inspired.

The other two reliable sources of "revelation" are the *wisdom of the universe that surrounds us* (filled with the divine essence), and the *universe that is within us* (our heritage, memories, predispositions, innate wisdom, family traits, and so forth).

Followers of Asatru feel that by putting these three guides together, they are able to arrive at and live by sacred truth.

Worship Services

Local religious communities are called *Kindreds*. A priest is called a *Gothi*; a priestess is called a *Gythia*.

The most common religious ritual, the *Blot* (pronounced "*bloats*"), is an offering or sacrifice to the gods. In ancient times, this involved animal sacrifice. Today, worshippers offer drink or food to the gods, after which, the kindred present consume the offering.

The *Sumbel* is a ritual in which worshippers individually greet and toast the gods or an ancient Norse hero or one's ancestors. One may also tell a story or share a song or poem. He or she then drinks from the horn, which is passed around.

Profession (sometimes called *Adoption*) is a simple ceremony officiated by a Gothi or Gythia, in which one makes an exclusive commitment to Asatru by giving an oath of allegiance and kinship to the gods of Asgard, Aesir, and Vanir.

Important Dates

The main holy days in Asatru are similar to those in other so-called neopagan faiths—the summer solstice and winter solstice (June 21 and December 21), and the spring equinox and fall equinox (March 21 and September 21). Yule (December 21) begins the winter solstice.

Other special celebrations include:

The Charming of the Plow (February 1)—to celebrate the Norse goddess Freya and the Disir (other fertility goddesses)
Merry-Moon (May 1)—a spring festival dedicated to Njord, the Norse god of winds, sea, and fire, and Nerthus (a Germanic fertility goddess)
Harvest or Freyfaxi (August 1)— the first harvest and celebration of Frey (the god of sun and rain)
Fogmoon (November 1)—a celebration of war dead and Ragnarok (the great battle that will end the world)

"The well-being of mankind, its peace and security, are unattainable unless and until its unity is firmly established."
—Bahá'u'lláh, founder of the Bahá'í faith

Number of Followers

Five to seven million distributed among 2,100 ethnic and tribal groups who reside in more than 230 countries and territories. Only Christianity has followers in more countries.

Major Figures/Prophets

The Bahá'í star

- **The Bab,** "the Gate," (1819–1850)—Siyyid 'Ali-Muhammad Shirází

- **Bahá'u'lláh,** "the Glory of God," (1817–1892)—Mírza Husayn 'Alí

- **'Abdu'l-Baha** (1844–1921)—son of Bahá'u'lláh

- **Shoghi Effendi** (1897–1957)—grandson of 'Abdu'l-Baha

Short History

The term "Bahá'í" literally means "a follower of the Baha." Baha is short for Bahá'u'lláh, the man credited with founding the Bahá'í faith. It is widely held that the Bahá'í faith arose from Islam much like Christianity developed out of Judaism.

The genesis of the Bahá'í faith occurred in 1844 when Siyyid 'Ali-Muhammad Shirází, a merchant in Iran, announced that he was the *Bab* (which literally means "gate" in Arabic) through whom God would lead all people to truth. Some of his followers, called *Babis*, declared him to be the *Mahdi* (analogous in Islam to Judaism's Messiah). But mainstream Bahá'ís now view the Bab in the same way that Christians look upon John the Baptist—a prophet and forerunner, paving the way for one greater to come. The chief minister of the Shah (Iran's leader) had the Bab and some of his devoted followers arrested, tried for heresy, and executed in 1850 because of the religious unrest they incited.

After the Bab's death, Mírza Husayn 'Alí, the son of a prominent Iranian nobleman and a former disciple of the Bab, assumed the mantle of leadership. In 1863, as the government prepared to exile him to Iraq, he declared himself *Bahá'u'lláh*, which means "the glory of God," and officially founded the new belief system we know as the Bahá'í faith. From 1863 to 1892, Bahá'u'lláh wrote numerous books that are now among the sacred texts of the Bahá'í faith. He spent the remainder of his life

Belief	Bahá'í
Sacred Text(s)	The many writings of Bahá'í leaders, Bahá'u'lláh and 'Abdu'l-Baha
Nature of God	One God, Creator and controller of all things, called various names by various religions; so great he remains distant and unknowable
Jesus Christ	The sixth of the nine great manifestations of God—superseded by Muhammad and ultimately by Bahá'u'lláh; Christ is not God incarnate, and not the only way to God
Human nature	Immortal souls, in mortal bodies, that are able to journey toward perfection
About human need	The individual needs to cultivate the latent spiritual virtues in his/her soul. The world's greatest problem is division and discord; its greatest need is for unity
Salvation	Knowing and diligently following the teachings of Bahá'u'lláh
Afterlife	A perfect world of lights; illumined souls leave the body and continue their journey

in exile or in prison. He named his son as his successor.

Bahá'u'lláh's son, 'Abdu'l-Baha, became the sole interpreter of his father's writings. In the late 1800s, Bahá'í spread beyond the Middle East. Before his death in 1921, 'Abdu'l-Baha named his grandson, Shoghi Effendi, successor. An able administrator, Effendi created within the Bahá'í faith a representative form of government. He also oversaw the printing of an authorized translation of the Bahá'í scriptures and presided over a time of great international growth.

When Effendi died in 1957, leadership of the Bahá'í religion was transferred to the nine-member Universal House of Justice, based in Haifa, Israel, and a worldwide parliament. Serving in this parliamentary body are nine elected Bahá'í representatives from each country where the church is active. The purpose of these groups is to maintain and spread the faith, not to further interpret the writings of Bahá'u'lláh.

Basic Beliefs and Values

At the heart of the Bahá'í faith is the belief that God has revealed himself in human history through nine great manifestations: Abraham, Krishna, Moses, Zoroaster, Buddha, Jesus, Muhammed, the Bab, and the final great prophet Bahá'u'lláh.

The implications of this eclectic, fundamental belief are what we might expect.

The Bahá'í faith teaches or advocates:

- The purpose of life is to know and worship God, to spiritually progress until one attains the presence of God.

- There is one God, but many ways to seek/experience God.

- We must work to achieve the oneness of mankind and harmony among all faiths (a minimizing of theological differences).

- Religious devotion includes daily prayer, living morally (being trustworthy, honest, chaste, avoiding drugs, materialism, gambling, gossip, and so forth), and serving humanity by seeking to eliminate all forms of prejudice, poverty, conflict, and ignorance.

- Service to humanity is the highest goal. The faithful should strive to apply spiritual solutions to temporal problems—social, economic, educational, cultural—and ultimately bring about a utopian society on earth.

- Salvation (variously called oneness with God, eternal life, or the second birth) comes through knowledge of God, love of God, faith, philanthropic deeds, self-sacrifice, severance from this world, sanctity, and holiness.

As to the common assertion that the Bahá'í faith is nothing more than an aberrant offshoot of Islam, Bahá'ís insist that it is an independent religion that grew out of Islam in much the same way that Judaism paved the way for Christianity.

A star with nine points is a prominent feature in the Bahá'í faith. Nine—being the highest integer—is felt to best represent the great diversity and unity of spiritual reality: one God who can be found in many ways.

View of God

The Bahá'í faith teaches the existence of one God, a single supernatural Being. God is omnipotent as well as omniscient. To the Bahá'í, Allah or Yahweh or God or Brahma are simply different names for the same unique Being, one who is so above us that humans can never construct an accurate image of Him with our limited understanding. Devotees to the Bahá'í faith seek to learn about God's attributes or qualities through study, prayer, and meditation, but feel that God's true essence is transcendent, inscrutable, and unknowable.

Worldview

Bahá'ís believe that life is meaningless until one recognizes the existence of the Creator and his or her own spiritual nature. Having grasped this truth, one must then

The Bahá'í Gardens in Haifa, Israel

determine to carry out God's will and purposes. Thus, personal, individual commitment to spiritual progress is the calling of each person.

Bahá'ís further believe that a united, cohesive worldwide civilization is achievable through diligent effort. The faith teaches that it is incumbent upon enlightened individuals to work together to create a just, peaceful, harmonious "global society that fosters both individual and collective well being." The religion, believing this is the age in which ultimate world peace will be established, seeks to implement social, agricultural, educational, moral, and economic programs for the betterment of society. Bahá'ís are well-known for their advocacy of human rights and gender equality.

Bahá'í communities as a whole are well integrated into society. Bahá'u'lláh encouraged his followers to be fully involved with the rest of humanity. And most Bahá'ís lead lives that would not seem out of place in their native society, though they maintain a strong commitment to the high moral and ethical standards that are encouraged by the faith.

In Bahá'í belief, heaven and hell are not physical places, but spiritual allegories suggesting nearness to God or remoteness from him. Beyond this, Bahá'í understanding and teaching about afterlife remains somewhat vague and elusive.

View of the Afterlife

Bahá'u'lláh confirmed the existence of a separate, rational soul for every human. This soul does not die; it simply leaves the body to continue its journey through the spiritual world, a timeless extension of our own universe. Bahá'u'lláh explained: "The world beyond is as different from this world as this world is different from that of the child while still in the womb of its mother."

Sacred Texts

Bahá'ís are allowed, if not encouraged, to study the holy books of all religions. As one might expect, however, the writings of Bahá'u'lláh, the Bab, and 'Abdu'l-Baha are viewed with special reverence and believed to have ultimate authority. These writings form the corpus of sacred scriptures within the Bahá'í faith. Though Bahá'ís prize more than one hundred holy texts, the Kitáb-i-Aqdas ("most holy book") is uniquely significant. It is seen as the charter of a new civilization. Also read and revered are:

- The Bab's *Letters of the Living*
- Bahá'u'lláh's *The Seven Valleys*, *The Hidden Words*, and *The Book of Certitude*
- 'Abdu'l-Baha's *Tablets of the Divine Plan*

> *"The source of all good is trust in God, submission unto His command, and contentment with His holy will and pleasure. The essence of wisdom is the fear of God, the dread of His scourge and punishment, and the apprehension of His justice and decree. The essence of religion is to testify unto that which the Lord hath revealed, and follow that which He hath ordained in His mighty Book."*
> —Selections from the writings of Bahá'u'lláh
> on *The Spiritual Life*

Worship Services

Bahá'í houses of worship are the parallels of Christian churches, Jewish temples, or Muslim mosques. Currently there is a house of worship on every continent (except Antarctica). All eight daily houses have a distinct design, but must have nine sides and a central dome. Impressive on the exterior, the interiors are rather simple. There, followers gather for prayer and meditation, but there is more to the purpose of the buildings. These edifices stand as beacons of faith, but the concern is not that followers come there to worship. Rather, the Bahá'ís have focused on developing the institutions of community throughout the world through the lives of their followers.

All houses of worship are open to people of every religion. There are daily devotions, and at the North American House of Worship in Wilmette, Illinois, a Sunday service is held with prayers and music. The Bahá'í faith has no clergy. Bahá'í communities do sponsor a wide range of activities, though, from social events to economic development projects.

Important Dates

The Bahá'í annual calendar consists of nineteen months, each with nineteen days (for a total of 361 days). The centerpiece of Bahá'í community life is the Nineteen-Day Feast. Every nineteen days (the evening before the first day of each Bahá'í month), all Bahá'ís of a particular community meet at one of their houses or the local Bahá'í center. This feast is the local community's regular worship gathering—and more. It combines religious worship with grassroots governance and fellowship. While food and beverages may be served, the term "feast" is also meant to suggest that the religious community should enjoy a "spiritual feast" of worship, companionship, and unity. Bahá'u'lláh stressed the importance of gathering every nineteen days "to bind your hearts together," even if nothing more than water is served. During the devotional program, selections from Bahá'í writings, as well as scriptures from other religions, are read aloud. A general discussion follows and then a time of fellowship.

Bahá'ís observe a month of fasting (March 2–20) during which all followers, ages fifteen to seventy, abstain from food and drink between sunrise and sunset.

Special holy days include:

World Religion Day (the third Sunday in January) —commemorating the oneness of all faiths

Naw-Rúz—the Bahá'í New Year

The Ridván Festival (sunset April 21 to sunset May 2) —marking Bahá'u'lláh's time in the garden of Ridván and his announcement that he was the prophet promised by the Bab.

The Declaration of the Bab (May 22–23)—beginning two hours after sunset on the 22nd

Ascension of Bahá'u'lláh (May 29, 3 a.m.)

Martyrdom of the Bab (July 9, noon)

Birth of the Bab (October 20)

Birth of Bahá'u'lláh (November 12)

The Day of the Covenant (November 26)

Ascension of 'Abdu'l Baha (November 28)

"All that we are is the result of what we have thought:
it is founded on our thoughts, it is made up of our thoughts.
If a man speaks or acts with a pure thought,
happiness follows him, like a shadow that never leaves him."
—Gautama Buddha, *Dhammapada*

Major Figures/Prophets

- **Siddhartha Gautama** (about 560–480 BC)—founder of Buddhism, who lived in northeastern India (modern-day Nepal)

- **The Dalai Lama**—the spiritual leader of the sect of Tibetan Buddhism

- **Maitreya**—a future Buddha, whose arrival will usher in a new era for mankind

The Buddhist wheel

Number of Followers

Estimates range from 325 million to 400 million, making Buddhism the fourth largest world religion, behind Christianity, Islam, and Hinduism.

Short History

Siddhartha Gautama was reared in a sheltered, royal family in what is now Nepal, but what was then northeastern India. As a young prince he evaded his father's watchful eye, slipped out of the palace, and encountered for the first time the great suffering of the world—the plight of the elderly and the realities of disease and death. Haunted by these experiences and intrigued by a joyful religious beggar he had met, Gautama made his "Great Renunciation." He forsook his family and privileged life. He embarked on a search for answers to the mystery of suffering and for the path to spiritual enlightenment.

Six years later, as he was meditating under a bodhi tree near the Ganges River, Gautama learned the "Four Noble Truths": (1) all life is suffering; (2) the cause of suffering is desire or attachment to this world; (3) eliminating desire is the way to eliminate suffering; and (4) desire can be eliminated by following the Eightfold Path (a way of life that avoids the extremes of pleasure and self-denial).

This discovery resulted in Gautama becoming *Buddha* ("the Enlightened One"). The Buddha then formed a community of monks called the *Sangha*. For four decades he taught his followers the truths he had experienced. Upon Buddha's death, his body was cremated. The ashes were divided and distributed, displayed, and worshipped at various sites called *stupas* (sometimes called pagodas).

Major Differences from Christianity

Belief	Buddhism
Sacred Text(s)	The Tripitaka, a three-volume collection of Buddha's teachings; numerous other sutras, the Tibetan Book of the Dead
Nature of God	Some Buddhists are literally "godless" (that is, atheistic); others are animistic and polytheistic, worshipping assorted deities and celestial beings
Jesus Christ	Largely ignored by Buddhists in the East; sometimes regarded as an enlightened teacher by Western practitioners of Buddhism
Human nature	Humans do not have a permanent or unchanging soul but are an aggregate of five components: a physical body, feelings, ideas, dispositions, and consciousness
About human need	Deliverance from the endless cycle of death and reincarnation through the elimination of all human desire
Salvation	Reaching a state of nirvana (an end to suffering and rebirth by the elimination of all desire) through following the Eightfold Path and, perhaps, by obtaining the help of bodhisattvas
Afterlife	No heaven or hell; one is either reborn to suffer more (samsara, which means "endless wandering"), or one reaches nirvana, the end of all suffering

For two hundred years, Buddhism did not spread beyond India. Then King Ashoka, weary of war, converted to Buddhism, and commissioned the sending of Buddhist "missionaries." At about this same time (c. 250 BC), theological differences began to develop within Buddhism and new sects began to emerge.

Basic Beliefs and Values

We can summarize the essential beliefs of Buddhism by remembering the numbers *three*, *four*, *eight*, and *ten*.

First, Buddhism speaks of Three Jewels. These precious, foundational beliefs are *Buddha* (the one who discovered the way to enlightenment), *dharma* (Buddha's teachings about what is true), and *sangha*, (the spiritual community within Buddhism that embraces, practices, and promotes Buddha's dharma).

Second, the Buddha emphasized Four Noble Truths:

- *The reality of suffering*—Suffering is an unavoidable fact of life.

- *The root of suffering*—Suffering stems from craving, attachment/addiction or desire.

- *The removal of desire*—Suffering will never cease until one reaches nirvana (the "blowing out" of all desire).

- *The road to Nirvana*—We eliminate desire (that is, reach nirvana, the end to suffering) by following the Eightfold Path.

Third, Buddha's Eightfold Path consists of:

- *Right view* (or understanding/knowledge/belief)—Embracing the teachings of the Buddha.

- *Right resolve*—Aspiring to develop right intentions.

- *Right speech*—Speaking the truth in a careful, compassionate manner.

- *Right action*—Abstaining from wrong behavior.

- *Right livelihood*—Refusing occupations that cause others harm.

- *Right effort*—Cultivating positive thoughts.

- *Right mindfulness*—Developing clear perception.

- *Right concentration*—Learning the art of meditation.

Fourth, Buddhism prescribes the Ten Precepts (the first five precepts are for all Buddhists; all ten precepts are for monks):

- No killing of living things.

- No stealing.

- No unchastity.

- No lying.

- No intoxicants.

- No inappropriate eating.

- No participating in or attending singing, dancing, musical, or dramatic performances.

- No decorative accessories.

- No luxurious furnishings or bedding.

- No possession of silver or gold.

In the same way that Christianity features many denominations with varying beliefs, so, too, does Buddhism. The two dominant schools within the religion of Buddhism are Theravada Buddhism and Mahayana Buddhism. This chart summarizes the main differences between these branches:

Theravada Buddhism	Mahayana Buddhism
Name means "the way of the elders" (formerly called Hinayana Buddhism, a derogatory title that means "the teaching of the lesser way")	Name means "the great vehicle"
The earliest form of Buddhism	A newer form that developed around the time of Christ
Enlightenment reserved for the especially devout, such as the monks	Enlightenment within reach of the masses
The goal is to become an *arahat* (one who seeks and finds self-enlightenment)	The ideal is to become a *bodhisattva* (an enlightened one who helps others find enlightenment)
Spirituality an individual, independent pursuit	Spirituality a community, interdependent affair
Only one Buddha	Many manifestations of Buddha
Buddha a revered saint and wise teacher	Buddha a compassionate savior
The "conservatives" of Buddhism	The "liberals" of Buddhism
Practiced in Southeast Asia (Sri Lanka, Myanmar, Thailand, Laos, Cambodia)	Practiced in China, Nepal, Tibet, Korea, Vietnam, Japan

Within Mahayana Buddhism are found the distinct Buddhist schools of Zen, Nichiren, Tendai, and Pure Land.

A third more recent branch of Buddhism is located primarily in Tibet, and is therefore called Tibetan Buddhism or Tantric Buddhism. This form of the religion emerged about AD 700. It embraces the animistic occult practices and pantheon of deities of ancient Tibet. Guided by reincarnated spiritual authorities called lamas, Tibetan Buddhism uses The Tibetan Book of the Dead as a guide to seeking enlightenment and ending the cycle of rebirth. Tibetan Buddhism is popular and influential thanks to its leader, the Dalai Lama, winner of the 1989 Nobel Peace Prize.

View of God

Many Buddhists do not believe (or see the need to believe) in a Supreme Being—or at least not a personal, omnipotent Creator God who will one day restore all things. Nothing about Buddhism requires a relationship with such a deity. Consider this statement from the Buddha Dharma Education Association:

There is no almighty God in Buddhism. There is no one to hand out rewards or punishments on a supposed Judgment Day. Buddhism is strictly not a religion in the context of being a faith and worship owing allegiance to a supernatural being.

It is through self-effort that devotees of Buddhism believe they can discover truth and eventually achieve enlightenment. The concept of sin and the need for atonement (that is, forgiveness by God's grace) are foreign to Buddhism.

It should be noted that some Buddhists do, in fact, view the Buddha as a physical manifestation of the divine.

Worldview

Underlying Buddhism is the belief that there is no ultimate reality; everything is constantly changing.

Buddhists of all stripes advocate living a good, moral life so that one may reap good consequences—if not in this life, then in the next. This is the ancient idea of karma— the eastern concept that the person who does good accumulates for himself or herself good consequences, while the one who commits evil guarantees future unhappiness.

Despite the fact that Buddhism does not believe in a Creator God to whom human creatures must give account, it nevertheless is permeated by a strong insistence on moral justice. Devout Buddhists seek to live conscientiously and compassionately.

Perhaps because Buddhism offers a kind of do-it-yourself morality without ultimate accountability, it has managed to attract a number of celebrity converts. Among them are: actors Harrison Ford, Orlando Bloom, Richard Gere, Goldie Hawn, Keanu Reeves, basketball coach Phil Jackson, film producers/directors George Lucas and Oliver Stone, and singer Tina Turner.

View of the Afterlife

What comes after this life? Either nirvana (for the devout) or rebirth (for those with lots of bad karma still to undo). Buddhists believe we experience countless rebirths in new bodies or forms until we reach nirvana, which is the cessation of suffering by the elimination of desire, the state of perfect contentment and salvation.

An interior of a Buddhist temple in Korea

Sacred Texts

For Theravada Buddhists, the bible is the Tripitaka (which literally means "Three Baskets"), a massive collection of the Buddha's teachings. The three baskets are the "Discipline Basket" (rules for the Sangha, the community of monks, a collection called the Vinaya Pitaka); the "Teaching Basket" (discourses of the Buddha known as the Sutta/Sutra Pitaka); and the "Metaphysical Basket" (scholarly writings about Buddhist philosophy called Abhidhamma/Abhidharma Pitaka). Tibetan Buddhists emphasize The Tibetan Book of the Dead. Mahayana Buddhists embrace a large number of sutras (collections of rules or teachings), the three most important being the Lotus Sutra, the Heart Sutra, and the Diamond Sutra.

Worship Services

Theravada Buddhists hold services on a kind of "Sabbath Day" (called *Uposatha*), which are held on quarter, full, and new moon days (thus, about weekly). Buddhists often go to Buddhist temples or shrines on these days, and on other occasions, to pray. While there, worshippers will typically revere the statue(s) of Buddha. They may burn incense and make offerings. They often spin prayer wheels (hollow cylinders containing sacred scrolls, and often embossed with a mantra).

At other times and places, as with almost all Eastern religions, practitioners of Buddhism spend much time in meditation. Though this can involve a variety of techniques and looks, the goal in meditation is to quiet the mind—halting that ceaseless parade of thoughts, concerns, questions, ideas, and cravings. Buddhists seek to replace all this mental hyperactivity with an inner serenity. Only through this concentrated discipline can one hope to develop the spiritual awareness and cessation of worldly attachment that ultimately leads to true enlightenment. *Mudras* are hand movements or gestures employed during meditation that symbolize various Buddhist beliefs.

Another common practice among Buddhists is chanting or repeating *mantras*. A mantra is a short statement or oft-repeated sound believed to be sacred and inherently supernatural. Especially popular in Tibetan Buddhism, these verbal expressions are thought to invoke the power and protection of deities.

Important Dates

Buddhism is a festive religion, its celebrations and special days varying from country to country due to various cultural traditions, and from year to year, because the days are tied to the lunar calendar. Among the more prominent dates for Buddhists are:

Kathina—a periodic ceremony in which Buddhist lay people offer robes and gifts to monks and nuns as a display of gratitude

Losar (in early February)—a holiday commemorating the Tibetan New Year

Parinirvana (usually in mid February)—a day on which Mahayana Buddhists commemorate the death of the Buddha and his achievement of complete nirvana

Sangha Day (on the day of the full moon in March)— a festival that celebrates the Buddhist spiritual community

Wesak/Vesak (first full moon in May)—a celebration of Buddha's birthday

Dhamma (or Dharma) Day (full moon day in July)— a day for commemorating Buddha's first sermon

"Cao Dai is a universal faith with the principle that all religions have one same divine origin, which is God, or Allah, or the Tao, or the Nothingness, one same ethic based on LOVE and JUSTICE, and are just different manifestations of one same TRUTH."
—Cao Dai Web site description

Number of Followers

There are seven to eight million followers in Vietnam, and about thirty thousand members elsewhere, primarily in Asia, Australia, Canada, Europe, and the United States. Another online source lists six to ten million adherents worldwide.

Short History

Cao Dai, an integrative spiritual path based in Vietnam, states that its roots go all the way back to 2500 BC, when—it claims—God inspired the founding of the Jewish and Hindu faiths. Two millennia later, God initiated a second wave of religious revelation, with the establishment of Buddhism, Confucianism, Taoism, Christianity, and Islam.

Because of cultural differences and geographical distance, and due to each religion's failure to pursue, preserve, and propagate the truth, God's goal—a single, universal faith—was never realized. Thus, in 1920, according to Cao Dai disciples, the Supreme Being appeared to Ngo Van Chieu, the spiritually minded governor of Phu Quoc, an island in the Gulf of Siam (now Gulf of Thailand). God revealed Himself symbolically as Cao Dai (which means "high abode" or "roofless tower"), and gave this message to Ngo to be delivered to the world: "All religions should return to the one faith from which they originally derived." Ngo was given a vision of the all-seeing eye and told to use that as a symbol of Cao Dai. In 1924, Ngo returned to Saigon and began teaching this new philosophy of Cao Dai and its novel practices to interested followers.

Meanwhile, separately, various other influential civil officials in Saigon, while practicing spiritism, were granted visitations and revelations from a spirit claiming to be Cao Dai. These leaders came together at the end of 1925 and began laying the groundwork for the beginning of the Cao Dai religion.

When Ngo opted not to be part of the ecclesiastical hierarchy, Cao Dai ordered that Le Van Trung be appointed the leader (that is, *Giao Tong*)

Major Figures/ Prophets

Ngo Van Chieu
(1878–1926)—a government official and spiritist, to whom the Supreme Being appeared with a new revelation for a worldwide, universal religious faith

Le Van Trung—the first "Acting Pope" of Cao Daism

of the group. The official public declaration of the founding of the Cao Dai religion came on September 28, 1926.

This new faith grew rapidly among the masses in Vietnam, and its popularity threatened the French government, which used various measures to try to prevent its practice. For nearly fifty years, the movement resisted all suppression attempts by the government, insurgent communist groups, and the Catholic church.

In 1975, however, the communist-controlled government in Vietnam began a campaign to co-opt Cao Dai for its own purposes, with the goal of remaking it into a kind of state-run church. During the succeeding tumultuous years, many believers in Cao Dai began to spread the faith elsewhere (especially in the West) as they fled the troubled Southeast Asian region—especially the oppressive governments in Vietnam and Cambodia (the Khmer Rouge).

With newfound freedom, adherents living in freer cultures continue to work for the reunion of all religious people under the banner of Cao Dai.

Basic Beliefs and Values

Pulling philosophical and theological threads from Buddhism, Hinduism, Taoism, Confucianism, and Christianity, Cao Dai is a fairly recent attempt to weave an eclectic but unified worldwide faith. Its distinctive tenets are as follows:

Belief	Cao Dai
Sacred Text(s)	Written revelation is Tan Luat (Canonical Codes); oral revelation comes through Cao Dai spirit mediums
Nature of God	Monism—all things are one, everything is bestowed with God's Spirit.
Jesus Christ	Cao Daism recognizes the divinity of Christ and sees Christianity as one of the original and principal elements of Cao Daism; many Cao Daists worship Jesus as a manifestation of the divine in human form
Human nature	"God and humans are one" but material desires cause humans to lose the truth of the Supreme Being, who resides in every heart
About human need	"...observe love and justice in order to be unified with God."
Salvation	Enlightenment and re-unification of the self with the Nameless Divinity
Afterlife	Similar to Hinduism—bad karma results in reincarnation; one breaks free from this cycle and finds nirvana by cultivating the True Self, which is God within

Major Differences from Christianity

- All religions teach the same basic principle and have one origin; though they call God by different names, all worship the same God.

- The Supreme Being, mankind, and the universe are one. "By introducing the words 'God is you, and you are God,' Cao Dai adds a new dimension to the concept of religion," says one online source.

- Materialism blinds people to the fundamental truth of divine oneness.

- The goal of Cao Dai is to help humankind achieve ultimate reunification with the Supreme Being ("The All That Is") through cultivation of the True Self.

- Disciples of Cao Dai cultivate the True Self (that is, pursue union with God) through either of two paths or sects: exoterism (outer methods) or esoterism (inner methods).

- Exoterism involves external behaviors like practicing good (such as, engaging in at least one ceremony of worship per day at home and two worship services per month at a local temple; or a regimen of vegetarianism at least ten days per month) and avoiding evil (that is, not doing to others what you don't want them doing to you).

- Esoterism involves internal practices like meditation and purification of the soul, for the purpose of eradicating the inferior self and developing the true, divine self.

- People should love one another and not discriminate against one another. Pursuing genuine love and justice for all is the foundation for personal spiritual liberation and for ultimate harmony on earth.

Cao Dai is not a separate religious entity, but is properly the encompassing of all religions. Its goal is not to convert those of other faiths but to unite all faiths. It is the true universal religion. As an organization, the group has a hierarchy similar to the Catholic Church (a "pope," but none since 1934; cardinals, archbishops, bishops, and priests).

The Personal Code of Conduct

All Cao Dai disciples are expected to follow these rule
1. Do not kill living beings.
2. Do not lie.
3. Do not be sexually immora
4. Do not be intoxicated.
5. Do not sin by word.

View of God

The group known as Cao Dai worships the Supreme Being they claim revealed Himself as "Cao Dai" (literally "high place") in 1920 to Ngo Van Chieu.

Adherents describe this Supreme Being as follows:

- The Source of everything, the everlasting Creator
- One and the same God as Allah, Jehovah, Brahman, and so forth
- Manifested at various times in divine beings such as Jesus, Lao-Tze, Confucius, and so forth
- Inhabiting everything and everyone
- All-seeing (thus the Cao Dai symbol of the wide-open eye)
- One with each human spirit
- Desirous of bringing everything—all peoples and all religions—together into one harmonious whole

View of the Afterlife	Sacred Texts
Hinduism's contribution to Cao Dai is evidenced most clearly in the religion's view of the afterlife. Adherents embrace the concepts of karma (present actions determine future consequences), reincarnation (bad karma requires the "penance" of additional lifetimes), and ultimate nirvana for those who overcome bad karma through the faithful devotion that leads to reunification with the True Self.	Cao Dai adherents believe they can receive divine revelation and guidance orally through mediums and spiritists. They sometimes even rely upon Ouija boards or similar objects. They also revere the written resource called Tan Luat, which contains the Canonical Codes of the group.

Worldview

Cao Dai champions the following values and lifestyle: duty toward family and society; love and justice for all; the brotherhood and sisterhood of mankind; renunciation of luxury and riches; worship of God, the Father of all; and commitment to a lifestyle of "spiritual evolution" that leads to oneness with the ultimate.

As it is commonly practiced, Cao Dai also relies on spiritism and séances—attempted communications with the dead, especially deceased ancestors. Some practitioners even engage in ancestor worship. One spirit thought to communicate frequently in séances is the famous French writer Victor Hugo (*Les Miserables* and *The Hunchback of Notre Dame*). Perhaps due to his own dabbling in spiritualism, some Cao Daist adherents regard him as the first great ambassador for Cao Dai to the Western World. Other famous "saints" admired by adherents of the Cao Dai religion (though they themselves were never members of this faith) include William Shakespeare, Napoleon Bonaparte, and Joan of Arc.

The "Holy See" at Tay Ninh, Vietnam

Worship Services

Cao Dai disciples (called *adepts*) who follow exoteric practices worship daily at home. At their altars, they worship the one true god Cao Dai, symbolized by the divine eye, and assorted manifestations of God, representing various religions (for example, Jesus who represents Christianity; Lao Tze, the founder of Taoism, and so forth).

Twice monthly, adepts worship at a temple. The principal temple of exoteric Cao Daists—called the Holy See—is in Tay Ninh, Vietnam (some sixty miles from Saigon). The primary temple for followers of esoteric Cao Dai is in Can Tho, Vietnam (in the Mekong Delta).

Worship services in the Tay Ninh temple are elaborate affairs, open to visitors and tourists, and filled with dancing, chanting, and borrowed symbolism from various religious traditions. The building itself is an eye-catching structure—combining Muslim turrets with stained glass and bright paint.

Important Dates

The Declaration of the Founding of the Cao Dei Religion (October 7, 1926)—was signed by twenty-nine founding members
There are no specific feasts or sacred days associated with Cao Dei.

> *"Chinese folk religion can be roughly defined as belief in three relation-*
> *ships . . . between man and nature which includes all natural phenom-*
> *enon and all supernatural beings, between one person and another . . .*
> *in any kind of social setting . . . [and] between life and afterlife.*
> *"During the course of defining and redefining these three relationships, the*
> *Chinese ancestors employed all kinds of ideas, concepts, beliefs and icons (both*
> *native and imported) to establish Chinese folk religion. The end product is*
> *very colorful in appearance, rich in concept and bold in expression. Pan-*
> *theistic in principle, Chinese religion is all-inclusive in its scope."*
> —Arthur Yaopo Chiang

Number of Followers

The indigenous folk religion of China is thought to have about four hundred million practitioners, mostly common people.

Major Figures/Prophets

As old as the ancient Chinese culture and as diverse as China itself, Chinese Traditional (or Folk) Religion cannot be attributed to any one religious founder, moral philosopher, or political leader. Its roots are lost in the mists of time, and its evolution is the result of many influences and faith traditions.

A Feng Shui spiral in Los Angeles' Chinatown

Major Differences from Christianity

Belief	Chinese Traditional
Sacred Text(s)	None
Nature of God	Polytheism—hundreds of folk gods and goddesses, plus demigods, immortals, and "saints"
Jesus Christ	Jesus is not part of this religious belief or practice
Human nature	Though immortal, humans are dependent upon the help of others (departed ancestors and the pantheon of gods)
About human need	Need protection from harm and favor from the gods in order to live a long life of happiness, good luck, and prosperity
Salvation	Not rescued from sin, but ultimate reunion with ancestors and gods in an undefined peaceful afterlife
Afterlife	Some kind of continuing existence—either as disembodied spirits in another spiritual realm or perhaps reincarnated (depending on Buddhist and Taoist beliefs)

Short History

Chinese culture is marked by a long and varied history of religious tradition. For thousands of years and hundreds of millions of citizens, vestiges of primitive mythology and folk religion (for example, ancestor worship) have been blurred and blended with assorted principles and practices borrowed from Confucianism, Taoism, and Buddhism to create a broad, eclectic spirituality called Chinese Traditional Religion.

As such there is no single founder, no unified doctrinal statement or concise creed, no official hierarchy or headquarters or website. Chinese Traditional Religion is like China itself—ancient, sprawling, diverse, and mysterious.

Basic Beliefs and Values

Since Buddhism and Taoism (and to some extent, Confucianism) are discussed in separate chapters, the focus here will be on the older traditions and rituals strictly associated with primitive Chinese folk religion.

It is difficult to make broad descriptive statements that will apply neatly across the board to all adherents. Suffice it to say that Chinese Traditional Religion is marked by the following beliefs, values, and practices:

- A pantheon of deities, immortal beings, and "saints."

- Veneration of one's ancestors—Done by some in hopes of attaining a favorable life and a peaceful afterlife (some regard departed ancestors as guardian angels), by others out of a sense of filial duty and respect. Ancestors are honored by visiting their graves and providing simple necessities (in or near their coffins) for their comfort in the afterlife.

- Prayers.

- Herbal medicine.

- Superstitious rituals—One example is the presence of "door gods"—these guardians of the entrance to the spirit world are often assigned (as indicated by the presence of statues and idols) to police and protect the entrance of Chinese homes, restaurants, or businesses.

- Exorcism of troublesome spirits (especially in remote areas).

- Divination/consultation of mediums.

> Any of these beliefs and practices may be incorporated into one's practice of Buddhism, Taoism, or Confucianism.

- Feng shui—Arranging the furnishings in one's home or office to harness the *Tao* (or life force) that flows through the universe.

- Astrology—Veneration of the sun, moon, earth, stars.

- Religious artwork—One example is the picture of the kitchen god Tsao Chun (often appearing with his wife) that hangs above the stove in many Chinese kitchens. Once a year Tsao Chun ascends into heaven to report on the behavior of family members to the Jade Emperor, king of the gods. Misbehaving souls have been known to smear Chun's mouth with sugar or honey in a kind of bribe attempt—hoping He will "sweeten" his report!

View of God

Traditional Chinese religion reveres hundreds of mythical beings and deities. Among these gods, goddesses, and demigods (who are arranged in a kind of hierarchy) are:

- **The Jade Emperor**—king of the gods
- **Baosheng Dadi**—a divine physician
- **The Three Gods**—Happiness, Wealth, and Longevity
- **The Eight Immortals**—artistic and literary figures who were deified posthumously
- **Cai Shen**—the great blue-whiskered cat who bestows fortune and wealth

- **Ch'eng Huang**—a collection of deities who are assigned to judge the dead
- **Kuan Yin/Miao Shan**—the devout, unmarried daughter of an ancient Chinese emperor, who was blessed with healing powers and is the protective goddess of women and children
- **Tu Di Gong**—"God of the earth" who protects local places and is immortalized frequently in roadside shrines
- **Wen-Chang**—the god of students and scholarship (who is most popular at exam times)
- **Zhusheng Niangniang**—the goddess revered by those who want children or want their child to be male

Worldview

Chinese Folk Religion attempts to explain the operation of natural and supernatural processes. It is also seen as beneficial for preserving historical traditions, passing on cultural standards, remembering one's national heritage, contributing to societal stability, and maintaining domestic and generational continuity.

View of the Afterlife

At death, one's spirit is carried to one of the Ch'eng Huang, the gods who assess one's life. The virtuous get to experience a Buddhist-type paradise; the unworthy are sentenced to hell for a short time. After punishment, these chastened souls live in oblivion, preparing for their next reincarnation. They then begin the cycle of rebirth all over again.

Sacred Texts

There is no Scriptural canon. Beliefs are passed down orally through families and embedded in the Chinese culture (especially in rural areas).

Worship Services

Chinese Traditional (or Folk) Religion is not an organized religion with official clergy or any sort of identifiable ecclesiastical structure. One can visit Buddhist temples in China, but there is no such thing as a Chinese Traditional Religion temple (such as a church building, synagogue, mosque, or other place of worship). In a similar way, other than the ancient rituals, often practiced at home by individuals and families, and the events held on special Chinese holidays, there are no weekly, regular worship services to attend.

Important Dates

In addition to the holy days of Buddhism or Taoism, many Chinese observe the following holidays:

Chinese New Year (first day of the first month of the Chinese calendar) (January/February)—this major holiday involves the cleaning and decorating of houses, the giving of red envelopes (*hong bao*), fireworks, lanterns, bonfires (to chase away evil spirits, called *kuei*), dancing in elaborate dragon or lion costumes, and eating certain foods that are believed to bring good luck

Lantern (Shang Yuan) Festival—a Taiwanese "second New Year" springtime event, featuring decorative lanterns and family activities

Farmer's Day—an early spring festival marking the passing of winter and the commencing of spring plowing and planting. Celebrants engage in a piñata-like ritual called "Whipping the Spring Ox." This involves whacking a colorful paper cow until "the five grains" pour out, drinking spring wine, and worshipping the spring deity/earth god.

Dragon Boat Festival (mid-autumn)—a pageant of lively, colorful boat races intended to ward off evil spirits and disease

Autumn Moon Festival (late September)—a celebration of family unity, this festival involves eating mooncakes together

Ghost Festival (the fifteenth day of the seventh lunar month)—a solemn traditional holiday that commemorates the annual emergence of ghosts and ancestral spirits from the lower world. Participants offer food and burn paper money ("ghost money") to please these visitors. They also release paper boats and lanterns on waterways to give direction to lost spirits.

Qing Ming Jie (Grave Cleaning/Tomb Sweeping Day, early April)—a remembrance of one's ancestors, this observance includes prayers, offerings of food and libation. Failure to care for the spirits in this way may result in hungry ghosts who wreak havoc on the living.

"Why do Christian Scientists say God and His idea are the only realities, and then insist on the need of healing sickness and sin? Because Christian Science heals sin as it heals sickness, by establishing the recognition that God is All, and there is none beside Him—that all is good, and there is in reality no evil, neither sickness nor sin. We attack the sinner's belief in the pleasure of sin, alias the reality of sin, which makes him a sinner, in order to destroy this belief and save him from sin; and we attack the belief of the sick in the reality of sickness, in order to heal them. When we deny the authority of sin, we begin to sap it; for this denunciation must precede its destruction."

—Mary Baker Eddy, Retrospection and Introspection 63:1,
in *Science and Health with Key to the Scriptures.*

Number of Followers

Christian Science, the belief system propagated by the Church of Christ, Scientist, does not report the number of its adherents. Various researchers estimate from 150,000 to 400,000 Christian Science faithful.

Major Figures/Prophets

- **Mary Baker Eddy** (1821–1910)—discoverer and founder of Christian Science. It has been said that she overcame the challenges of poor health and financial and emotional hardship by pioneering a "reliable, widely practiced system of prayer-based healing" (the official Church of Christ, Scientist Web site).

Short History

Mary Baker Eddy, the above-mentioned founder of the Christian Science faith, was born in 1821 in Bow, New Hampshire, into a strict religious home. From birth through middle-age, her life was a nonstop series of physical illnesses, familial tragedy, and personal and emotional debilitation.

Eddy sought and experimented with all sorts of traditional and nontraditional cures, even as she pursued spiritual relief through personal Bible study and prayer. In her forties, Eddy met Phineas P. Quimby, an eccentric, self-taught philosopher and hypnotist, who advocated "New Thought"—the concept of natural healing using the untapped potential of the human mind. When his teachings failed to give Eddy long-term relief (especially after she slipped on an icy sidewalk in 1866, severely injuring herself), she reportedly turned in final desperation to the New Testament. While reading the gospel accounts of Jesus healing the sick, she claimed complete and miraculous deliverance from her assorted ailments. Eddy concluded that it is by the power of the divine Mind, not the human mind, that we discover God's goodness, presence, and power.

Through further study of the Bible, Eddy refined and recorded her beliefs. Her unique Bible interpretations and conclusions ultimately became the book entitled *Science and Health with Key to the Scriptures*, published in 1875. When Eddy began propagating these ideas—which she believed to be a rediscovery of simple, primitive gospel Christianity—existing Christian churches were nonreceptive and nonwelcoming. Meanwhile, readers of *Science and Health* began gathering to discuss its teachings and to share their stories of God's miraculous healing.

In 1879, Eddy formally established the First Church of Christ, Scientist, in Lynn, Massachusetts (also known as The Mother Church, now located in Boston).

In the final three decades of her life, Eddy wrote other books, launched a prolific publishing enterprise, and oversaw the development and organization of the vast religious enterprise that today claims two thousand branch Churches of Christ, Scientist, and Christian Science societies in more than eighty countries around the world.

Belief	Christian Science
Sacred Text(s)	The Bible, but only as it is read and interpreted by using *Science and Health with Key to the Scriptures*, by Mary Baker Eddy
Nature of God	God is an impersonal, all-powerful force called divine Love, Father-Mother, ultimate Mind, All-in-all
Jesus Christ	"Jesus Christ is not God, as Jesus himself declared, but is the Son of God" (*Science and Health*, 361:12-13); the human Jesus and the divine Christ are separate entities
Human nature	Humans are not material or physical, but the spiritual children of God: "The true nature of each individual as a child of God is spiritual"
About human need	Realizing God's infinite goodness and experiencing healing (physical, moral, mental, and emotional) through Christian Science prayer
Salvation	Not something to be obtained, but to be realized: "Life, Truth, and Love understood and demonstrated as supreme over all; sin, sickness and death destroyed" (*Science and Health*, 593:20–22)
After-life	Heaven and hell are not literal places, but are states of either right thinking or a blinded mind, respectively

Major Differences from Christianity

Basic Beliefs and Values

Christian Science teaches these primary doctrines and ideas:

- *Spirit (God) is the only ultimate, true reality*—Material things deceive us into believing that they are ultimate, but these physical things and substances are not "real" in the sense that God is real. They only seem essential, vital, fundamental, and enduring. Likewise, sickness, death, and sin are not "real."

- *"It's all in your mind"*—Illness is illusory. It is a kind of mental trick. Healing begins when one understands that illness can be traced to subjective problems in the mind, not objective issues in the body. This hard-to-grasp concept is, perhaps, analogous to people who dream that they are falling or about to drown, but are somehow able in their dreams to realize, "This isn't actually happening—it's only a dream" and then wake up safe and sound. Christian Science attempts to "wake up" those who have been lulled into thinking that this physical, earthly, material existence is ultimate.

- *Healing* (whether physical, emotional, or mental)—Is experienced through refocusing one's human mind on the positive and true teachings of Christian Science and praying accordingly, perhaps with the help of a Christian Science Practitioner (see below). Praying, in Christian Science practice, is not so much asking God for specific things, as it is shedding common human illusions about reality and bringing one's mind into agreement with the Divine Mind.

- *Jesus is not God*—He did not die on the cross, nor did He physically rise from the dead. He was one who possessed and perfectly displayed the Christ spirit, and is thus our "Way-Shower."

Membership in the group requires the following:

- Agreement with the six tenets of The Mother Church (written by Mary B. Eddy)—Beliefs in the Bible, God, destruction of sin and unreality of evil, salvation through Christ's atonement, and spiritual resurrection, plus the promise to "watch, and pray for that Mind to be in us which was also in Christ Jesus; to do unto others as we would have them do unto us; and to be merciful, just, and pure."

- The dissolution of all other existing church ties.

- One must be twelve years of age.

View of God

Christian Science advocates an all-powerful God, which it variously names: Father-Mother, All-in-all, Mind, Spirit, Soul, Truth, Life, Love, and Principle. Many of Mrs. Eddy's theological statements (for example, "All is Infinite Mind and its infinite manifestations, for God is all in all.") suggest a kind of pantheism, similar to Hindu belief. God is not independent and distinct from creation, but rather permeates it as an impersonal force.

Christian Science doctrine insists that, as spirit, God could never become a fleshly, material human. Thus Christian Science rejects orthodox Christian Trinitarianism— one God existing eternally as three coequal, coeternal persons (Father, Son, and Holy Spirit). Christian Science considers that historic view as polytheistic, and thus sees Jesus not as God incarnate but as a man who nobly embodied the ideal of Christ-like perfection. Also, the one evangelical Christians call "the Holy Spirit" is regarded by followers of Mary Baker Eddy as an impersonal, powerful divine intelligence.

Worldview

Christian Science can be classified as one of the "mind science" or "new thought" religions. Its teachings are similar to the United Church of Religious Science, Unity School of Christianity, and certain New Age belief systems. It is also somewhat dualistic in its strict division between the spiritual versus the physical.

> Because of their heavy emphasis on spiritual healing, many Christian Science followers refrain from utilizing standard healthcare.

While the church does not forbid its members from consulting doctors or having surgeries, many adherents do not take medicines, painkillers, accept blood transfusions, or submit to medical testing. This shunning of medical intervention has stirred controversy, especially when Christian Science parents have refused to have their children vaccinated or hospitalized in cases of critical illness.

View of the Afterlife

Christian Science teaching here is vague. Regarding death, Mrs. Eddy wrote: "The universal belief in death is of no advantage. It cannot make Life or Truth apparent. Death will be found at length to be a mortal dream, which comes in darkness and disappears with the light." (*Science & Health* 42:5). Apparently, upon the cessation of this earthly existence, one's spirit is united with God.

The historic Christian teaching of a future judgment day is opposed by Christian Science teaching: "No final judgment awaits mortals, for the judgment-day of wisdom comes hourly and continually" (*Science & Health* 291:28).

Heaven is typically described in Christian Science writings and teachings as a

Sacred Texts

The seminal book explaining Christian Science beliefs is *Science and Health with Key to the Scriptures*, written by Mary Baker Eddy. She also wrote the *Manual of The Mother Church*, which sets forth the organizational details of the church. The Christian Science Publishing Society publishes a Pulitzer Prize-winning daily newspaper (*The Christian Science Monitor*), a monthly journal (*The Christian Science Journal*), a weekly magazine (*The Christian Science Sentinel*), and quarterly Bible lessons and instructional curriculum.

state of mind, as ultimate harmony of being. It is not a literal place or destination. Likewise, hell is not regarded as an actual place, but a condition.

Worship Services

The Christian Science Mother Church in Boston broadcasts its weekly service. Christian Science branch churches offer Sunday services that are open to the public. These gatherings involve readings and music. Sunday school is offered for children and teens. Wednesday "testimony meetings" are also held.

Christian Science has no clergy. In 1895, Mary Baker Eddy proclaimed the Bible and her explanatory text *Science and Health with Key to the Scriptures* as "pastor" for worldwide Churches of Christ, Scientist. All ministry is conducted by lay members of the faith.

Christian Science *practitioners* are members who have undergone special training and serve the church full time by praying for situations brought to their attention by Christian Science adherents and those outside the church. Though practitioners can explain Christian Science beliefs, they do not counsel; theirs is strictly a prayer ministry. Because practitioners are self-employed, they charge fees for their services.

Christian Science *nurses* are members who offer simple physical care (but no medical treatment) to those who are seeking healing through Christian Science. They may, for example, give baths, dress wounds, or provide mobility and dietary assistance. Like practitioners, Christian Science nurses also charge fees for their services.

Christian Science Reading Rooms are found worldwide (about 1,900 in number). They double as bookstores and research centers "for the exploration of spiritual healing, prayer, and spirituality." Open to the public, they sponsor special activities and community events.

Important Dates

Most adherents of Christian Science observe the traditional holidays observed by Christians: Easter, Thanksgiving, and Christmas. There are no holy days unique to Christian Science.

The church has its annual meeting each June at The Mother Church in Boston.

*"Satan is a symbol, nothing more. . . . Satan signifies our love of the world-
ly and our rejection of the pallid, ineffectual image of Christ on the cross."*
—Anton LaVey

*"We are the first above-ground organization in history openly dedicated to the
acceptance of Man's true nature—that of a carnal beast, living in a cosmos which is
permeated and motivated by the Dark Force which we call Satan. Over the course of
time, Man has called this Force by many names, and it has been reviled by those whose
very nature causes them to be separate from this fountainhead of existence. They live in
obsessive envy of we who exist by flowing naturally with the dread Prince of Darkness."*
—Statement from Church of Satan

Number of Followers

Official membership in the Church of Satan is reportedly between five thousand and fifteen thousand members. However, the number of self-proclaimed Satanists who dabble in occult practices and read *The Satanic Bible* is much greater, probably several million worldwide.

Major Figures/Prophets

- **Magus Anton LaVey** (1930–1997) —founder of the Church of Satan in 1966, author of *The Satanic Bible*

- **Blanche Barton** (1959–present)— high priestess from 1997–2002; now has the title of Magistra Templi Rex; long-time companion of Anton LaVey and mother of his third child, a son named Satan Xerxes LaVey (1993–present)

- **Magus Peter H. Gilmore**—high priest of the Church of Satan since 2001

Belief	Church of Satan
Sacred Text(s)	*The Satanic Bible* and related works by Anton LaVey
Nature of God	No belief in a Supreme Deity; each person is his/her own god
Jesus Christ	Not regarded as God or Savior; not revered; mocked as a symbol of the weakness and failure of Christianity
Human nature	Fleshly (material) beings, not spiritual
About human need	Freedom from moral restraints, indulgence with personal responsibility
Salvation	Achieving a powerful lifestyle of self-interested hedonism
Afterlife	This life is all there is: live it up!

Major Differences from Christianity

Short History

Anton LeVey founded the Church of Satan in 1966. Beyond that fact, most details of the early history of the church are sketchy and debated.

The official story is that LaVey, an organist for burlesque shows on Saturday nights and for tent revival meetings on Sunday mornings, was repulsed and angered by the hypocrisy of the "Christian" men who frequented both settings. Consequently, on April 30, 1966 (a pagan holiday known as *Walpurgisnacht*), LaVey shaved his head in the fashion of ancient executioners and announced the formation of the Church of Satan.

The seal of Baphomet, an inverted pentagram

Over the next few years, he published various Satanic books: *The Satanic Bible* (1969), *The Compleat Witch* (1970—later reprinted as *The Satanic Witch*), and *The Satanic Rituals* (1972).

Some researchers dispute some details of this official story, claiming that LaVey was a bright and charming small-time huckster who lectured on the occult and paranormal activities for little money. At the prompting of a publicist friend, LaVey realized he could make a bigger splash (and a lot more money) by starting a controversial church centered on the occult. Was LaVey a true believer in the principles he espoused? Or was he a master marketer who set out to shock and titillate others for personal gain? Probably the answer to both questions is yes.

LaVey's success spawned or inspired other similar Satanic organizations. In 1975, Michael Aquino founded the Temple of Set. The First Church of Satan, another offshoot of the Church of Satan, is led by John Allee, and accepts many of the ideas of Aleister Crowley (1875–1947), a British pioneer in occult practices.

LaVey died in 1997, leaving his companion, Blanche Barton, in charge of the church. She turned over the administrative reins in 2001 to Peter H. Gilmore.

Basic Beliefs and Values

The Church of Satan declares only two possible options in life: the left-hand path or the right-hand path.

The right-hand path refers to traditional religion, which elevates the spiritual search and promotes the worship of external deities through adherence to strict moral codes. The left-hand path refers to traditions that celebrate the carnal and earthly, and promote the advancement of self and the quest for personal power.

Here are a few observations about the left-hand path traveled by adherents of the Church of Satan (what they believe and do):

- God does not exist.

- Satan—a literal, actual devil—does not exist. Rather, like a sports team's mascot, the name/idea of Satan is appropriated as a mere symbol. He represents man's independent, carnal nature. It is this "satanic" spirit that is believed to be the underlying force that fills and energizes the universe.

- *The Satanic Bible* (1969) includes the "nine satanic statements":

1. Satan represents indulgence instead of abstinence!

2. Satan represents vital existence instead of spiritual pipe dreams!

3. Satan represents undefiled wisdom instead of hypocritical self-deceit!

4. Satan represents kindness to those who deserve it instead of love wasted on ingrates!

6. Satan represents responsibility to the responsible instead of concern for psychic vampires!

7. Satan represents man as just another animal, sometimes better, more often worse than those that walk on all-fours, who, because of his 'divine spiritual and intellectual development,' has become the most vicious animal of all!

8. Satan represents all of the so-called sins, as they all lead to physical, mental, or emotional gratification!

9. Satan has been the best friend the Church has ever had, as he has kept it in business all these years!

- Satanists do not see themselves as championing "evil." Instead, they view good and evil as subjective terms and believe that normal, natural drives have been wrongly labeled as "sin." Satanists don't think in traditional categories of right and wrong; they choose to embrace whatever beliefs and practices they regard as personally beneficial.

- Satanists regard Christianity's teachings to be a "con game"—a way of insuring that everyone ends up being in sin and thus, in need of spiritual salvation that only the Church can provide. They insist that those who indulge in the so-called "seven deadly sins" (lust, pride, greed, envy, anger, gluttony, and sloth) in healthy moderation will enjoy life. Satanists do not believe in resisting internal impulses, but going along with them. Their motto is: "Indulgence—*not* compulsion!" They encourage gratification, not mortification, of fleshly desires.

- Church of Satan members practice magic. Satanists commonly use occult rituals involving curses and spells in an attempt to try to harness power for personal gain.

- The "nine satanic sins" to be avoided are: stupidity, pretentiousness, expecting others to treat you fairly and kindly, self-deceit, following the herd, losing perspective, forgetfulness of past orthodoxies, counterproductive pride, and loss of an aesthetic sense.

- In Satanism, there is no mercy or forgiveness. On the contrary, Satanists believe in a strong sense of justice called *Lex Talionis*, an eye for an eye. LaVey's "eleven satanic rules of the earth" include: "If a guest in your lair annoys you, treat him cruelly and without mercy," and "When walking in open territory, bother no one. If someone bothers you, ask him to stop. If he does not stop, destroy him."

View of God

Members of the Church of Satan do not believe in God. If anything, "God" is just a name given to the impersonal—evolutionary—force that permeates and balances the universe. In the Church of Satan, each person is his or her own god, given over to the goal of achieving mastery and control over his/her own life.

Worldview

Satanism, as practiced in the Church of Satan, has these goals: (1) a world free from the baggage and lies of Christianity; (2) a life governed by reason and logic, rather than faith and superstition; (3) a libertarian ("live and let live") social agenda, expressed in political views; (4) a championing of the idea of individuality; and (5) a nonproselytizing, nonaltruistic lifestyle violently opposed to any notion of self-sacrifice.

Frequent references to the "survival of the strong" suggest a strong evolutionary mindset. These are coupled with deploring weakness and despising mediocrity and ignorance.

Worship Services

The Church of Satan adamantly claims that it does not believe in nor worship Satan. They state, "The reality behind Satan is simply the dark evolutionary force of entropy that permeates all of nature and provides the drive for survival and propagation inherent in all living things." It could be said that Church of Satan members worship self, hedonism, and individual freedom.

Members gather for "services," where they engage in magic rituals (both private and corporate). They often dress in black robes bearing the Baphomet symbol (an inverted pentagram, containing the head of a goat, surrounded by Hebrew letters). They employ magic spells in an attempt to influence the behavior of others and the outcome of certain events.

"Black Masses" (subversive parodies of the Roman Catholic mass) are not a regular event as is commonly believed. (A few credible witnesses say that LaVey celebrated these infrequently, and sometimes in almost a kind of tongue-in-cheek manner, to shock and garner publicity and notoriety.) Reports of ritual abuse, human sacrifice, Satanic orgies, and so forth, are continually alleged, but conclusive evidence of such behavior has never been produced.

Beginning Satanists are taught to engage in a simple ritual in front of a black candle. They give themselves over to the spirit of unbridled indulgence and independence, chanting, "I am ready, oh, Dark Lord. I feel your strength within me and wish to honor you in my life. I am one of the Devil's Own. Hail Satan!" By concentrating on a mental image of Satan, they are told they can conjure Satan into their lives.

View of the Afterlife	Sacred Texts
Satanists have no belief in any afterlife. "We think that we live only once, and life is thus too short to waste our time on shoddy goods and behavior," said Peter Gilmore, high priest of the Church of Satan.	Revered texts include *The Satanic Bible, Satanic Rituals, The Satanic Witch, The Devil's Notebook,* and *Satan Speaks*— all written by Anton LaVey.

Important Dates

In keeping with Satanism's fierce commitment to self-interest and self-gratification, the most important holiday is said to be the individual church member's birthday. Other days of interest to Satanists are:

Walpurgisnacht (April 30)	**Halloween** (October 31)
Summer (June) and winter (December) solstices	Spring (March) and fall (September) equinoxes

"God is within you. You don't need to seek Him. Be of good cheer. You have noth-
ing to get. Everything that is, is within. God is within you and is your near-
est and dearest. In fact, He is you and your existence is the way to Him."
—Dadaji

Major Figures/Prophets

- **Amiya Roy Chowdhury** (1909?–1992)—also known as "Dadaji," beloved elder brother, was born in East Bengal (now Bangladesh).

Short History

The birth date of Amiya Roy Chowdhury is un-known. (The years between 1906 and 1912, inclusive, have been suggested.) What is known is that Amiya was born into an aristocratic Hindu family. His father was a doctor and his mother was a kind and devout woman.

Amiya's birth was allegedly accompanied by supernatural signs (mystical dreams and a divine fragrance filling the Chow-dhury home). He was a precocious child, often asking difficult spiri-tual and theological questions to the religious leaders who frequented the Chowdhury home. According to Dadaji's official biography, the boy was charming, with a wisdom far beyond his years. At age six he is reported to have explained the (Hindu holy books) Gita and Bhagawata to his father. About the same time he vio-lated longstanding Hindu customs and cultural tradition by dining with a Muslim neighbor. The boy used this occasion to confront social inequity and to preach an early version of one of his enduring messages: truth is one, humanity is one, language is one, and religion is one.

It is claimed that Amiya left home at age nine. He traveled widely, returning home after a couple of years, where once again he tangled with Hindu leaders over their religious practices. Whenever he met holy men (yogis, sadhus, and renunciates), he questioned the purpose of their asceticism.

As a young man, Amiya supposedly became enamored with music. He began singing and toured India, giving concerts. The Dadaji Web site claims he also pro-duced movies, played on a world-class soccer club, and met with Stalin, Mussolini, and Churchill. It further alleges that he began to be seen in multiple locales at the same time.

In the 1940s, Amiya relocated his family to India, just ahead of the Muslim revolts in East Pakistan. He became a successful businessman, experiencing success

Number of Followers

Because founder Dadaji eschewed every attempt to gather a following or start an official movement and because he did not arrange for a successor, it is impossible to say how many devotees Dadaji currently has.

[44]

in banking, insurance, and even worked for a time as a university professor.

In 1967, Amiya became known as "Dadaji," (a name that translates as "beloved elder brother"). He began a series of worldwide travels, revealing himself and teaching his anti-religious establishment message. Many miracles and supernatural signs are attested to Dadaji—such as healings, resurrections of the dead, and alterations of weather.

By 1987, Dadaji had become reclusive, his health reportedly failing. On June 7, 1992, he died. He specifically refused to provide for any kind of successor.

Basic Beliefs and Values

It could be argued that Dadaji as a religion is essentially a polemical faith. Its beliefs are largely reactions against prevailing religious practices. Dadaji, the elder brother, insisted that in true religion there is/are:

- No organization to join.
- No institution to support.
- No donations required.
- No rituals required.
- No temples to be built.
- No penance necessary.
- No expensive spiritual courses to complete.
- No mechanical muttering of mystic syllables.
- No ascetism or austerity.
- No physical restrictions.
- No religious classes.
- No gurus or intermediaries needed.

Belief	Dadaji
Sacred Text(s)	None, though followers read and/or listen to Dadaji's teachings in written form, and on audio/videotape
Nature of God	God is within; is dearest friend and inner guide
Jesus Christ	Not acknowledged, much less emphasized
Human nature	Spiritual and physical beings; human bodies are channels for experiencing God's love
About human need	At birth, we forget our true divine nature. As ego expands, our awareness of divinity fades
Salvation	Look within and find God, Truth, and Love
After-life	Life is eternal; the body consists of matters which dissolve in time to their original form, but the self does not dissolve

Major Differences from Christianity

[45]

He stated: "I want to tell you, do not accept me as your guru. God is in you. Do not seek a guide or instrument. No mortal being can ever be a guru. All these God-men, all, each and every one are bluff, full of bluff. Their only interest is to collect money and make institutions. God alone is the Guru. Don't bother running after gurus, yogis, or priests. No person can initiate or guide you to God. Look within."

Dadaji resisted attempts by followers to turn his teaching into an organized religious faith. "There are so many people who told me they would give me ashram [buildings and properties for a religious community]. All the universe is my ashram. No need for all these things. Why should I go for buildings? Ashram is also one kind of cheating. In the name of Him we have no right to take anything. Is there anybody who can challenge that in the world?"

One interesting and unique aspect of Dadaji is the so-called experience of Divine Fragrance. Occasionally, and without warning, devotees are said to be able to catch a whiff of a delightful aroma (a mixture of rose scent and sandalwood). This mysterious phenomenon is sometimes intense and sometimes short-lived. It can happen when one meets Dadaji through his books (which are available on the Internet as free downloads).

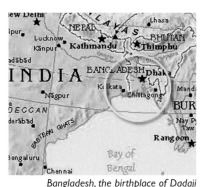
Bangladesh, the birthplace of Dadaji

View of God

God, also known as the Supreme or *Mahanam* ("God's name within"), is inside each person. The Dadaji religion teaches that we are full of God, even pregnant with God. When we forget this basic truth, life becomes void of peace and joy.

Though Dadaji insisted, "I'm nobody," the Dadaji Web site says that "he possessed Infinite Supreme Wisdom" and that "He is Supreme Love Incarnate."

View of the Afterlife

Dadaji teaches that, at death, the soul or mind (that is, God) leaves the body. It comes back in a different body, "until one's *Prarabdha* [destined unfolding process of one's life] is full, until one is merged with God." Says Dadaji, "Life has no death. Life is Eternal. What you call death or end of life is actually a phase and is concerned only with the body. Body consists of matters which dissolve in time to their original form. But Self has no dissolution."

Worldview

Perhaps the worldview of Dadaji is best expressed in his own words: "Take refuge in none but God. Just try to remember Him and do your duty. Your work is your penance, your sacrifice, your worship. So go ahead, no need for worry. Live a natural life. Don't deny and don't indulge. Be of good cheer and enjoy! We have come here to relish His Love and to enjoy His Play. Just try to remember Him with love and remain in a natural state."

Sacred Texts

There is no holy book. In addition to Dadaji's published books and unpublished manuscripts, adherents of Dadaji give their attention to his teachings through his transcribed talks and conversations, audio tapes, and videotaped messages.

Worship Services

Dadaji did not advocate or look with favor upon religious rites, formal services of worship, organized prayer meetings, meditation rituals, offerings, and so forth. He insisted that God is not encountered through these common, official religious practices. One does not have to visit a church, temple, shrine, or mosque to find God.

On the contrary, one worships by living a simple, natural life, enjoying everything and everyone in His creation. The key is remembering His name wherever one is. The spiritual and physical are not separate entities. All of life is spiritual.

Important Dates

During Dadaji's life, an event called the Annual Gathering of God Lovers was held in the month of October. Other than this, in keeping with Dadaji's unorthodox, contrarian views, no special holidays were observed.

"Imagine a model society where people live in harmony with the land and each other; a society which boasts a zero percent crime rate and not one single act of vandalism; where people live in the absence of fear; where the young and the old are cared for; where nurturing the beauty inside of each person is of utmost importance; and where no one ever needs Prozac. Fairy tale or reality? Tucked in the Alpine foothills of northern Italy sits Damanhur . . ."
—Randy Peyser

Major Differences from Christianity

Belief	Damanhur
Sacred Text(s)	None
Nature of God	God is an impersonal force that permeates everything and everyone; we are all part of God, and God is within each person
Jesus Christ	Not emphasized in Damanhur
Human nature	All humans possess a divine spark or nature, an unlimited "God-potential"
About human need	Need to recognize and awaken our true divine nature, so as to bring about a renaissance of peoples and cultures on the earth
Salvation	By nourishing our inner potential, we can discover, develop, and use our gifts and fulfill our life purpose by blessing the community
Afterlife	As part of the divine cosmic spirit, we are eternal; we have past lives, and we experience reincarnation after death

Number of Followers

It is reported that there are thousands of Damanhur members all over the world. There are forty-four small communities (or communes), each with about twenty members, located in and around Valchiusella, in the alpine foothills of northern Italy.

Major Figures/Prophets

- **Oberto Airaudi, "Falco"** (1950–present)—founder of the Damanhur Federation or Community. A native of Balangero, Italy, Airaudi is a visionary and spiritual leader, with a long-time interest in meditation and paranormal activities.

Short History

Take some New Age spiritual beliefs and some magical, occult practices. Add a big dose of optimism and human potential philosophy. Mix this with a high regard for the arts and concern for the environment. Throw in a communal dynamic and a democratic political structure. Place all this into an exotic geographical setting, the jewel of which is an underground engineering marvel. The result is Damanhur, one of the most unusual religious experiments in human history.

The Dammanhur Community is located in the Italian Alps north of Turin

One source reported that Damanhur founder Oberto Airaudi, or "Falco," demonstrated unique spiritual abilities (including the ability to heal) from an early age. He devoted himself to a rigorous, ongoing regimen of experimentation, study, travel, and spiritual research. Ultimately, Airaudi was able to reawaken his "inner master" (that is, his divine nature). Damanhur is named after the Egyptian city of Damanhur which was the site of a temple dedicated to Horus.

Today, Airaudi remains an active student of philosophy, human potential, and various spiritual pathways. He has supposedly cultivated skills in hypnosis, levitation techniques, and how to engage in soul travel. He is regarded by admirers as a spiritual Master, healer, and artist.

In the early 1970s, Airaudi dreamed of establishing a model community of artisans and professionals in Northern Italy for the purpose of spiritual, artistic, and social research. Central to that dream was designing and building a grand cathedral to rival the great religious structures of medieval times. This cathedral would be a place of healing for all peoples. Airaudi purchased property in the Italian Alps, thirty miles north of Turin. He and his followers decided to attempt to build their temple underground (because no laws forbade such a construction project).

Using his own money from a successful insurance business, Airaudi and his small band of followers began secretly digging in 1978. As the story goes, when authorities learned of this effort, the Italian army was mustered to "destroy the terrorist cult under the mountain." However, upon entering the stunning edifice, soldiers could only stare in awe. The judge who signed off on the raid reportedly became an adherent of Damanhur. The project was declared an artistic wonder. Over time, even the United Nations officially praised the Damanhur experiment.

Now, the Damanhur Federation is a collection of small communities. Its "Temples of Mankind" are renowned for their exquisite beauty and craftsmanship. The group has its own constitution, a council that resolves conflict, schools, businesses, its own currency (called the *credito*, which assumes the same value as the euro), and even a daily newspaper.

Basic Beliefs and Values

Damanhur, according to its Web site, insists that people can control their own destiny by "awakening the inner Master through study, experimentation, the full expression of individual potential, and the elimination of dogmatic attitudes." It is an attempt to create an ideal society, a kind of utopia on earth.

By any and every standard, the goals are noble and lofty: true brotherhood and harmonious relations; a just society built on equality and freedom; a strong work ethic; robust scientific inquiry; never-ending philosophical/educational pursuit; a continuous dogma-free, esoteric spirituality; and great emphasis on artistic freedom and expression.

Says the official Web site: "The aims of Damanhur are: the freedom and re-awakening of the Human Being as a divine, spiritual, and material principle; the creation of a self-sustaining model of life based on ethical principles of good communal living and love; harmonic integration and cooperation with all the Forces linked to the evolution of Humankind."

Here are some of the unique beliefs and ideals of the group:

- *Becoming a united community* (called "the Spiritual People")—linked not by blood or racial ties, but by a common commitment to artistic, cultural, and philosophical expression, positive thinking, generous sharing, genuine solidarity, and the goal of reviving human consciousness on planet Earth.

- *Communal living*—built on reciprocal trust, respect, personal responsibility, clarity and acceptance. Marital arrangements vary from lifetime partnerships to one-year renewable contracts.

- *Participation in smaller groups*—called "The Ways," which research, through music, teaching, dance, ritual, and healing exercises, various theories about spiritual advancement.

- *Membership in Damanhur*—requires acceptance of the group's constitutional values and ends whenever a member loses desire to belong; citizenship requires a six-month trial period.

- *Name changes*—members typically adopt an animal and/or plant name to reflect the belief that all species are interconnected. Thus, founder Airaudi took the name Falco (or "falcon").

- *Spiritual value of work*—work should benefit the entire community. According to its home Web site, "Every task is precious and carries the same dignity."

- *No spiritual dogma*—only spiritual theories and hypotheses that are tested by members in the course of everyday life; spiritual experience should happen not just on weekends, but in the course of one's normal life and work.

- *Inner discipline of meditation*—adherents seek to practice this around the clock.

- *Planet as a "sentient being" to be respected and preserved*—goal is a true eco-society, complete with renewable energy and eco-architecture. Members work to protect the environment and utilize technologies that avoid pollution and waste. "Music of the Plants" is an audio experimentation that Damanhur devotees are convinced demonstrates that plants have the capacity to "make music."

- *Continuing education for members*—offered through Olami Damanhur University and other schools with short courses in many fields, including time travel, divination (especially use of Tarot cards and astrology), past lives research, a form of psycho-spiritual healing called "heart touch," paranormal ability (including telepathy, dream interpretation, clairvoyance, communication with animals, plants and "subtle beings"), pranatherapy (a form of spiritual healing in which trained practitioners harness the intelligent, positive energy of the cosmos and channel it into patients), and hypnotic therapy (for changing perceptions and behavior).

Sacred Texts

Being an antidogmatic group, Damanhurians do not have a holy book they revere in the way that Christians regard the Bible or Muslims view the Qu'ran. *The Book of Synchronicity* (November 2007) by founder Oberto Airaudi is a translation of an ancient book of magic.

View of God

Adherents of Damanhur believe that "God" is within. We do not need external help. Rather, we must awaken to the divinity within—the limitless cosmic force that makes all things possible and enables us to live harmoniously, creatively, and constructively.

Worldview

Because the world is ever changing and evolving, the Damanhur Community plays the "Game of Life." This is the title given to the practice of intentionally introducing new and different philosophies and situations into group life. This regular, intentional act of "shaking things up" forces the group to innovate and create, to adapt, to play, to experiment, and in the process, to grow and enjoy challenging interaction and teamwork with one another.

Damanhur shuns passivity. Members commit to "transform themselves and the planet through concrete and informed action. . . . It is not enough to sit down and meditate an hour a day to be an evolved human being. It is necessary to work and manifest spiritual achievements through concrete actions that make a difference" (from the manifesto of the independent political movement of Damanhur named *Con te per il Paese*, "With you for the Country").

View of the Afterlife

Damanhur, like other groups that hold to New Age beliefs, sees humanity as possessing a divine spark, each individual bearing a portion of the eternal cosmic force. Because of this, we are eternal creatures, with past lives and future incarnations. There is no literal heaven or hell. The emphasis is on living to the full now—using this life to realize one's full potential, to create for and contribute to the good of all.

Worship Services

Followers regularly visit the "Temples of Mankind" (sometimes called the "Eighth Wonder of the World") to meditate and connect with the Divine. The Temples are an underground complex of rooms and gathering halls, filled with beautiful statuary and artwork. The Temples include the Hall of Mirrors, the Hall of Water, the Hall of the Earth, the Labyrinth, and the Hall of Metals. The group reports, "Passing through the rooms and along the corridors of the Temples is a journey inside the self, a spiritual pilgrimage open to all creeds and convictions."

A small group of Damanhurian devotees began secretly digging (by hand) into the Italian mountainside in 1978. In keeping with the group's evolutionary ideals, the temples are continually being enhanced and enlarged (the current structure represents only ten percent of the overall temple plan). The Hall of Mirrors boasts the largest Tiffany glass dome cupola in the world.

Important Dates

The Damanhurian Community, "the Spiritual People," gather together annually (usually at the end of August) for a special day of celebration and festivity and for a group photograph. It is a day devoted to the People.

Other key dates include:

Global Peace Meditation Day (May 20)
Spiritual Birthday of Damanhur (May 29)—includes special rituals and artistic performances

"There is a happiness in Deism, when rightly understood, that is not to be found in any other system of religion. All other systems have something in them that either shock our reason, or are repugnant to it, and man, if he thinks at all, must stifle his reason in order to force himself to believe them. But in Deism our reason and our belief become happily united. The wonderful structure of the universe, and everything we behold in the system of the creation, prove to us, far better than books can do, the existence of a God, and at the same time proclaim His attributes."

—Thomas Paine

Major Figures/Prophets

Deism, as a theology/philosophy, was not established; rather it developed over centuries due to the influence of prominent thinkers. Key among these are:

- **Lord Herbert of Cherbury** (1583–1648)—the English thinker who advocated the superiority of human reason over divine revelation

- **Voltaire** (1694–1778)—the antidogmatic French writer and deist philosopher who famously wrote this statement during the Enlightenment: "It is perfectly evident to my mind that there exists a necessary, eternal, supreme, and intelligent being. This is no matter of faith, but of reason."

Number of Followers

The number of people who hold to a deistic worldview is unknown. This is because Deism is not an established religion, but rather a philosophical and theological outlook. It is probably accurate to say that most Deists remain aloof from all forms of organized religion, though some choose to affiliate with the Unitarian-Universalist church because of its tolerant views.

- **Immanuel Kant** (1724–1804)—the influential German philosopher who popularized free thought, meaning autonomous inquiry using reason, without the constraints of external authority

- **Thomas Paine** (1737–1809)—the prolific pamphleteer of the Revolutionary era who championed deistic ideals in his landmark book, *The Age of Reason*

- **Thomas Jefferson** (1743–1826)—principal author of the Declaration of Independence and third President of the United States, an advocate of deism, as evidenced by his "rewriting of the Gospels" so as to exclude all references to the miraculous

Short History

By the seventeenth century, the cultures of Europe were awash in Renaissance thinking. A profound philosophical and theological shift had taken place since the Middle Ages. The age of discovery had opened eyes to the diversity of world cultures. The Protestant Reformation, the scientific revolution spurred on by Copernicus, Galileo, and Newton, and the rise of biblical criticism resulted in many people questioning, and ultimately rejecting, the long-standing teachings and dominant role of the church. Intellectual pursuit was the rage. This "Age of Reason" was facilitated largely by philosophers and thinkers such as Immanuel Kant and Voltaire, who held great sway over those in positions of social and political influence.

By the eighteenth century, both Europe and the American colonies were hotbeds of so-called Enlightenment thinking. Reason was king. Toleration was a new rule. In intellectual circles and academic institutions, rational thought and scientific inquiry (not religious faith in divine revelation) were increasingly seen as a superior and more reliable authority in life.

It was within this environment that Deism—the idea of a benevolent Creator, knowable only from a distance through nature and inquisitive reason—began to flourish and spread.

Belief	Deism
Sacred Text(s)	None, though Deists have great respect for the writings of Thomas Paine, particularly *The Age of Reason*
Nature of God	There is a universal creative force which is the source of the laws and designs found throughout nature. It is beyond the world, but not active in the world
Jesus Christ	A benevolent moral teacher, but not divine and not a miracle-worker; neither virgin-born nor resurrected
Human nature	Responsible moral agents created by God with the capacity to discover the truth of God through rational study of His creation
About human need	Use reason to live by morals and ethics that are good for all
Salvation	"Salvation" is freedom from the dogmatic restraints of man-made religion through rational inquiry
Afterlife	No one knows for sure what happens after death, but nature gives hints that existence continues in a different form

Major Differences from Christianity

[55]

A number of America's founding fathers (for example, Thomas Jefferson, Benjamin Franklin, Thomas Paine, and Ethan Allen) embraced such deistic ideas. M. Paul Hazard referred to holders of such views as "rationalists with a nostalgia for religion." This faith-flavored reliance on human reason is reflected in their writings, even in important documents such as the Declaration of Independence and the Constitution.

Basic Beliefs and Values

There is no official creed among Deists since they are fiercely opposed to dogma and thought-control. However, some broad observations about the foundational premises of Deism can be made:

Thomas Paine, one of the many vocal Deists of the 18th century

- Faith is regarded as unnecessary and in many instances dangerous; reason points indisputably to the existence of God—an intricately designed universe requires a Designer.

- God speaks, not through special revelation (holy books) but through general revelation (the natural world of creation); human reason, given by God, is mankind's guide to living.

- True religion consists of doing justice, loving mercy, and seeking the best of all men.

- Evil in the world is due to ignorance and/or the unwillingness to embrace God-given reason and personal responsibility for one's own actions.

- It is important to oppose religious superstition, bigotry, and arrogance, even while granting others the freedom to believe whatever they wish to believe.

- Miracles are antirational and therefore impossible. It is not that God cannot do such things; it is that He has chosen not to—creating instead a world that runs by natural laws and principles.

- It is crucial to retain an open mind, to be a free thinker, to constantly question dogmatic ideas.

- All people are equal.

Worldview

Deists see the world as the work of an intelligent designer. They see our role as living rationally, with integrity, practicing kindness to fellow human beings. The pursuit of knowledge and scientific inquiry are prized. Superstition and ignorance are to be decried.

As a theological, philosophical, and practical approach to life, Deism can be summarized by words and phrases such as: Don't be irrational. Put aside your foolish superstitions. Think! Reason! Rely on your God-given common sense. Don't believe everything you hear. Question authority. Never stop seeking and learning. Stop blaming God or waiting for Him to intervene. Take responsibility for your own life.

View of the Afterlife

Most Deists retain a vague sense (or hope?) of immortality. Consider the words of Thomas Paine: "I consider myself in the hands of my Creator, and that he will dispose of me after this life consistently with His justice and goodness. I leave all these matters to Him, as my Creator and friend, and I hold it to be presumption in man to make an article of faith as to what the Creator will do with us hereafter."

The World Union of Deists asserts:

Contrary to [the] self-serving attitude of the revealed religions, Deism teaches that no one knows for certain what happens after death. If anything at all, it teaches that, based on the creation we are all a part of, we shouldn't worry about it. That instead, we should be concerned for the present and future of planet Earth and humanity. That we should work hard to improve life and also enjoy it here and now. Why should we worry about death when we have so much to do in life?

View of God

God is the intelligent and powerful Creator. Many Deists regard God as distant, unknowable, and uninvolved in human affairs. Albert Einstein, for example, described his deistic beliefs this way: "My religion consists of a humble admiration of the illimitable superior spirit who reveals himself in the slight details we are able to perceive with our frail and feeble minds. That deeply emotional conviction of the presence of a superior reasoning power, which is revealed in the incomprehensible universe, forms my idea of God." Because Deists reject the divinity of Christ, they are non-Trinitarian.

Sacred Texts

Deism rejects the notion that God has revealed Himself in special scriptures like the Bible, the Koran, or the Book of Mormon. It scoffs at the suggestion that any books are divinely inspired, holy, or inerrant. Creation itself is the "Word of God."

The Festival of the Supreme Being, a Deist holiday, in revolutionary France

However, Deists do base their convictions on the arguments of prominent deist thinkers in books such as *The Age of Reason* (Thomas Paine).

Worship Services

Deism has no clergy and deems religious professionals unnecessary. Common sense in studying the created order of things is how one finds divine guidance and inspiration.

Prayer consists primarily of thanksgiving, since God is thought to work through natural processes and laws, not through intercession and supplication.

Important Dates

Because it is not an official religion, Deism has no official holidays. Some Deists celebrate Christmas and Easter; others do not.

"[They] know much about the stars and celestial motions, and about the size of the earth and universe, and about the essential nature of things, and about the powers and authority of the immortal gods; and these things they teach to their pupils."
—Julius Caesar, referring to the Druids

Major Differences from Christianity

Belief	Druidism
Sacred Text(s)	No definitive, authoritative text; truth is found in ancient Celtic oral traditions and in subjective, personal experiences
Nature of God	Mostly polytheistic (many gods and goddesses) and animistic (deity inhabits common things)
Jesus Christ	Jesus not important and not emphasized (though some Druids do refer to the tolerance and compassion of Christ)
Human nature	We are interconnected material beings with souls, one part of the vast natural order or sacred fabric of life
About human need	Need to purposefully cultivate sacred awareness, wisdom, creativity and love (of nature, of peace, of beauty)
Salvation	Learning to live happily in this world with respect for others and the earth and with ethical integrity
Afterlife	Repeated reincarnations, with "rest stops" in the otherworld, another realm or dimension that exists beyond our senses

Number of Followers

Because of similar beliefs and rituals, practitioners of Druidry are often lumped together with adherents of Wicca, Asatru, Shamanism, and Heathenism, under the umbrella terms "neopaganism" or "paganism." This not only makes for an eclectic, pick-and-choose spirituality but also makes it difficult to give even an approximate number of followers of modern Druidism.

Like their ancient ancestors, modern Druids are not a formal, highly organized group given to keeping detailed membership lists. Groups frequently form and dissolve, merge, and disband. Affiliations remain loose and tenuous, many viewing Druidism as more of a philosophical pursuit and fraternal activity than a formal, long-term religious allegiance. Despite those organizational realities, anecdotal evidence seems to suggest that Druidism is growing in popularity in Northern Europe and North America.

Major Figures/Prophets

Shrouded in ancient history, Celtic Druidism has no known founder. The modern Druid revival is often attributed to:

- **John Toland** (1670–1721)—an Irish philosopher who lived in the early 1700s and was the founder of The Druid Circle

- **Henry Hurle**—the British organizer of the Ancient Order of Druids in 1781

Short History

A fanciful depiction of a druid

Druidism dates back to the time of the Celts (500 BC to AD 100). The Druids were the common priesthood of the assorted Celtic tribes, functioning as messengers between humans in this world and the gods in the otherworld. In addition to their role as spiritual leaders, these learned Druids acted as tribal historians and teachers, as well as legislative and judicial leaders. Such broad influence gave the Druids a quasi-royal status among the Celts.

When the Romans conquered and occupied most of Europe by the second century, they sought to eradicate Druidic beliefs. With the spread of Christianity, the religion almost completely died out in the fifth century. Catholic cathedrals were sometimes erected on ancient Druid sacred sites.

In the seventeenth and eighteenth centuries, assorted attempts were made (primarily in England) to reconstruct Druidism. These groups did not endure. The last hundred years have seen another revival of interest in this ancient Celtic religion. Some modern Druids seek to recover and practice the pure beliefs of ancient Druidism, while others work to create a new Druidism, blending old beliefs with new ideas.

Basic Beliefs and Values

One of the most influential modern Druid groups, "A Druid Fellowship," calls itself "Neopagan Druidry" and describes the term this way:

Neopagan Druidry is a group of religions, philosophies, and ways of life, rooted in ancient soil yet reaching for the stars. We are part of the larger Neopagan movement, one of the world's most vital and creative new religious awakenings. Like much of that movement we are polytheistic nature worshippers, working with the best aspects of the Pagan religions of our predecessors within a modern scientific, artistic, ecological, and wholistic context using a nondogmatic and pluralistic approach.

One could summarize Druidic beliefs as follows:

- Reality/life is fundamentally "spiritual."

- Druidism has no fixed dogma. With no inspired scripture and no abiding, governing authority, Druidic beliefs are fluid and individualistic. No one person or group is seen as having a monopoly on truth.

- Ancient Druidic worship focused on the elements of the natural world: earth, fire, water, and air. Modern Druids continue this great reverence for nature as divine or sacred, often becoming involved in ecological movements.

- Ancient Druids practiced divination (predicting future events). Many modern Druids practice forms of magic.

- Druids believe in the immortality of the soul/reincarnation (either in human form or rebirth as an animal or some inanimate natural object).

- Druids pursue three goals: wisdom, creativity, and love.

- Many Druids believe in honoring their ancestors.

- Toleration of diversity in viewpoints and beliefs is vital. Followers of Druidism are free to express their spirituality in whatever ways they choose.

Says one Druidry source:

People are drawn to Druidry because they can practice and study it on its own, or in combination with other spiritual paths. Each spiritual way has gifts to offer, and some people find that they can combine the Druid and Christian approaches. Others combine their Druidry with Wicca or Buddhism, while others find in Druidry itself all the spiritual nourishment they need.

Stonehenge, England, regarded as a holy site by modern Druids

There are some strict Druids who want to create a pure and separate Druidism. Adherent Cahan Tiarnan claims, "One cannot be a Christian, Muslim, or anything else, and a Druid. They will contradict each other."

View of God

Ancient Druidism was both polytheistic and animistic. The chief god among the ancient Celts was *Dagda*, the "father of all." *Cernunnos*, "the horned one," was revered as the lord of animals, and the god of crops, fruit, and money.

Theological tolerance among modern Druids allows for the whole gamut of beliefs about deity: animism (the belief that everything in nature, even inanimate objects like rocks and wind, possesses a divine spirit), polytheism (the belief in many gods and goddesses), pantheism (everything is deity and deity is everything), duotheism (god and goddess), even monotheism (the belief in one God or Spirit), and so forth.

Worldview

A love for and reverence of nature leads most Druids to become involved in efforts to care for the earth. Modern Druids tend to stress vigorous intellectual debate, personal responsibility, volunteerism, and political activism.

Perhaps John Michael Greer, author of *Druidry: A Green Way of Wisdom*, best summarizes modern Druidism:

What does it mean to be a Druid today? Above all else, Druidry means following a spiritual path rooted in the green Earth. It means participating in a living Western spiritual tradition drawn from many sources, including surviving legacies from Celtic wisdom teachings, but embracing the contributions of many peoples and times. It means learning from archaic traditions, from three centuries of modern Druid scholarship, and from the always changing lessons of the living Earth itself. It means embracing an experiential approach to religious questions, one that abandons rigid belief systems in favor of inner development and individual contact with the realms of nature and spirit.

View of the Afterlife

Modern Druids believe in reincarnation and in the otherworld, a reality that exists beyond our physical senses. We can experience the otherworld during this life via dreams, visions, trances, or while meditating. We will ultimately travel to this place to rest there between our various incarnations.

Sacred Texts

Druidism sprang out of a Celtic culture steeped in folklore and ancient rituals. Though the Celts had a written language it was not widely used. In short, the mythical, religious, and philosophical ideas of Druidism were passed down orally, meaning modern practitioners of Druidism have no written scriptures.

Contemporary Druids have written more about their beliefs. The Henge of Keltria, for example, has a *Book of Ritual* that is revered by members of that group. Many other books about the Celts and Druids have been published in recent years. Much information has been posted on the Internet.

Worship Services

Druids meet together to share experiences and celebrate festivals of the year. Ivan Macbeth states, "As Wiccans have covens and Christians have congregations, so Druids have groves. The grove is a name chosen in honor of the trees, great beings of nature, friends, teachers, and providers of life."

Because water is thought by strict Druids to be a gateway to the gods, Druidic rites are often held in parks or near bodies of water—"holy" wells, rivers, lakes, bogs. Sacred oak groves are also a common Druid gathering place. Stonehenge, the mysterious circle of giant stones on the Salisbury Plain in England, is revered by modern Druids, who believe it to be an ancient temple. Dating from about 3000 BC, this structure may have functioned as a giant solar calendar.

Important Dates

Given their reverence for the earth and love of the natural order, most Druids celebrate the summer solstice (June 21/22), winter solstice (December 21/22), spring equinox. (March 21/22), and autumnal equinox (September 21/22). (These dates are for those living in the northern hemisphere.)

Also significant to the Druid calendar are the following festivals:

Samhain (November 1)—the traditional beginning of the Celtic New Year

Imbolc (February 1)—an honoring of the Mother Goddess

Beltane (May 1)—a celebration of spring

Lugnasash (August 1)—a harvest gathering

"The theology of Druze religion is called hikma, *and its main theme is that God incarnated himself in the Fatmid caliph al-Hakim, who they claim disappeared in 1021. While most Muslims believe he died in 1021, the Druze believe that al-Hakim is waiting to return to the world in order to bring a new golden age to true believers . . . . The Druze call themselves* muwahhidun, *'monotheists.'"*
—Encyclopedia of the Orient

Number of Followers

The *Druze* (as they are commonly called by others), or the *Mowahhidoon* (as they refer to themselves), number between half a million to one million adherents. It is a minority sect in every place it is practiced, mostly in the Middle East—Syria, Lebanon, Israel, and Jordan—and a small number who have immigrated to North America.

Major Figures/Prophets

- **Tariq al-Hakim**—an eleventh century Egyptian caliph (ruler) and an Islamic reformer, who was viewed by his followers first as a prophet, and then as the very incarnation of God Himself. His sudden and mysterious disappearance in 1021 contributed to his divine aura.

- **Hamza ibn 'Ali ibn-Ahmad**—the Persian architect of the

Belief	Druze
Sacred Text(s)	Kitab Al Hikma ("Book of Wisdom"), sometimes called Rasahl al-Hikma ("Letters of Wisdom")
Nature of God	Is one; God is the omniscient and omnipotent Creator; al-Hakim is the final incarnation of God
Jesus Christ	Revered as a prophet, along with other great men of religious and philosophical history (or by some, revered as an incarnation of divine intelligence, but not God)
Human nature	Man is an ancient spirit (inhabiting a series of bodies) on a journey through time, until the day when all spirits unite with the cosmic mind
About human need	Renounce all incomplete religions and recognize al-Hakim as the one visible God
Salvation	Druze believe they are "saved" by living devoutly as enlightened members of the faith
Afterlife	Heaven and hell are spiritual realities, not literal places; a follower experiences reincarnation until ultimate union with God or separation from Him forever

Major Differences from Christianity

Druze movement; devoted follower and close associate of al-Hakim, who championed the divinity of al-Hakim, prompting mainstream Muslims to label the group heretical.

- **Muhammad bin Ismail ad-Darazi**—the leader from whom the religion is thought to derive its name of "Druze."

- **Jethro**—the father-in-law of Moses, and one of their chief prophets. Many Druze make annual pilgrimages to his tomb in lower Galilee.

Short History

The entire Druze movement—its history and beliefs—is shrouded in secrecy and ambiguity. Scholars believe the faith originated in the eleventh century, thanks to al-Hakim, an Egyptian caliph (985–1021). Whether al-Hakim was attempting to reform Islam or author an entirely new faith is debated.

What is clear—from what little can be known about those who call themselves the Mowahhidoon—is that their beliefs appear to be a theological smorgasbord. There are elements of Greek Platonist philosophy, hints of Gnosticism and Islam, and nods to Judaism and far eastern religions.

Basic Beliefs and Values

Outsiders view the faith as a late offshoot of Islam that incorporates neo-Platonic ideas, Judaic mysticism, Hindu mythology, and assorted Iranian religious traditions (including Zoroastrianism). Adherents see themselves as possessors of the original and only true faith. They view other religions as later, impure, incomplete imitations.

Here are some of the unique features of the Druze:

The Druze Star

- They are strictly monotheistic and Unitarian.

- Their purpose is two-fold: (1) to strive for a favorable reincarnation by living purely, and (2) to wait for the reappearance of al-Hakim, believed to be an incarnation of God, who will inaugurate a Golden Age for the devout.

- They follow the Druze Code of Conduct: truthfulness, loyalty to the brother-hood, renouncing other religions, avoiding evil (including alcohol, tobacco, and eating pork) and evildoers, believing in the divine unity of mankind, and devotion and obedience to al-Hakim.

- They are secretive about their doctrines and rituals for fear of persecution in countries where they are a minority.

- Most Druze follow a practice called *taqiyya* ("dissimulation"), whereby they conceal their true beliefs and outwardly participate in whatever religion is practiced in the area in which they live.

- Women are allowed into the secret inner circle of the faith, and some re-searchers claim Druze even regard women as spiritually superior.

- Polygamy and marriage to anyone outside the sect is forbidden. Marrying outside the Mowahhidoon faith is thought to be grounds for divine retribu-tion in one's next reincarnation.

- There is no such thing as joining or converting to Druze—one must be born into the sect.

View of God

God is *al-Aqui al-Kulli* ("Universal Intelligence" or "Divine Essence"). The Druze view al-Hakim as divine. They sometimes pray to and refer to him as "our Lord."

Worldview

The Druze believe this world is corrupt and that they are the pure religious rem-nant. They look forward to a future golden age, when al-Hakim will return and usher in God's kingdom. Until that time, they live privately, guarding their religious iden-tity, and even fighting ferociously when threatened.

Sacred Texts

Given the secrecy of the Druze, it is difficult for outsiders to know with certainty the group's doctrinal details. Only the devout are given access to Druze holy books. The best-known text is called *Kitab al-Hikma* ("Book of Wisdom"), which is actually multiple volumes.

In addition, the Koran and the Judeo-Christian Bible are said to be respected and regarded as useful. Also, the writings of al-Hakim seem to be especially revered: *Al-Naqd al-Khafi* ("Copy of the Secret") and *Al-Juz'al-Awwal* ("Essence of the First").

View of the Afterlife

The Druze believe in instant reincarnation at death. Heaven and hell are not literal places but spiritual conditions. Hell is an estrangement from God and results in repeated reincarnations. Heaven is the final escape from the cycle of reincarnation.

Worship Services

The Druze gather for corporate prayer on Thursdays (not on Fridays, as is the practice in Islam) in modest temples called the *khalwa*. Nominal adherents are called *juhhal* ("the ignorant") and are not privy to the deep secrets of the faith. The most devout Druze are initiated into the secrets of the religion and are called the *Uqqal*. The elite members of the Uqqal are called the *Ajawid*.

Important Dates

Because the Druze fiercely guard their religious doctrines and beliefs, and since they are prone to hide their practices, there are no public Druze holidays. As stated above, they try to blend in with the prevailing religions where they live, meaning they participate in most Muslim rituals and holidays (except Ramadan and Hajj—the pilgrimage to Mecca).

"Dreams touch every level of our life. They may let us glimpse the future, or give suggestions for healing, or share insights into our relationships. Above all, they can and will steer us more directly toward God."
—Sri Harold Klemp

Number of Followers

Students of Eckankar (which means "co-worker with God") are called *chelas* (pronounced CHEE-LAHS) or *ECKists.* Though Eckankar doesn't publish membership figures, conservative estimates put the number of adherents at fifty thousand. Followers study at over three hundred Eckankar centers in more than a hundred countries around the world.

Major Figures/Prophets

- **John Paul Twitchell** (1908–1971)—a former Scientologist and founder of Eckankar in 1965; he called himself the "971st Living Eckankar Master"

- **Darwin Gross** (1928–current) —the successor to Paul Twitchell; his reign as the 972nd Living Eckankar Master ended in controversy

- **Harold Klemp** (1942–current) —a native of Wisconsin and former divinity student, Klemp discovered Eckankar in the 1960s. In 1981 he became Sri Harold Klemp, the Mahanta, the Living Eckankar Master, the spiritual leader of Eckankar; Klemp's spiritual name is *Wah Z,* "the Secret Doctrine"

Major Differences from Christianity

Belief	Eckankar
Sacred Text(s)	The *Shariyat-Ki-Sugmad* ("Way of the Eternal") by Paul Twitchell; other books by Harold Klemp
Nature of God	Sugmad—the formless, infinite Divine Spirit
Jesus Christ	Not emphasized prominently in this belief system; but regarded as a spiritual teacher who utilized soul travel
Human nature	Each person is a creative, divine spark of a loving God; each has a body, but is an eternal soul.
About human need	To gain experience, find truth, and learn how to give and receive love in order to find our way home to God
Salvation	Self-realization that leads to God-realization (via guidance from the Mahanta/Living Eckankar Master); this enables one to work off all bad karma in this lifetime
Afterlife	Death is not a finality; hell is not an Eckankar concept because of the group's belief in reincarnation

Short History

Eckankar, the "Religion of the Light and Sound of God," was founded by Paul Twitchell in 1965 in Las Vegas.

Twitchell, who had previously been a Scientology "clear" and a student of yoga master Kirpal Singh, advocated what he described as an ancient program of "soul transcendence" through spiritual exercises that would usher one into the presence of "the Divine Light and Sound." He claimed this teaching had been passed down through a long series of Eckankar masters, of which he was the 971st.

In 1971, Twitchell died, leaving the Eckankar movement in the care of Darwin Gross. Gross guided Eckankar from 1971 to 1981 (some sources say to 1983), until Harold Klemp took the reins of the organization following a bitter personal and legal battle for control. Followers of Gross maintain that Klemp excised all references to Gross from Eckankar's official history and publications.

Under Klemp's leadership, Eckankar relocated from San Francisco to suburban Minneapolis and built a temple complex.

Basic Beliefs and Values

Some of Eckankar's distinctive teachings and features are as follows:

- *Leadership*—The Mahanta is regarded as the wise spiritual power that inhabits the Living Eckankar Master. This Master is respected but not worshipped. His role is to help spiritual novices and apprentices gain wisdom and experience the Light and Sound of God. He is not a savior, but a way-shower.

- *Light and Sound of God*—The Holy Spirit is the divine current that flows from God and sustains life, and is manifested in both light (for example, burning bushes, stained glass, candles, and so forth) and sound (for example, chanting and singing); Eckankar aims to teach adherents how to recognize God's Light and Sound.

- *Membership*—Official membership in Eckankar is said to link one with the Mahanta, the Living Eckankar Master, who is able to guide seekers home to the heart of God. Anyone is welcome to join. Adherents of other faiths may join Eckankar without dissolving their existing affiliations. Memberships are available to those eighteen and older, for an annual fee. For this price, members receive the quarterly publication called *Mystic World*, plus monthly Eckankar discourses—sacred letters written by the spiritual leader of Eckankar.

- *Initiation*—During the first year of membership, most ECKists experience their first initiation, usually in the form of a dream. A second initiation is often requested after two years of membership. ECKists claim this process leads to greater spiritual awareness and a new sense of spiritual stability and strength.

- *Dreams*—Eckankar believes dreams are a window to the deep needs of the soul and the life-changing realities of the spiritual realm; it teaches ECKists how to gain spiritual insight by learning to interpret dreams; the Mahanta is the Dream Master who can guide followers through dreaming to spiritual discovery and enlightenment.

- *Soul Travel*—An experience that helps one regain a spiritual viewpoint and a higher state of consciousness when life becomes overwhelming; this ability is developed by engaging in various spiritual exercises, all of which can be learned in Eckankar classes and workshops.

- *Singing HU*—Eckankar teaches that HU is an ancient name for God, a word that both represents the love of God and serves as an expression of love for God. By singing HU, one is lifted spiritually, making one happier and more aware of God's love.

- *Prayer*—for ECKists, prayer is contemplation not intercession or petition. "We don't try to tell God what to do. We listen to hear what God's Voice is saying to us" (Sri Harold Klemp).

View of God

God is referred to as *Sugmad* by ECKists, and regarded as neither male nor female. People connect to God through an Eckankar current, which may take the form of sound or light. The sound is thought to be God's voice, beckoning followers to come home. The light is considered a beacon to light the path home to God.

Worldview

Since the goal of Eckankar is individual spiritual growth, even difficulties are viewed in a positive manner. They are further opportunities to practice the disciplines of Eckankar and make progress in the journey toward self-realization and God-realization.

Eckankar's teachings about soul travel, dream interpretation, and pondering past lives mean ECKists tend to approach life in an almost adventurous manner. They exude a positive, upbeat manner, but do not proselytize actively.

The goal in everyday life is to become a coworker with God and serve others with love, kindness, compassion, and understanding.

Sacred Texts

ECKists consider Paul Twitchell's *The Shariyat-Ki-Sugmad* their main holy text. They describe the book this way: "Through *The Shariyat-Ki-Sugmad* you will discover an answer to every human question ever yet, or to be, devised. Its pages tell what life really consists of and how to live it. Eckankar is ancient wisdom for today. Its teachings, which resurfaced in 1965, emphasize the value of personal experiences as the most natural way back to God. Whatever your religious background, they show how to look and listen within yourself—to expand your consciousness and enjoy spiritual connectedness. See for yourself—perhaps for the first time—how to lead a happy, balanced, and productive life."

View of the Afterlife

Similar to Hindus and Buddhists, ECKists believe that wrongs done (passions such as anger, lust, greed, materialism, and pride) accumulate as a kind of spiritual debt (karma). This debt must be paid in future lives before one can experience reunion with God. When this karma is finally and fully paid, the reincarnation cycle ends. Eckankar additionally claims to help people recall their past lives.

Worship Services

The Temple of Eckankar (also known as the "Golden Wisdom Temple"), completed in 1990, is located on 174 acres in Chanhassaen, Minnesota. Harold Klemp, the spiritual leader of Eckankar, says that the temple is "the starting place for the soul's dream of reaching God." It offers daily tours and hosts weekly classes, workshops, seminars and discussions about past lives, soul travel, and the meaning of dreams. On the first Sunday of each month, a 10:00 a.m. worship service is held in the eight hundred-seat sanctuary. This gathering is intended to open one's heart to God's love and features creative arts, "dynamic" speakers, and singing HU, an ancient name for God.

Important Dates

There are no specific holidays cited as unique to Eckankar. One online source states that ECKists observe the following:

Founder's Day (September 17)
Spiritual New Year (October 22)

"Falun Dafa is practiced according to the evolution principle of the Universe. Therefore what we cultivate is Great Law and Great Tao."
—Master Li Hongzhi, in *Zhuan Falun*

Major Differences from Christianity

Belief	Falun Dafa/Falun Gong
Sacred Text(s)	*Zhuan Falun* and *Falun Gong* by Li Hongzhi
Nature of God	Because the movement insists it is not a religion, it makes no overt references to God
Jesus Christ	Christ is not emphasized; founder Li Hongzhi is revered by followers as a great, enlightened teacher, but not a savior or deity.
Human nature	Confused, susceptible to alien beings bent on corrupting the human race; unnecessarily unhealthy and unenlightened
About human need	Need to pursue physical health, cultivate moral virtue (truthfulness, kindness, and tolerance) and develop untapped spiritual/mental potential
Salvation	Practicing Falun Gong, which means to tap one's inner strength and achieve a higher realm of spiritual awareness and existence
Afterlife	Emphasis is on living better and with more awareness in this life

Number of Followers

Falun Gong claims eighty million Chinese adherents, and another twenty million worldwide. (The Chinese government puts the number closer to between two million and three million.)

Major Figures/Prophets

- **Li Hongzhi** (1951 or 1952–present)—called "Master Li" by Falun Gong followers, he was born in northeastern China in either 1951 or 1952. (Hongzhi claims May 13—also the supposed birthday of Buddha—1951; the Chinese government says he was born on July 7, 1952.) Hongzhi's approved biography reports his training by Buddhist and Taoist masters as a child. The BBC calls him "a former trumpet player." Mr. Li has lived in New York since 1998.

Short History

Established in 1992, Falun Dafa (that is, "the great wheel of universal laws or principles") is a popular, but controversial Chinese spiritual movement that practices Falun Gong (which means the "cultivation of the wheel," referring to the Buddhist wheel of Dharma, page 17). Technically, Falun Dafa is the name of the group, and Falun Gong refers to the practices of the group; however, the group is commonly called Falun Gong.

In early 1999, the Chinese government launched a crackdown against various spiritual movements and religious groups. On April 25 of that year, some ten thousand Falun Gong practitioners responded by protesting peacefully in front of the Communist Party headquarters in Beijing. The size of this protest alarmed authorities, resulting in the group being branded as a cult and outlawed in July 1999. Since

Li Hongzhi, founder

that time, many Falun Gong leaders and followers have been harassed, arrested, and sentenced to prison terms. This religious persecution has prompted an international outcry and demand for religious freedom in China. Founder Li Hongzhi relocated to New York just before this severe crackdown.

Basic Beliefs and Values

Like the majority of those living in Eastern Asian cultures, practitioners of Falun Gong practice a form of *Qi-gong* (also spelled ch'i or chi, and pronounced "chee"). Qi (which means "steam" or "breath") refers to the basic element of creation, the essential life force and energy in every form of existence. This energy can be accessed, channeled, or cultivated through slow, deliberate movements and stretches, accompanied by meditation.

Li Hongzhi teaches that the Falun, or wheel, which is the center of spiritual energy, is localized within each person's navel. This wheel spins in concert with the universe and both absorbs energy from the universe and emits negative elements from the body. Practitioners who faithfully follow the regimen prescribed by Master Li believe they awaken and strengthen this Falun.

Falun Gong advocates five exercises, a combination of bodily movements—performed to the accompaniment of music—and stillness. It also encourages a healthy lifestyle (often vegetarianism) and various meditative practices. The movement further adds a vague spiritual emphasis on reaching higher dimensions. Thus, Falun Gong, followed in the manner prescribed by Master Li, is believed to result not only in good physical health and mental renewal, but also in spiritual transcendence.

The emblem of Falun Dafa/Falun Gong was designed to symbolize in miniature the universe, as described by the teachings of Buddhism and Taoism. Hongzhi teaches that all truth and religious belief are subsumed within these two fundamental schools of thought. The emblem consists of two concentric circles. In the center circle is a large symbol that many Westerners would call a Nazi swastika. However, this ancient symbol, called a *manji*, is widely considered a sign of good fortune in China and is intended to represent the "Buddha School." In the outer, larger circle are four smaller, curvier manji symbols interspersed with four *taiji* ("Yin-Yang") symbols. Two taiji are red and blue; the other two are red and black. The difference is meant to suggest the various dimensions and manifestations of spiritual reality. These four taiji are meant to represent the "Tao School."

View of God

Falun Gong websites are adamant that the movement is not a religion, despite its use of certain Buddhist and Taoist phrases. References to a Supreme Being are nonexistent. Rather than encouraging the worship of a deity and requiring adherence to a strict list of sectarian rules, Falun devotees insist their emphasis is on cultivating the universal moral virtues of truthfulness, benevolence, and tolerance, and pursuing physical health and mental wholeness.

Enlightened followers of Falun Dafa are said to be able to see with their "celestial eye" that this Falun emblem is rotating in a clockwise direction. Says Hongzhi, in lecture five of *Zhuan Falun*, "The whole universe is in motion, and so are all galaxies within it."

Some deeper Falun Gong teachings read like a Star Wars/Jedi-Master training course, with discussions of telekinesis (the ability to move objects without touching them), flying, walking through walls, entering new dimensions, time-shifting, and even transforming substances. One of Hongzhi's more bizarre teachings is that demonic space aliens are here on the earth engaged in an attempt to destroy the human race. Li believes this effort is being realized through many of the practices of modern science and medicine. He insists that illness is the result of karma, not viruses or pathogens. Medical testing, which is limited to this physical dimension only, is incapable of isolating the true cause of sickness. In light of this belief, Falun Gong members sometimes shun medical treatment, a fact that has aroused the ire of the Chinese government.

View of the Afterlife

There are no explicit references to heaven or eternity in basic Falun Dafa teaching or in Falun Gong practices. The emphasis is on bettering one's experience in this life.

Sacred Texts

Adherents read and study the writings and lectures of Li Hongzhi, especially Zhaun Falun. While these texts are viewed as helpful for growth, they are not considered absolutely necessary.

Worldview

The Falun Dafa/Falun Gong movement is rooted in ancient Chinese folklore and practices and represents an amalgamation of Buddhist principles, certain teachings of Taoism and Confucianism, with a few tenets of New Age thinking thrown in.

Adherents (most living under a Communist regime that views all religious activity with suspicion) insist Falun Gong is not a religion in the pure sense, but more a practical, moral philosophy and a healthy lifestyle that can enhance and complement any spiritual pursuit.

Worship Services

Rather than organizing and attending weekly services, those who practice Falun Dafa/Falun Gong incorporate its teachings and practices into their daily lives. The movement is very loose, unstructured, and unorganized. There are no temples, no religious hierarchy, no clergy, no headquarters, no requirements or costs to join.

Important Dates

Probably because of Falun Gong's fierce desire to avoid appearing to be an organized movement, official and unofficial sources do not make reference to any kind of religious calendar, nor do they highlight certain days as being special religious holidays.

"We affirm that every Being contains the 'Sacred Flame,' a Spark of the Divine, and that Awareness of the Sacred Flame within constitutes the highest level of Self-Knowledge and the Experience of God simultaneously. This act of Awareness, which is held to be liberating, transcendent and experiential, is called Gnosis."
—The Apostolic Johannite Church

Major Differences from Christianity

Belief	Gnosticism
Sacred Text(s)	The Nag Hammadi texts, which include the so-called Gnostic Gospels (discovered in 1945)
Nature of God	The Supreme God is largely unknowable; the God of the Bible is a lesser god who is spiteful, cruel, and evil
Jesus Christ	Christ was sent by the Supreme God to save the human race by revealing secret knowledge; primarily a messenger and an example; only "appeared" to take on a body and only "seemed" to die on the cross
Human nature	Divine spirits imprisoned in material bodies
About human need	Need liberation from ignorance, deception, and the trap of evil matter through firsthand knowledge of God and the things of God
Salvation	By *gnosis* (Greek word meaning "knowledge") of the inner soul and secret things of God
Afterlife	Only those possessing (or at least seeking) divine knowledge will be reunited with God; all others will be annihilated

Number of Followers

Since Gnosticism manifests itself more often as a set of ancient, underlying philosophical ideas (and less often as an official religion or organized group), it is difficult to state accurately how many people hold Gnostic beliefs or engage in Gnostic behaviors.

Major Figures/Prophets

Some of the influential thinkers, theologians, authors, and philosophers who have contributed to Gnosticism's development and spread are:

- **Philo of Alexandria** (20 BC–AD 50)—Jewish philosopher who attempted to harmonize Judaism with Greek philosophy

- **Simon Magus** (c. AD 35–40)—a sorcerer and influential spiritual leader encountered by the original apostles (see Acts 8:9–24)

- **Cerinthus** (c. AD 100)—proponent of the idea that the Christ-spirit descended on the man Jesus at His baptism and left Him at the crucifixion, thus denying the divinity of Jesus

- **Basilides** (early second century)—a teacher in Alexandria, Egypt, who advocated a Christian dualism tinged with Zoroastrian beliefs

- **Valentinus** (100–160)—aligned Christian teachings with Greek Platonism, becoming a proponent of the dualistic idea that our imperfect world is the work of Jehovah, a lesser god (and not the Supreme Being)

- **Marcion** (110–160)—an early promoter of the Gnostic idea of dualism

- **Mani** (216–c. 277)—the founder of Manichaeism, a dualistic and ancient Gnostic religion with elaborate theories about the origins of the cosmos

- **Elaine Pagels** (1943–present)—an influential Princeton University religion professor; author of *The Gnostic Gospels* and *Beyond Belief: The Secret Gospel of Thomas*

- **Dan Brown** (1964–present)—author of the best-selling book *The Da Vinci Code*, a novel that purports to be rooted in historical fact, and that popularized the idea that Gnostic beliefs about Christ were suppressed by the Church

Dan Brown, bestselling author whose book The DaVinci Code *popularized Gnosticism*

Short History

Gnosticism (nahst-i-sih-sum) is derived from the Greek word *gnosis,* which literally means "knowledge." It refers to an experiential, relational knowledge of the divine. Unlike spiritual belief systems that have a founder and a defining moment, Gnosticism's history is long and murky. It might be likened to a snowball that has rolled down through time, morphing slowly as it accumulated new ideas, aspects, and players.

The roots of Gnosticism are believed to lie deep in the soil of assorted ancient cultures and religions. Egypt, Babylon, India, Persia, China, and Greece contributed philosophical and spiritual seeds to this mystical, syncretistic religion.

However, Gnosticism as a movement did not exert widespread influence until the late first century to early second century. This is evident because during the early first and second centuries on into the fourth century, the writings and rulings of the early church fathers were filled with denunciations of the ideas now grouped together to form Gnosticism. In fact, until the discovery of the Nag Hammadi codices (the writings of ancient Gnostics) in 1945 in Egypt, the only information about Gnosticism came from the anti-Gnostic writings of the early church fathers. Two prominent examples are Irenaeus, who wrote *Against Heresies* in AD 180, and Tertullian, who around AD 200, penned many works against Gnostic ideas, including *The Prescription Against Heretics, Against Marcion, Against the Valentinians,* and *Against Praxeas.* Many of the great church councils dealt with serious theological controversies generated by Gnostic teachings.

The Mandeans (in Iran and Iraq) are thought to be the only Gnostic sect that has existed continuously since the first century. Members of this sect number only a few thousand.

With the publication of the Nag Hammadi library in the 1960s and 1970s, there has been a revival of scholarly and public interest in Gnosticism.

Basic Beliefs and Values

As a philosophy, basic Gnostic teachings include:

- God is found in the self or in the "I" (that is, human souls are divine sparks from the upper world).

- Human souls/divine spirits are trapped in the evil physical, bodily realm. This pitting of the material against the spiritual is called *Dualism.*

- The pursuit of secret knowledge; *gnosis* means "knowledge," and only an elite group of seekers are granted the privilege of acquiring this knowledge.

Some religions that embrace one or more of these tenets of Gnosticism include a few sects within Sufi Islam, Kabbalah, Sikhism, and Buddhism, plus a few denominations in the broader Christian tradition.

As a stand-alone religion in and of itself, Gnostic beliefs can include:

- The Supreme God of the universe (possessing both male and female traits) created a group of divine yet finite beings called *Aeons*. One of these, named Sophia (meaning "Wisdom"), gave birth to a lesser god, or Demiurge, who then created the imperfect, messed-up world in which we live. This lesser god is the so-called Jehovah of the Bible, the God of Abraham and Moses. Gnostics view this god with disdain, regarding him as fundamentally prideful, uncompassionate, jealous, petty, and rigid.

- Christ was not truly human, but only "seemed" to have a body (an idea called *Docetism*).

- The divine Christ was resurrected spiritually before the physical death of the man Jesus on the cross (an idea first propagated by Cerinthus).

- The serpent in the Garden of Eden (see Genesis 3), far from being an evil seducer, was actually a noble helper, trying to help the human couple gain necessary knowledge (belief held only by some Gnostic sects).

- The conviction that they possess the little-known secrets of God and the true, long-lost message of Jesus.

View of God

The true Supreme God is hidden and practically unknowable. This Godhead transcends the universe. The God worshipped by Christians is a lesser god (Demiurge) who created the imperfect, evil world in which we live.

Worldview

Gnosticism is dualistic. It sees the material world as evil and the invisible realm of the spirit as good. It teaches that the world did not become evil because of some supposed sin by humanity in the Garden of Eden; rather, it was imperfect and inferior from the start, because it was the work of a lesser god.

Gnosticism also sees humans as essentially divine, but ignorant and blinded—sparks of God trapped in fleshly prisons.

The implications of these beliefs cause many knowledge-seeking Gnostics to embrace asceticism (shunning all physical pleasures, because the body is evil, and one should be devoted only to the spiritual). Other Gnostics practice libertinism or hedonism, reasoning that since the body is inferior to the spirit, it doesn't matter what one does physically, so long as one seeks and acquires ultimate spiritual knowledge.

View of the Afterlife

Death releases human souls from the prison of the human body. Ignorant souls who do not bother to seek true spiritual knowledge and live only for physical, fleshly pleasure will be lost forever. Seekers who diligently pursue truth may be saved (even if they never gain the ultimate gnosis). The spiritually enlightened (that is, possessors of true knowledge) will be saved and reunited with the Supreme God, no matter how they lived.

Worship Services

There are a few organized groups and/or congregations that identify themselves as Gnostic, but most adherents hold their beliefs privately. Gnostic churches practice sacraments, and in many ways function the same way as traditional churches do.

Sacred Texts

In 1945, an Egyptian peasant unearthed a stone jar containing thirteen leather-bound, papyrus books, containing fifty-two (some sources say fifty-one) separate works. The majority of these works was not previously known to exist. These writings are now known collectively as the Nag Hammadi library. These "Gnostic Scriptures" are believed to have been buried between AD 360–390. Translated into English in the late 1960s and 1970s, these texts have sparked much research, speculation, and debate. Conservative mainstream Christians deride them as spurious works of heresy. Others believe them to reveal long lost secrets of the true teachings of Jesus and the early church.

Important Dates

Holidays are not emphasized, but a few Gnostic congregations follow a traditional liturgical calendar.

"*A growing number of anthropologists and archeo-mythologists . . . argue that the prevailing ideology of belief in prehistoric Europe and much of the world was based on the worship of a single earth goddess, who was assumed to be the fount of all life and who radiated harmony among all. . . . The last vestige of organized goddess worship was eliminated by Christianity. . . . [I]t seems obvious that a better understanding of a religious heritage preceding our own by so many thousands of years could offer us new insights.*"
—Al Gore, *Earth in the Balance*

Major Differences from Christianity

Belief	Goddess Worship
Sacred Text(s)	No definitive "holy writ," but many instructive modern writings (and the goddess as an ever-present inner guide)
Nature of God	A mixture of polytheism and pantheism; many goddesses that all emanate from a feminine force that both permeates and is the universe
Jesus Christ	No consensus belief; for some He was a myth, for some a moral teacher who elevated women, for others an enlightened guru/example who recognized His own divinity
Human nature	Both male and female, but patriarchal religions and cultures have suppressed the feminine, oppressing women and denying their own femininity
About human need	Need to abandon the prevailing patriarchal structures and return to humanity's original matriarchal spirituality
Salvation	Awakening to and embracing the healing, feminist energy that permeates life
Afterlife	No consensus belief, except that the soul, which is divine, is immortal

Number of Followers

A recent survey found that two hundred thousand to three hundred thousand women practice goddess worship in the United States. There may be many more who dabble in it because it empowers women.

Major Figures/Prophets

A few of the more prominent goddesses worshipped through the ages are:

- **Gaia** (also known as Mother Earth, the Great Goddess)—the Greek goddess who personifies the earth
- **Sophia**— the Gnostic soul or spark that emanates from the feminine aspect of God
- **Diana**—the Roman goddess of the hunt, the moon, and of chastity
- **Freyja**—a fertility goddess in Norse mythology
- **Isis**— a fertility goddess worshipped in ancient Egypt
- **Venus**—the Roman goddess of love and beauty and fertility
- **Aphrodite**—the Greek goddess of love and beauty and fertility
- **The Virgin Mary**—the mother of Christ, whom some regard as divine

A few of the influential contemporary figures within goddess worship are:

- **James Lovelock** (1919–present)—British scientist who proposed the Gaia hypothesis (that is, the notion that the earth is not only eternal, but is a living, breathing organism; Mother Earth)
- **Starhawk** (1951–present)—prominent author, feminist, and witch in Berkeley, California
- **Sue Monk Kidd**—bestselling author of *The Secret Life of Bees* and *The Dance of the Dissident Daughter* (a memoir of her journey from Christian faith to the belief in the Sacred Feminine)
- **The living goddesses of Nepal** (also known as *kumaris*)—little girls, between the ages of two and puberty, chosen on the basis of their beauty, worshipped by both Hindus and Buddhists, and thought to watch over the country's health and economic prosperity.

Short History

Goddess worship, its adherents claim, originated in ancient primitive societies. French cave paintings, for example, said to be twenty thousand to thirty thousand years old and believed to be from the Paleolithic Era, depict a matriarchal world. Dependent upon bountiful harvests, successful hunts, fruitful flocks, and abundant off-

An ancient wall painting of Isis

spring to carry on the traditions of the tribe, these early human cultures are thought to have believed in a life-giving force of fertility. Regarded as feminine, this force, this "goddess" of the earth and of nature was sought, honored, and called upon for blessing and help. Archaeologists have unearthed thousands of naked, well-endowed "goddess statues" that seem to suggest a reliance upon and reverence for one or more feminine deities.

Influential feminist historians speculate that during the centuries that this ancient European goddess culture was in place, the various inhabitants lived mostly in peace, and that men and women enjoyed equality. However, the invasion of Indo-Europeans from the East is said to have introduced a more aggressive, male-dominated worldview. The gods of these invaders were masculine; rather than reverencing nature, these new peoples "raped" the earth. Rather than being peace-loving, these newcomers were war-like. The role of women in society changed drastically, and not in good or beneficial ways. Matriarchal culture became patriarchal.

By the time history began to be recorded, women occupied a secondary, often subservient role in most cultures. As pagan religions gave way to the rise of the great monotheistic faith traditions (such as Judaism, Christianity, and Islam), feminine influence in religious and societal matters was minimized. As one online source puts it, "The God, King, Priest, and Father replaced the Goddess, Queen, Priestess, and Mother."

Modern goddess worship is a phenomenon that seems to have been sparked by the revival of interest in Wicca (page 240) in the mid-twentieth century. The women's rights movement in the late 1960s and early 1970s, coupled with the explosion of New Age (page 154) beliefs and practices in the 1980s, has launched a rapidly growing belief in feminist spirituality.

Basic Beliefs and Values

Goddess worship is not a centralized, monolithic movement. It is a patchwork quilt of individuals and organizations coming from assorted starting points. This means beliefs, emphases, and practices among goddess worshippers vary greatly. Adherents have diverse influences, individual passions, and unique motivations that may include any or all of the following: feminism, environmentalism, Wicca, Jungian psychology, New Age beliefs, and so forth. One must be careful not to make sweeping statements; for example, it would be inaccurate to assume that all goddess worshippers practice Wicca, or that all feminists are goddess worshippers.

Given this great diversity, goddess worship takes many forms. Yet some general observations can be made:

- The "goddess" is widely regarded as the sacred, feminine, positive energy force that permeates the world.

- Goddess spirituality is polytheistic—the goddess is thought to be represented by countless female deities (see above list), who are nurturing, mysterious, and loving like the earth, or like a mother.

- Goddess worship is typically viewed as the ancient and original belief system in the world. Unlike modern, male-dominated religion that is often aggressive and destructive, goddess worship is seen as uniquely capable of giving birth to peace and harmony.

- Goddess worship is usually tinged with a pantheistic worldview: "The symbolism of the Goddess is not a parallel structure to the symbolism of God the Father. The goddess does not rule the world; She is the world" (Starhawk).

- All the deep, necessary knowledge of the universe is within, and one needs only to seek truth within.

- Women should reclaim their rightful place as the priestesses of their own lives; the indwelling divine intuition means no intermediaries are needed.

- Men are encouraged to embrace goddess spirituality, but this will require their giving up power, exercising humility, and surrendering to the sacred feminine that is without and within.

- In some goddess worship sects, there is an overt emphasis upon nudity and sexual fulfillment through magic or Hindu tantric practices. This adds greatly to its allure.

View of God

Adherents of goddess worship believe that a divine energy permeates the universe, and each person is an essential expression of this power. Goddess spirituality insists this ultimate force is not a "he" but a "she." In the words of historian Merlin Stone, "In the beginning, people prayed to the Creatress of Life, the Mistress of Heaven. At the very dawn of religion, God was a woman."

Says Reverend Ava of the Goddess Temple of Orange County, California, "When our only God is a scary, punitive, remote Father in the Sky, it's hard for people to feel the nurturing, protective, compassionate aspect of the divine, and to show that loving face to one another. Even though the more recent New Testament/Christian God is often referred to as compassionate and loving, the actual underpinning of our overall societal beliefs about God seems still to be the Old Testament God of punishment, wrath and fear. And he's way up there in the sky somehow, far away, transcendent, not inside, not part of us."

Among goddess worshippers, God is referred to in multiple ways: Holy Spirit, the Eternal, Great Mother, Goddess, Ground of Being, or the Sacred Feminine Power for Good.

Worldview

Why is goddess spirituality so popular? What is its draw? It challenges male-dominated power structures and empowers women. It is esoteric and sometimes erotic. It promises a spirituality that understands women's unique needs and corresponds to their experience. It is ecologically and environmentally sensitive, pledging to heal the earth and bring peace to humanity.

Worship Services

Individual goddess worshippers often choose a goddess, erect small home altars, and then devote themselves to a lifetime of knowing, worshipping, and serving the goddess they have selected.

View of the Afterlife	Sacred Texts
Views on the afterlife vary. Few goddess worshippers believe in a literal heaven or hell. Most hold pantheistic beliefs in reincarnation or reabsorption into cosmic oneness, because the divine soul within is eternal.	Goddess worshippers do not embrace a single holy book; however, many contemporary writings enjoy a wide readership. Among the more influential books are: *The Spiral Dance* by Starhawk, *Drawing Down the Moon* by Margot Adler, and *The Once and Future Goddess* by Elinor Gadon.

There are also a few formal congregations of goddess worshippers, such as the Goddess Temple of Orange County, California. These women, who are of "The Sacred Feminine, priestessing the earth towards peace and prosperity," have Sunday services for women, as well as hosting workshops and seminars.

Important Dates

Depending on one's background (Wicca, Hinduism, New Age, and so forth), different holy days are celebrated. A single "Goddess Worship" calendar does not exist.

> *"Integration and assimilation into gajikané [that is, non-Roma] society have always threatened the preservation of Romani customs, traditions, and language. The Roma ability to adapt to new environments in order to survive has been responsible for the loss of many customs forgotten with time. Understanding these threats can prevent the further loss of a unique and misunderstood culture."*
> —The World Wide Web Virtual Library: "Roma/Gypsies An Introduction"

Number of Followers

"Gypsies" (also known as Romanies or Travelers) is the popular designation for the Roma (literally meaning "people"), whose ancestors migrated from India to Asia and Europe. An accurate count is impossible to determine, not only because a number of Roma continue to practice the nomadic lifestyle of their forefathers but also because they often choose to remain in their own exclusive Romani-speaking subcultures on the fringes of society. Estimates range from ten million up to twenty million worldwide, the largest concentration living in central and eastern Europe.

Belief	Gypsies
Sacred Text(s)	Since it is common for "Gypsies" (also known as *Roma*) to become adherents of the prevailing faith in the areas in which they live, fundamental beliefs vary significantly—from Christianity (including Eastern Orthodoxy) to Islam. Whatever religion they practice, they typically retain ancient customs and superstitious practices.
Nature of God	
Jesus Christ	
Human nature	
About human need	
Salvation	
Afterlife	

Major Figures/Prophets

None are given.

Short History

Researchers have concluded that the modern-day Romani people are the descendants of a Hindu people group from Northern India/Pakistan (the Punjab region). Migrating north and west to southern Europe (beginning about AD 1000), many Roma became goddess worshippers of Kali, holding for a time to a belief system similar to Wicca (page 240).

Over succeeding centuries, the Roma continued this constant relocation and migration, gradually assimilating (at least religiously) into European culture. Specific beliefs tended to vary according to where groups of Roma settled. Many converted to Christianity or Islam.

Some two hundred thousand to five hundred thousand Gypsies are believed to have been murdered during the Nazi Holocaust.

Basic Beliefs and Values

As stated, Roma typically embrace the dominant religion of the culture in which they happen to live; however, many supplement any adopted spiritual belief with traditional "Gypsy" supernatural beliefs, taboos, and practices. These may include:

Gypsy children in Eastern Europe

- Faith in omens and curses (called *amria*).

- Fortune-telling (that is, spiritual advising of non-Roma by a woman called a *drabardi*), often using tarot cards.

- Healing rituals that often involve use of herbs, or acts such as shaking a tree to transfer one's fever to the tree.

- Superstitious reliance on good luck charms (for example, horseshoes), talismans, and amulets to prevent misfortune or ward off illness.

- Widespread belief in ghosts (*mulo*), who are regarded as "living dead," possibly seeking to exact revenge on those who harmed the deceased; thus, when a Roma dies, relatives and friends often gather to settle grievances or ask forgiveness.

- To keep evil spirits from entering the body of the deceased, wax is often inserted into the nostrils; to help the departed in the next world, valuables and tools are sometimes placed in the coffin; other possessions are destroyed or sold to non-Roma.

View of God

There is no one view of God. Muslim Roma worship Allah; Christian Roma adhere to biblical notions of the Almighty.

Worldview

The Roma in most locales tend to keep to themselves in family/clan groups. This leeriness is almost certainly due to a long, documented history of persecution (including many state-sponsored pogroms) and cultural ostracism by the majority population. The designation "Gypsy," originating from a now-debunked theory that the Roma people were of Egyptian descent, is looked upon as a pejorative term.

The Romani chakra, a wheel with sixteen spokes, is the official symbol of the Roma people since 1971. It was chosen for two reasons: it resembles a Hindu chakra wheel, commemorating the group's Indian heritage; and it looks like a wagon wheel.

View of the Afterlife

The Roma views of the afterlife vary, depending on the religious system to which a Roma adheres. Whatever their official "faith," many still cling to traditional Gypsy beliefs, which include reincarnation (coming back as humans or animals), or even returning to earth as a ghost to settle affairs with one's former enemies in life.

Sacred Texts

These are determined by the religious tradition a Roma embraces. There are no traditional "Gypsy" holy books.

©iStockphoto.com/David Cannings-Bushell

A typical Gypsy wagon in England

Worship Services

Worship services depend on the faith tradition to which a Roma belongs. Wedding ceremonies are simple. For example, in previous generations, the couple would jump over a broomstick in front of family witnesses. Marrying a non-Roma is frowned upon. Many Roma prefer to baptize their infants in running water.

Important Dates

Two Roma festivals or holidays are worth noting:

Saintes-Maries de la Mer (May 24–26)—an annual pilgrimage to the Camargue region of France by Roma worldwide to pay homage to Sara-la-Kali ("Sarah the Black" who, according to Romani legend, was the servant of the Virgin Mary when Mary journeyed to France following the death of Christ)

Sainte Anne de Beaupre (July 26)—a festival in Quebec, Canada, that honors Saint Anne

"Krishna consciousness is not something imposed on the mind. On the contrary, it's already inside of each of us, waiting to come out, like fire in a match. Chanting Hare Krishna brings out that natural, pure state of mind. . . . Krishna and His energy are fully present in the sound of the mantra, so even if we don't know the language or intellectually understand how it works, by coming in touch with Krishna, we'll become happy, and our life will become sublime. Hare Krishna Hare Krishna Krishna Krishna Hare Hare / Hare Rama Hare Rama Rama Rama Hare Hare"
—Hare Krishna Web site description

Belief	Hare Krishna-ISKCON
Sacred Text(s)	Bhagavad-Gita, the Vedas
Nature of God	One God, Krishna ("all-attractive"), who lives within all
Jesus Christ	Not an incarnation of God, but an enlightened teacher who taught his disciples to meditate
Human nature	An immortal, non-material, or spiritual self, which is part of the Godhead
About human need	Realization not repentance; enlightenment, not forgiveness; devotion, not grace
Salvation	*Mukhti* ("liberation") through *bhakti* ("devotion")
Afterlife	Reincarnation, until one is ultimately freed from the cycle of rebirth and death

Major Differences from Christianity

Number of Followers

Hare Krishnas, as they are commonly known, claim that worldwide there are ten thousand temple devotees and two hundred and fifty thousand congregational devotees. Other sources set the figure as high as one million followers worldwide. They report there are sixty rural communities, fifty schools, and sixty Krishna-owned restaurants. They sometimes refer to themselves as *Gaudiya Vaisnavas*, due to their roots in the Gaudiya Vaisnava Hindu tradition.

Major Figures/Prophets

- **Sri Caitanya Mahaprabhu** (1485–1533)—a fifteenth-century Hindu reformer and saint, who was revered by his followers as a direct incarnation of Krishna

- **Srila Bhaktivinoda Thakura** —a nineteenth-century Hindu theologian, who taught the principles of Krishna consciousness to a modern audience

- **Bhaktisiddhanta Sarasvati Thakura**—the son of Bhaktivonoda Thakura, and a guru in his own right
- **His Divine Grace A. C. Bhaktivedanta Swami Prabhupada** (1896–1977)—also known as Srila Prabhupada, the official founder of the International Society for Krishna Consciousness (ISKCON) in 1966 in New York City

Short History

Long before the twentieth century, when Hare Krishnas were recognized for shaving their heads, chanting in red saffron robes, and selling magazines at airports, the ideals of Krishna consciousness were championed. In the 1400s, an Indian reformer named Sri Caitanya, and his associates, the Six Goswamis (that is, influential teachers or gurus) of Vrindavana, were the catalysts for a new and wildly popular devotional movement growing out of the Gaudiya Vaisnava branch of Hinduism. From the Hindu Vedas and other scriptures, they collected and compiled hundreds of volumes on the philosophy of Krishna consciousness. Sri Caitanya even came to be revered as a direct incarnation of Krishna.

A.C. Bhaktivedanta Swami Prabhupada

Several centuries later, another Vaisnava theologian named Srila Bhaktivinoda Thakura gave the movement new impetus. His son, a guru named Bhaktisiddhanta Sarasvati Thakura, is credited with mentoring Srila Prabhupada and instructing him to spread Krishna consciousness in the West.

Thus, in 1966 in New York, the International Society for Krishna Conciousness, or ISKCON, was officially founded by the then seventy-year-old A. C. Bhaktivedanta Swami Prabhupada, also known as Srila Prabhupada.

In 1967, Prabhupada traveled to San Francisco and began seeking disciples there. The group received great media attention when celebrities like George Harrison (of Beatles fame) and poet Allen Ginsberg dabbled in the movement.

In 1970, Srila Prabhupada formed a Governing Body Commission (GBC) to help manage the growing ISKCON. Before he died in 1977, he arranged for executive authority for the group be passed to this Commission. The GBC decides ISKCON's major strategies and guidelines by democratic voting and in consultation with temple presidents and other leaders.

Basic Beliefs and Values

"The mission of this nonsectarian, monotheistic movement is to promote the well being of society by teaching the science of Krishna consciousness according to Bhagavad Gita and other ancient scriptures," states an online source.

Hare Krishnas believe that unenlightened people live evil lives and accumulate bad karma that results in endless reincarnation (physical rebirth). By chanting Krishna's name constantly and giving oneself to His service, by following the tenets of ISKCON through many reincarnations, devotees can eventually eliminate bad karma and find release from the rebirth cycle.

By far the most significant belief/practice of Krishnas is the practice of chanting the Krishna mantra: *"Hare Krishna Hare Krishna Krishna Krishna Hare Hare; Hare Rama Hare Rama Rama Rama Hare Hare."* This discipline is employed in the effort to free one's mind from all other distractions and to enable one to focus solely on Lord Krishna (the "all-attractive"). This is the essence of Krishna consciousness, the way to bring out the natural, pure mind, ridding oneself of material dirt and accumulated bad karma. Devotees are expected to repeat this mantra 108 times daily, using a kind of rosary called a *japa mala*.

In addition to chanting, initiates into the Hare Krishna movement agree to engage in all of the following: yoga, vegetarianism, an ascetic lifestyle, and soliciting donations for ISKCON. Followers also must abstain from intoxication, gambling, illicit sexual activity (all physical pleasures distract one from spiritual pursuit), and the eating of meat, fish, or eggs. Oftentimes converts change their names and cut off contact with family and former friends. This kind of *bhakti* ("devotion") is considered the path to *mukhti* ("liberation").

View of God

God is Lord Krishna, the "all-attractive," a personal creator, "the prime entity." The souls of all living things are part of Krishna, and He lives within all. He has unlimited names such as Rama, Buddha, Vishnu, Jehovah, Allah, and so forth. ISKCON teaches that what Krishna does for His own pleasure (intoxication, fornication) is prohibited to His devotees. Contrary to what some outsiders think, Hare Krishna devotees do not worship Srila Prabhupada. He did not think he was God, stating that men who claim to be God are dogs.

Worldview

Hare Krishna devotees seek to propagate spiritual knowledge in society so as to achieve real unity and peace in the world. They also strive for a simpler, more natural way of life.

The emphasis on purity—abstaining from worldly pursuits—is intentional. Gambling consumes the mind (and the mind must remain clear for spiritual meditation and realization). Intoxicants bend and cloud the mind. Meat-eating involves violence against other spiritual and living (albeit less intelligent) beings. Illicit sex brings entanglement, exploitation, and illusion. They practice asceticism not for its own sake but in order to be able to focus on eternal things.

View of the Afterlife

When it comes to beliefs about the life to come, Hare Krishnas follow in the ancient tradition of Hinduism, which involves many, many lives and a long cycle of death and rebirth. Death is not final; it is merely another transition to another body. The hope? One might, through enlightenment and pure devotion, eventually find freedom, which Hindus call *samsara*, from this reincarnation process.

A Krishna parade in London

They believe that what a person does in this life helps them on the way to the next life. In the next life, one can go up or down, or become free of the cycle.

Sacred Texts

Devotees of Krishna believe that fifty centuries ago, Lord Krishna came into the world to enlighten a great warrior named Arjuna. When Arjuna became overwhelmed and even despondent on the brink of a great battle, Lord Krishna spoke the words that comprise the book known as Bhagavad Gita. This eternal transcribed wisdom answers mankind's deepest questions about who we are, what is our purpose, and how we can become free.

ISKCON adherents revere Srila Prabhupada's translations and commentaries on Hindu scriptures, especially his translation, Bhagavad Gita, ("As It Is")

Worship Services

The *sankirtana* movement is the name given to the practice of congregational chanting of the holy name of God. This "maha-mantra" (believed to be the most effective practice for self-purification) is said to mean, "Please Lord, engage me in Your service."

ISKCON adherents practice "Krishna consciousness" in their everyday lives as they live and work. They also congregate in temples for worship.

Because of great public backlash, accusations of cult-watchdog groups, and some key legal rulings restricting their fundraising practices, Krishnas now maintain a lower profile than they did during their heyday in the late 1960s and early 1970s.

Important Dates

Hare Krishna adherents celebrate many holidays—some by fasting, others by feasting. Some of these special days include:

Appearance of Srila Bhaktisiddhanta Sarsvati (early February)—the guru/mentor of Srila Prabhupada, founder of ISKCON	**Gaura Purnima** (early March)—the appearance of Caitanya Mahaprabhu, the great Hindu reformer who advocated Krishna consciousness in the fifteenth century
Vyasa-puja (August/September, depending on the lunar calendar)—commemorates the anniversary of Srila Prabhupada's "appearance" (his birthday)	**Sri Krishna Janmashtami** (early September)—the appearance of Lord Krishna, the Godhead himself, the source of everything, on earth.
Appearance of Srila Bhaktivinoda Thakura (late September)—the nineteenth-century guru who revitalized interest in Krishna consciousness	**Disappearance of Srila Prabhupada** (November)—a remembrance of the founder of ISKCON on the day of his passing

"Give me your mind and give me your heart, give me your offerings and your adoration."
—Krishna in Bhagavad Gita 9:34

Number of Followers

Best estimates state that Hinduism has between eight hundred million and one billion followers worldwide. This makes it the world's third largest religion, trailing only Christianity and Islam in number of adherents. More than one million Hindus live in North America.

Major Figures/Prophets

There is no single founder of Hinduism.

Short History

Hinduism has no clear beginning date. This ancient religion that dominates Indian life evolved out of the merging of ancient cultural beliefs.

Some scholars say the word *Hindu* comes from *Hind,* an ancient Persian term for "India." Others say that it is derived from the Indus River and Indus Valley in what is modern-day Pakistan.

Whichever the case, the religion we call Hinduism seems to have come into being some four thousand years ago, perhaps through a clash of ancient cultures somewhere around northwest India. Some historians

Belief	Hinduism
Sacred Text(s)	The Vedas, ancient texts given by God; also the Upanishads and Bhagavad Gita
Nature of God	An impersonal, universal, eternal soul (Brahman) who created and is present in everything; manifested by as many as three hundred million deities
Jesus Christ	A great teacher or guru; He did not die for sin, nor did He rise from the dead
Human nature	Immortal, uncreated souls that journey through countless reincarnations toward eventual reunion with the Ultimate
About human need	Need to recognize one's divinity and break the vicious cycle of karma through ritual devotion to the gods
Salvation	Reaching the end of endless cycles of reincarnation through actions, knowledge, and devotion; ultimate salvation occurs when we are absorbed or merged into Brahman
Afterlife	Hindus who live well and achieve good karma are reincarnated into a better state; those who live badly accumulate bad karma which can only be atoned for through suffering

Major Differences from Christianity

believe the Dravidians of the Mohenjo-Daro civilization were overrun by the more aggressive Aryan peoples from ancient Persia. The amalgamation of these cultures that practiced polytheism and animism provided the basis for what eventually developed into Hinduism.

Ganesha, a popular Hindu deity

The Aryans expressed their religious ideas in mythic stories, chants, hymns, and prayers that were passed down orally, until they were written down in texts called the Vedas.

Over time, this Indo-Aryan culture also experienced an increasing stratification. Distinct classes emerged, based on color and birth. The highest and most powerful class was the priestly Brahmins. Next in line was the warrior class, then the merchant class, followed by the slave or peasant class. (This was the beginning of the Indian caste system, which also produced the so-called untouchables, those "lowest of the low" who have no caste or birth status.) Over the centuries these social and racial divisions became woven into the fabric of Hindu religious life, so that each caste developed its own dharma, or laws for living.

Around 600–500 BC, when the Brahmins were at the height of their power and controlled all Hindu religious rituals, the lower classes revolted. This upheaval not only resulted in the breakaway faiths of Buddhism and Jainism, it also introduced a fundamental change in the practice of Hinduism. Ritualistic action became less important. The quest for internal knowledge (that is, finding the God within through meditation) became more important. The Hindu holy text called the Upanishad was pivotal in this inner search.

Around AD 700, Hinduism began to be practiced in yet another way, through the path of *bhatki* ("devotion"). Adherents to this form of Hinduism selected certain gods for special adoration, from the three hundred million plus Hindu pantheon of gods.

Though the caste system is now officially illegal in India, it is still very much a part of Indian life and Hindu belief.

Basic Beliefs and Values

Most churches and Christian organizations can provide seekers a concise statement of their doctrinal beliefs. Hinduism has no such theological document. The authors of *The Penguin Dictionary of Religions* describe it this way: "Hinduism is not a unity, having no 'founder,' no single creed, no single universally accepted scripture, no single moral code or theological system, nor a single concept of god central to it. It is rather a tradition that embraces a wide variety of religious positions."

While it is difficult to make sweeping statements about such a wide-ranging belief system, we can state Hinduism's central emphases by explaining a few key words:

- *Brahman*—The Hindu word for "Ultimate Reality," the source of all things that permeates all things. The gods and deities worshipped in Hinduism are various manifestations of "the One."

- *Samsara*—The Hindu belief that one's immortal soul is continuously reborn (reincarnation).

- *Karma*—A Sanskrit word that means "actions," and conveys the notion that one's moral choices have a direct impact on one's quality of life in this life and in future incarnations.

- *Moksha*—The goal of Hinduism. This refers to liberation or release from the endless cycle of reincarnation (samsara). Some liken this to being in the presence of God; others see it as a kind of merging with the Ultimate, as a drop of water is absorbed into the ocean. Hindus believe there are three primary paths or ways to achieve this deliverance from the cycle of death and life:

  — *Action*, performing one's religious duties and, thus obtaining blessing;

  — *Knowledge*, seeking for the meaning of life through meditation and realization of the fundamental unity between the external Brahman and the internal *atman*, or divine self;

  — *Devotion*, worshipping certain deities and becoming one with them.

- *Dharma*—The ethical, dutiful "way of living" practiced by devout Hindus. Works include following dietary laws, observing the expectations of the caste system, and participating in sacrifices and rituals.

Most modern Hindus worship one or more deities, often represented by stone and wood idols. They both value and practice the holy habits of prayer and meditation. This involves chanting, breathing exercises/yoga, and saying the syllable "om" or "aum" before and after all prayers. *Yatra* ("pilgrimages") are sometimes undertaken, and these may culminate with bathing in the waters of certain holy rivers (such as the Ganges River, the Jumna, and so forth). This practice is believed to effectively wash away one's sins and garner the blessing of the deities. Disciplines practiced include commitments to truth, nonviolence, cleanliness, and sexual purity, resisting the desire to steal, avoiding corrupting influences, cultivating contentment, the reading of Hindu scriptures, and regular prayers.

To summarize, Hinduism is a mishmash of the cultural practices and religious rituals of countless people groups of the Indian subcontinent collected over three millennia.

View of God

Called "the Absolute" or "the One," *Brahman* (the Hindu term for "God") is a universal spirit, the impersonal Ultimate Reality. In the same way that drops of water form the sea, *atman* ("individual selves") are all part of Brahman. In a real sense, then, Hinduism teaches that humans are divine, part of the ultimate; however, most remain unaware of their divine status.

Hinduism says there are many manifestations of Brahman (that is, many gods and goddesses). The most "famous" Hindu gods are three in number and comprise a kind of Hindu trinity. They are Brahma (the creator), Vishnu (the maintainer/preserver), and Shiva (the destroyer and re-creator).

Vishnu is the god who is thought to maintain the balance between good and evil in the universe. When evil begins to hold sway, Vishnu is incarnated to restore divine order. He assumes the form of Krishna or Rama, or one of eight other forms.

Other gods are worshipped, depending on what special powers they are thought to possess and what needs a particular Hindu has.

Worldview

Hindus see life and the world with these presuppositions:

- Time and creation are cyclical.
- All of life is essentially spiritual.
- The physical world clouds our ability to grasp spiritual reality.
- Our choices and actions now have significant future consequences—the universe is just, and all are held accountable.

For the Western mind, which tends to think in logical terms, Hinduism is mysterious, mystical, and misunderstood. In actual practice, Hinduism is noncreedal and tolerant of other—even competing—religious truth claims. It says there are many spiritual paths. Is it polytheistic (the belief in many gods), pantheistic (the belief that everything is god), or monistic (the belief that all is one)? Yes, yes, and yes! Hinduism seems to allow for all of these theological positions.

In terms of salvation, Hinduism puts the responsibility squarely on the individual. He or she must perform the right actions, obtain the right knowledge/enlightenment, and show necessary devotion to one's chosen God. This is a highly subjective system that doesn't provide much spiritual certainty.

Most Hindus are peaceful and nonviolent. Many practice vegetarianism.

Krishna and his consort Radha

View of the Afterlife

Hinduism teaches that at death, one's soul (atman) is reborn or recycled into the world. This new incarnation might take human, animal, or plant form. Certain Hindu sects believe that one can be reincarnated even to an inanimate existence. This is the ever revolving wheel of samsara—the succession of lives that one must endure on the path to moksha (that is, the liberation and union with "the One").

The number of incarnations one experiences is directly tied to the principle of karma (Hindu's law of cause and effect). Callous and selfish living results in bad karma attaching to one's soul. Bad karma can only be undone by suffering (in another life) and striving (to follow the Vedas and principles of Hinduism). Living well in one's current life insures the reward of a better existence in the next life.

Sacred Texts

Hinduism relies on many writings, which fall into two basic categories: (1) *Shruti*—truth directly from the gods, revealed to/heard by holy men; and (2) *Smriti*—wisdom from Hindu sages. Making up the shruti are the Vedas (hymns dating back to about 1000 BC), the Brahmanas (priestly instructions), the Sutras (rules for the people), and the Upanishads (mystical and philosophical interpretations of the Vedas). The most famous of the smriti writings is the Bhagavad Gita, a discourse attributed to Lord Krishna.

Worship Services

Hindu temples are called *mandirs*. They are often ornate and elaborately decorated. Worshippers remove their shoes upon entering, because temples are viewed as the dwelling place of the gods, and every part of the mandir is regarded as holy. Temples typically feature various statues of the gods. Devotees bring offerings and may watch as priests lovingly wash and clothe these statues. (Hindus do not consider this idolatry because they believe each statue is actually inhabited by the god it represents.) Priests may occasionally read or recite the Vedas to gathered worshippers. However, this public worship in the presence of other Hindus tends to be more individual than congregational or communal.

Most Hindus also create shrines within their homes. Every day they engage in acts of worship and adoration called *puja*.

What about those red dots on the foreheads of many Hindu women? This mark, called a *bindi*, (which literally means "a drop") has many connotations. But essentially it is a traditional way of saying, "I am a married Hindu woman."

Important Dates

Hanuman Jayanti (January)— a festival in honor of the birthday of Hanuman, the Monkey God	**Holi** (late February/early March)— spring festival associated with Krishna; may feature pranks and high jinks
Mahashivaratri (February/March)— Festival of Shiva, a deity in the "Hindu trinity"	**Ganesha Chaturthi** (August/ September)—a celebration of the birthday of Lord Ganesh
Raksha Bandhan (July/August)— a celebration of Hindu brotherhood	**Krishna Jayanti** (July/August)— Birthday of Krishna
Navarati (or Navratri) (September/ October)—a celebration of the triumph of good over evil	**Divali** (late October/early November)— Festival of Lights, an important multi-day event that heralds the start of the Hindu New Year

"Incomprehensible to Muslims is the Christian belief of being 'saved' in which a person who asks Jesus into his or her heart automatically goes to heaven. . . . Islam teaches that you save or damn yourself every day through your belief, or lack of it, your actions, good or bad, and your overall record. . . . God, in His mercy, will forgive much and overlook much, but this doesn't absolve us our responsibility to try to be as virtuous as possible."
—Yahiya Emerick, President of the Islamic Foundation of North America

Major Differences from Christianity

Belief	Islam
Sacred Text(s)	The Qur'an is the final, one hundred percent reliable, unchangeable culmination of God's revelation; the *Hadith* (sayings and practices of Muhammad) is also a guide
Nature of God	God, or *Allah*, is one (no Trinity). He is all-powerful, just, all-knowing, and merciful
Jesus Christ	A revered prophet who worked miracles, was born of the Virgin Mary; not divine, not actually killed on a cross; returning one day to defeat the Antichrist.
Human nature	Each person has a soul or spirit that is imparted by angels to babies in the womb. No original sin, we are born good, but vulnerable because of our physical nature/animal desires
About human need	To surrender to Allah's will and serve Him in every part of life
Salvation	Depends on belief in Allah and keeping the laws of Islam; atonement or sacrifice for sin unnecessary; personal sin must be removed by making *tawba* (a four-step process of repentance)
Afterlife	Paradise or heaven is the place of eternal delight for the devout; hell is the place of horrible torment

Number of Followers

The best estimates show that there are between 1.2 billion and 1.4 billion Muslims in the world. Islam is widely regarded as the fastest-growing religion in the world. Between five and seven million Muslims make their home in the United States.

Major Figures/Prophets

Muhammad (AD 570–632)—born in the city of Mecca, in what is modern-day Saudi Arabia, he was raised by his grandfather, a Bedouin tribesman, following the death of his parents. Muhammad was a shepherd and successful merchant. Muslims do not consider him divine, nor is he regarded as a savior. He is believed to be God's final messenger or prophet.

Short History

Islam is an Arabic word that means "submission" or surrender of one's will to God. A *Muslim* is a devotee of Islam. *Mohammedanism*, a term sometimes used to refer to Islam, is offensive to Muslims, as it suggests worship of Muhammad.

According to Islamic tradition, Muhammad began receiving visions from Allah (God) when he was forty years old. He established the religion called Islam in AD 622, after a series of revelations given to him by the archangel Gabriel. Muslims believe that Muhammad was not being called to launch a new faith, but rather to clarify, codify, and—most importantly—purify the faith first revealed to Abraham, Moses, David, and Jesus. Muhammad preached to his neighbors in Mecca and ac-cumulated a small following. His teachings were the subject of initial criticism and persecution, probably because their strict monotheism and morality threatened an Arabian culture awash in polytheistic beliefs and immorality. Adherents to this fledg-ling Islamic faith left Mecca under Muhammad's leadership and moved to Medina, some 280 miles north. Eight years later, the group returned to Mecca, and Islam began to be accepted by the populace.

After the death of Muhammad in AD 632, two major factions arose within Islam—the Sunnis and Shi'ites. The "breakaway" faction became known as the *Shi'as*. Through the centuries they have developed different—some would say more harsh—interpretations of Islam's beliefs. Shiite Muslim-controlled countries or regions have an organized hierarchy: a supreme leader, called an *imam*, several *ayatollahs*, and mul-tiple local *mullahs*. These spiritual leaders also wield absolute civil power.

The vast majority (probably eighty to eighty-five percent) of Muslims worldwide are *Sunnis*. They are more inclined to separate politics and religion, and prefer a decentralized religious system. A smaller, mystical movement within Islam is called *Sufiism*.

Islam regards itself as God's final and most complete revelation to the world. All other religions are corruptions or incomplete versions of the truth. Islam shares certain beliefs and traditions with Judaism (strict monotheism, angels, a belief in a literal heaven and hell, honor for many of the same prophets, kosher standards, reverence for certain sacred writings, and so forth). Muslims and Christians agree on Christ's virgin birth, the fact of a coming judgment and literal heaven and hell, but not much else.

Basic Beliefs and Values

Islam has seven* core beliefs:

- *Belief in God*—Muslims call him Allah (see further explanation below).

- *Belief in Angels*—Muslims believe angels are made of light energy and can materialize in various forms. Unlike Christianity, which teaches the existence of fallen angels (that is, demons), Islam teaches that all angels serve Allah.

- *Belief in the revealed Books of God*—Muslims revere the Qur'an (God's dictations to Muhammad) and the Sunnah ("the way of the Prophet"), sayings of Muhammad that were collected in a book called the Hadith. They also read and respect the Torah, the pages of Abraham, the Psalms of David, and the Gospel of Jesus. However, the Bible used by modern-day Christians is regarded as inauthentic and full of errors.

- *God's many prophets*—Muslims honor all the major religious figures of Judaism and Christianity, including Abraham, Moses, David, Solomon, Job, and Jesus. (Islam has a different interpretation on their lives and missions than has Christianity.)

- *Last Day*—Islam is marked by a pervading belief in a coming judgment day, in which all acts, good and evil, will be recompensed.

- *Divine measurement*—This is called *qadr*, and is not the same as "fate" or "destiny" or "fatalism," but rather the belief that whatever Allah decrees will come to pass. Muslims see no contradiction between Allah's knowledge and sovereign control of all things and human responsibility for choices and actions.

- *Life after death*—Islam has a very developed theology of the afterlife: resurrection to either heaven or hell. Heaven will be a place of exquisite delight and pleasure; hell will be terrible beyond words.

(*Some Muslims and religious scholars combine beliefs five and seven above, resulting in a total of six core beliefs.)

Muslims practice five essential tenets of faith. These are often called the "Five Pillars of Islam":

- *Expressed faith in the oneness of God and Muhammad as his prophet*—The verbal declaration of this creed is called the *Shahadah*.

- *Prayer five times a day (Salah)*—This takes place just before sunrise, midday, mid-afternoon, just after sunset, and after nightfall

- *Alms for the needy (zakat,* meaning "to purify")—This letting go of worldly goods is believed to help free one's soul from greed and gluttony. This charitable giving amounts to two and a half percent of a debt-free, adult Muslim's annual wealth.

- *Self-purification through fasting (Sawm)*—From sunrise to sunset, every day during Ramadan, the ninth month of the Muslim calendar. Only small children, the sick, the mentally ill, and the elderly are exempted.

- *Pilgrimage to Mecca (Hajj)*—This journey, to honor the life of Muhammad and to recommit oneself to Allah, is expected of all physically healthy, financially able, mentally sound, adult Muslims at least once in life.

There is much current debate within Islam about the meaning of *jihad* ("struggle"). Some peaceful Muslims interpret this term to refer primarily to the moral fight of trying to follow Allah's ways. They see any kind of exertion for Allah as a kind of jihad. They cite Qur'an 6:151, which says, "Don't take a life which Allah has made sacred except by way of justice and law: thus does he command you that you may learn wisdom." They interpret this as forbidding the taking of any life except for just causes: capital punishment in certain heinous crimes, fighting in wartime, or self-defense.

Radical Muslims interpret jihad as calling for physical struggle and aggressive conflict with those who do not embrace Islam (or, in other words, those who do not submit to Allah). They cite a statement in the Qur'an that says, "Fight the unbelievers wherever you find them."

Conversion to Islam is a simple procedure. One simply recites a two-line statement, called the *Shahadah* ("Testimony of Faith"): "There is no God but Allah, and Muhammad is His Prophet" in the presence of two witnesses. For Muslims this act is believed to effectively accomplish the erasure of past sins. This is the Islamic version of being "born again." Forced conversions are prohibited in Qur'an 2:254.

View of God

Islam embraces a strict monotheism (Allah means "the one and only God"). Islam teaches that God is all-seeing, all-powerful, eternal, and uncreated, the Creator of all. Islam abhors any teaching of polytheism or any physical representations of God. It rejects as blasphemy the Christian belief in the Trinity (one God existing eternally as three Persons). Muslims believe Allah is one and the same as the God of Abraham, Moses, and Jesus, but it rejects the notion that God has a special, permanent covenant with the Jews.

Muslims speak of *taqwa*, a consciousness of Allah in one's life. Following the practices of Islam is believed to increase this divine awareness and foster self-control, since God is watching our every action. Muslims strive to know what God is like by studying the qualities embodied in the "ninety-nine names of God" set forth in the Qur'an.

The Kabaa, a Muslim holy relic, in Mecca

Unlike the distinctively Christian idea of God as an affectionate, personal heavenly Father whose Spirit lives in us, Islam's Allah is a more distant and separate master. Followers are slaves or servants, not children.

Worldview

Islam regards itself less as a set of beliefs and more as a way of life. All created things fall into one of two categories: either they are surrendered to God's will or they are resistant to God's will. In short, Muslims believe there is God's way and the wrong way. Inanimate objects (mountains, rivers, comets, and so forth), animals, and plants are inherently surrendered. That is, they "do" what they were created to do. By fulfilling their natural roles, they are innately "Muslim." It is only within the realm of humanity and spiritual beings that we find created entities that resist God's rule.

In Islam belief, each human has a soul or spirit (called *ruh* by Muslims) that comes from Allah and is imparted by angels on babies in the womb. *Jinns* are invisible, spiritual creatures that exist in another dimension. *Shaytan* is an evil jinn who seeks to corrupt and ruin humans (similar, but not identical to the evil one Christians refer to as "Satan").

Allah endows each person with a moral guide, a kind of conscientious inner compass (Muslims call it a *fitrah*). Life is about learning to respond humbly to this guidance, which means traveling a three-stage journey: (1) moving from the animal self, where the focus is on basic instincts and fleshly desires; (2) passing through the accusing self stage, during which one begins questioning his or her purpose and seeking truth; and (3) finally, the restful self stage.

View of the Afterlife

Islam teaches that during our lives Allah keeps a detailed record of each person's good and bad deeds. At death our souls lie in the grave until resurrection day. On the day of judgment, God will assess our lives using the criteria of belief, behavior, and motives.

Depending on what this "divine audit" reveals, and how much mercy Allah decides to show, each person is sent to either heaven or hell. According to Yahiya Emerick, author of *The Complete Idiot's Guide to Understanding Islam*, Muslims believe in the existence of a narrow bridge that spans the chasm of hell and leads to paradise. The bridge is jagged and razor-like. The righteous fly right over this bridge with no complications. Less devout souls are cut and bruised during this harrowing journey (but healed once they reach the other side). Sinners trip and are snagged. They fall into the pit at some point along the way. Heaven for devout Muslims will be a paradise. Abstention from sinful pleasures in this life will be rewarded with guilt-free indulgence in the life to come.

Sacred Texts

The Qur'an (also known as the Koran in English) means "The Reading" and is the Muslim holy book. Muslims believe this text is the literal word of God revealed to the prophet Muhammad by the angel Gabriel. It consists of 114 chapters arranged in order of length.

The Hadith, a book of sayings of the Prophet Muhammad, is also prized by Muslims, being seen as a kind of living application of the Qur'an.

The original Torah, scrolls of Abraham, Psalms of David, and Gospel of Jesus are revered, but these texts as recorded in the Bible are considered altered and corrupted.

Worship Services

In addition to their daily prayers, which can be said anywhere as long as one is able to bow toward Mecca, Muslims gather on Friday afternoons at mosques for a congregational worship/prayer service.

The word *mosque* means "the place of bowing down." (Actually, it may have originated from King Ferdinand and Queen Isabella of Spain, who once vowed that they would smash Muslim prayer houses like one swats mosquitoes.) At these services an *Imam* (the religious leader of an Islamic community) may give a sermon.

Important Dates

Islam has three major holidays:

Ramadan—the month of fasting, ending with **Eid-al-Fitr** ("the feast that breaks the fast"), a day of celebration and feasting

al-Hajj—the month of pilgrimage, culminating in **Eid-al-Adha** ("The Feast of Sacrifice"), a day commemorating when Allah spared Ishmael (the half-brother of Isaac), a time of gratitude and generosity toward the poor

Mawlid an-Nabvi —the Prophet Muhammad's birthday

"Endowed with conduct and discipline,
Who practices control of self,
Who throws out all his bondage,
He attains the eternal place."
—Mahavira (from Uttaradhyayana Sutra)

Major Differences from Christianity

Belief	Jainism
Sacred Text(s)	A variety of texts that include or expand the teachings of Mahavira
Nature of God	No god to worship, only the twenty-four enlightened spiritual teachers; some Jains also worship Hindu gods
Jesus Christ	Jainism does not acknowledge Jesus as the Savior of the world
Human nature	Eternal souls reborn again and again on path to enlightenment
About human need	Ridding one's soul of bad karma and collecting good karma; done by acquiring right knowledge, having right faith, and exhibiting right conduct
Salvation	Living according to rigid Jain principles eliminates bad karma and eventually liberates the soul
Afterlife	Reincarnation: a cycle of birth, death, and rebirth until one experiences *moksha* (liberation)

Number of Followers

There are approximately four million Jains, mostly in India. Some sources estimate as many as one hundred thousand Jains now live in North America, and a fast-growing population exists in England.

Major Figures/Prophets

- **Vardhamana Mahavira** (599-527 BC)—Also known as Mahvi ("the Great Hero"), founder of Jainism in the mid-500s BC, though he was the twenty-fourth in a line of teachers of Jain principles
- **Queen Trishala**—mother of Mahavira
- **Gautamswami**—a well-known, brilliant Brahmin who became a disciple of Mahavira

Short History

Jainism was established in Kundalpur, India, by Vardhamana Mahavira, who lived between 599 and 527 BC. Around the age of thirty, he left his royal family, gave up all his worldly possessions (including his clothing!) and became a wandering monk. Disillusioned by all existing religions, he spent the ensuing twelve years seeking truth by living an austere life of hunger, deep silence, and meditation. In the end, Jain tradition says Mahavira achieved enlightenment (liberation, perfect knowledge, spiritual power, and bliss). He is reported to have fasted to death.

A major schism within Jainism occurred about six centuries after Mahavira's demise. Two competing sects emerged: *Svetambara* (founded by Sudharma, "the white robed one") and the more strict *Digambara* ("sky-clad") led by Visakha, whose monks renounce all possessions, even clothes. Each group claims its own sacred texts.

Basic Beliefs and Values

The word *Jain* is derived from the Sanskrit word *jina*, which means "one who conquers." Thus the goal of Jainism is to conquer suffering through the liberation of the soul from the body. Devout Jains regard strong emotions as negative diversions, keeping them from attaining true knowledge and freedom. By utilizing strict self-control and by engaging in meditation, Jains seek to eliminate desires like love and hate, experiences of pleasure and pain, attitudes of attachment and aversion.

Jains believe in *karma*, a kind of cause-effect principle with respect to the soul. The law of karma says that good thoughts and actions result in good consequences, and negative thoughts and actions accumulate for the guilty party in future pain and suffering. Jains believe that bad karma actually accumulates on the soul, tainting it and weighing it down.

In attempting to eliminate bad karma, devout Jains (especially monks and nuns) adhere to five great vows:

- *Ahimsa*—The protection of all life through nonviolence.
- *Satya*—Truthfulness.
- *Asteya*—Non-stealing.
- *Brahmacharya*—Chastity/nonadultery.
- *Aparigraha*—Non-possessiveness/detachment.

Practicing these principles is seen as the path to free one's *jiva* ("soul") from the cycle of birth, life, pain, misery, and death. This liberation, called *moksha*, signals the gaining of omniscience and takes many reincarnations/lifetimes. Once freed from the weight of bad karma, each jiva ascends to the height of the universe and there enjoys eternal bliss and knowledge. This state is called *nirvana*.

In the attempt to free their souls, devout Jains will become *sadhus* ("holy men") and *sadhvis* ("holy women"). These "monks" and "nuns" of Jainism live strict spartan lives. As much as possible they strive to live separate from the world. They often own only the most basic possessions (for example, a robe, a broom for gently sweeping away insects so as not to harm them, a walking stick, a bowl for food). They beg for food, live mostly outdoors, and abstain from killing any living thing (ahimsa, see above). Devout monks and nuns are even known to wear masks to keep from inadvertently inhaling gnats and small insects. One obvious implication of this devotion and belief is that Jains practice vegetarianism.

Lay adherents of Jainism (those who are not monks or nuns) are less ascetic. They engage in business (as a general rule, the Jain population in India tends to be wealthy) and anticipate becoming holy men and holy women in a future reincarnation.

In summary, Jainism is an ascetic, pacifistic religion with many similarities to Hinduism and some to Buddhism.

Unlike Hinduism, which believes in one great spiritual reality (the Brahmin) of which we are all part, Jainism teaches that each living being possesses a distinct, eternal, uncreated, infinite soul, or jiva. Our souls reside inside a series of temporary physical bodies.

View of the Afterlife

The Jainism view of the afterlife can be summed up in two words: reincarnation and rebirth. Heaven is less a real, literal place and more a state of mind (nirvana). Hell is actually eight hells that get increasingly colder as one descends. Following punishment of the soul there, one is reborn yet again to continue the arduous path to liberation and enlightenment.

View of God

Jains do not profess belief in one supreme God who controls all. Instead, they revere twenty-four enlightened *tirthankaras* ("spiritual teachers"). Mahavira was and is worshipped by many Jains.

Worldview

According to Jainism, the universe is uncreated; it has no beginning and no end. Karma is the good and evil on the soul that accumulates during a series of lifetimes. Nonviolence is of the utmost importance in one's thoughts and actions. Violence contributes to bad karma which adversely affects one's future life.

The Mirrored Temple in Calcutta, India

Sacred Texts

The Purvas (now lost) are accepted by both major sects of Jainism as sacred. The Jainworld Web site lists sixteen "Scriptures–Sacred Books."

These various writings include rules for ascetic living, doctrines, history, teachings of the twenty-four tirthankaras, hymns, literature, description of karma, and discussions of passions. The two major sects within Jainism favor different texts.

Worship Services

Upon visiting a Jain's simple household shrine or a formal Jain temple (often exquisitely ornate), a person would see an image or idol of a Jina, or a tirthankara (though the enlightened ones are not believed to be present in these images). The lay worshippers remove old offerings, anoint the image with water, yogurt, or milk, recite prayers, and then present fresh offerings (uncooked rice, flowers, fruit, incense, flame, and so on). They engage in *Puja*, a ritual that features intense concentration and prayer. Monks and nuns do not participate in temple worship because it is too material, involving objects from this world.

Each day, devout Jains pray the *Navkar Mantra*, a brief salutation to the perfect souls who have achieved nirvana.

Samayika is a meditative ritual. *Pratikraman* is a ritual done morning and night to repent of violence or duties left undone.

Yatra ("pilgrimage"), while not obligatory, is a popular form of worship and devotion among Jains. The devout followers travel to places where one of the tirthankara gained enlightenment.

Important Dates

Of the various events on the Jain calendar, three stand out:

Mahavir Jayanti (March/April)— the birth of Mahavira

Paryushan (August/September)—this eight-day festival features fasting, reflection upon one's conduct the previous year, discourses in the temple, and concludes with prayers of repentance, seeking forgiveness (not from an almighty god, but from living beings one has harmed).

Diwali (late fall)—a more celebratory feast in honor of Mahavira's enlightenment; also called the "Festival of Lights"

"YOU are my witnesses," is the utterance of Jehovah, "even my servant whom I have chosen, in order that YOU may know and have faith in me, and that YOU may understand that I am the same One. Before me there was no God formed, and after me there continued to be none. I—I am Jehovah, and besides me there is no savior."
—Isaiah 43:10–11 (*New World Translation*, the official Bible of Jehovah's Witnesses)

Number of Followers

The Watchtower Bible and Tract Society reports 6.7 million active Jehovah's Witnesses, including 1 million in the United States and almost 250,000 new converts in 2006. Other sources give a much lower figure.

Major Figures/Prophets

- **Charles Taze Russell** (1852–1916)—a clothing merchant in Pennsylvania, founder and first president of the Watchtower Bible and Tract Society, the parent organization of the Jehovah's Witnesses church

- **Joseph F. Rutherford** (1869–1942)—the second president of the Watchtower Society, known for adopting the name "Jehovah's Witnesses," and for instituting the group's famous door-to-door witnessing strategy

Belief	Jehovah's Witnesses
Sacred Text(s)	The Bible, in the *New World Translation*, a publication that rephrases certain passages in order to coincide with their doctrine
Nature of God	God, who is properly called Jehovah, is One; He is loving, holy; no such thing as the Trinity.
Jesus Christ	Not eternal and not Almighty God; Jesus is the first creation of Jehovah. Before his incarnation, Jesus was Michael, the archangel, through whom Jehovah made the universe. He lived a perfect life, and died to make atonement. His body was not resurrected, only his spirit
Human nature	Mortal souls, that, despite sin, are still capable of choosing to do good
About human need	Need to strive to do God's will and remain pure in his eyes
Salvation	Christ's death offers the opportunity for the faithful to earn their salvation through good works; salvation can be lost
Afterlife	Only 144,000 will live as spirits in heaven; the "Great Crowd" remain on earth, where they must obey God perfectly for one thousand years, or be annihilated.

Major Differences from Christianity

- **Nathan Knorr** (1905–1977)—the third president of the Jehovah's Witnesses, presided over the publishing of the official Jehovah Witness translation of the Scriptures (1961)

A Watchtower issue from the early 20th century

Short History

Growing up in the Congregational Church, young Charles Taze Russell bristled at the historic Christian teachings of the Trinity and hell. For a while, he dabbled in Adventist theology, drawn especially by their teaching that the wicked will be annihilated and not punished eternally. In his late teens, with no formal Bible or seminary training, Russell began formulating his own theological system, based on his personal study and interpretations of the Bible. A centerpiece of his belief was the conviction that Christ would return in 1874. When this didn't happen literally, Russell decided that the Lord must have come in a spiritual and invisible way.

In 1879, Russell launched his own magazine (*Zion's Watch Tower and Herald of Christ's Presence*—later called simply *The Watchtower*) to promote his beliefs. He financed this venture out of his own pocket (he managed a lucrative men's clothing chain). Soon he was making more prophetic announcements, declaring that Armageddon would happen in 1914, which would destroy the wicked and usher in God's kingdom.

While waiting for the end, Russell officially established the Watchtower Bible and Tract Society (1896). In 1909, he relocated the group's headquarters to Brooklyn, New York. Russell initially believed the outbreak of World War I was the beginning of Armageddon, but he died in 1916 without seeing his prophecies come to pass.

Leadership passed to the group's legal advisor, a lawyer named Joseph F. Rutherford. He immediately predicted that Armageddon would occur in 1925. Undeterred when his prophecy failed, Rutherford renamed the group "Jehovah's Witnesses" (taken from Isaiah 43:10). He also mandated widespread door-to-door proselytizing for the faithful. Rutherford set several more dates for Armageddon, but died in 1942, still waiting for the end to come.

Subsequent Jehovah's Witnesses leaders continued to set dates for the end of the world. As the years passed, they were also forced to come up with various creative explanations for all their prophetic inaccuracies. In 1961, under the leadership of third president Nathan H. Knorr, the Jehovah's Witnesses produced their own English translation of the Bible, *The New World Translation of the Holy Scriptures*.

Basic Beliefs and Values

Despite their claim to be the only true Christian church, the beliefs of Jehovah's Witnesses place them well out of the Christian theological mainstream. Here are some of their unique doctrines and practices:

- *Jesus*—God's first creation, meaning he is not coeternal with God. He was God's "master worker" in creating everything else. Christ is also God's chief spokesman. Jehovah's Witnesses believe that in 1914, Jesus was given authority over Jehovah's kingdom. Enthroned in the heavens at that time, he has been ruling ever since. In the end, Jesus will serve as Judge. He will separate the "sheep" (those who are his loyal followers) from the "goats" (those who refuse Jehovah's kingdom). He did not die on a cross, but on a pole or a stake. The cross was, Jehovah's Witnesses insist, a symbol in ancient false religions. They do not wear crosses or use them in worship.

- *Satan*—an angel who wanted the worship that belongs only to God. In attacking God's character and deceiving God's creatures (Adam and Eve), Satan became God's chief enemy. He continues to mislead people through false religion, spiritism, and internal sinful desires. He and his wicked angels were banished from heaven in 1914—which explains why life on earth has been so terrible since then (wars, famines, increasing lawlessness). These are actually signs that Jesus is ruling and that we are in the last days.

- *Creation*—Jehovah created the earth perfectly with the intent of humans living righteously and happily on it forever. Adam and Eve's sin ruined this paradise. Jesus came to rectify this situation; however, before God's purposes for earth can be realized, wicked people must be removed.

- *Armageddon*—God's future plan for bringing an end to all wickedness and restoring the world to the way it was meant to be. Following Armageddon, millions will be resurrected to live on the earth. Christ will rule as king on the earth for one thousand years. During this time, earth will be remade into paradise. Those who obey Jehovah will continue to live on earth forever. Those who refuse his rule will be destroyed. At the end of this millennium, Jesus will hand the kingdom back to his Father. Only 144,000 faithful men and women from the earth will ultimately go to heaven to rule with Jesus.

- *Religious Practices*—Because Jesus always talked about the kingdom (Luke 8:1), true Christians must do likewise. This is why Jehovah's Witnesses engage in faithful door-to-door proselytizing. Prayers should be offered only to God, in the name of Jesus. New converts must be baptized by immersion. There is to be no use of images, pictures, or symbols in worship.

- *Daily Practices*—Jehovah's Witnesses refrain from civic involvement (military service, voting in elections, pledging or saluting the flag). They do not observe holidays—not even Christmas and Easter. Birthdays are also not celebrated by Jehovah's Witnesses. This is because they believe these celebrations and customs come from ancient false religions. According to their official Web site: "The only two birthday celebrations. . . in the Bible were held by persons who did not worship Jehovah." Believing that the soul is in the blood (see Leviticus 17:11), devout members refuse all blood transfusions.

View of God

According to Jehovah's Witnesses, there is one true Creator God. His name is Jehovah. He alone is worthy of our worship. He is loving, just, wise, and powerful. He is also merciful, kind, forgiving, generous, and patient. Though God is a Spirit, He has a body.

Jehovah God is one. Jehovah's Witnesses do not believe in the Trinity. Jesus is God's created Son, and the Father is greater than the Son (see John 14:28). They also believe that the Holy Spirit is not a person, but a force.

Worldview

Because they believe in the imminent end of the world (Armageddon), and because they see their faith as the only true expression of Christianity, Jehovah's Witnesses work tirelessly to share their convictions with others. They are simple, peaceful people who strive to live as model citizens.

Sacred Texts

The *New World Translation of the Bible*, published in 1961, is regarded by Jehovah's Witnesses as the only trustworthy translation of the Scriptures. Many verses have been reworded from accepted traditional Bible translations, changing their theological meaning to make them consistent with Jehovah's Witness doctrine.

Awake! magazine, published in 81 languages, is aimed at potential converts. *The Watchtower* magazine, published in 158 languages, is written to instruct faithful Jehovah's Witnesses in church doctrine. Some 22 million copies of each issue are printed. Only *Watchtower* articles and other approved Jehovah's Witness Bible lessons are studied at local gatherings, ensuring organizational control and uniformity of belief.

Worship Services

Jehovah's Witnesses typically meet three times per week to study the Bible. Adherents gather in buildings called "Kingdom Halls." These are almost always simple structures, constructed by members of the church. Kingdom Halls are void of religious images, symbols, or art. These Bible studies feature prayer and singing, but no offering.

Each local congregation is led by a group of elders—unpaid volunteers who do the teaching and who shepherd the flock. The entire church is directed by the New York-based "governing body," consisting of a president and twelve other men. This body makes all policy and determines all activities of the Watchtower Society.

Important Dates

The one holiday Jehovah's Witnesses celebrate annually is the "Memorial of Christ's Death." This solemn observance of the Lord's Supper is held around the time of Easter and Passover, depending on when these events fall in the calendar.

View of the Afterlife

Regarding eternity, Jehovah's Witnesses ascribe to the following:

- Believe that only 144,000 of the most devout will live as spirits with God and Jesus in heaven.

- Look forward to Armageddon, when wickedness will come to an end and God's kingdom on earth will begin.

- Following Armageddon, all people will be resurrected and judged by Jesus Christ; the righteous "Great Crowd" will live in a restored "Garden of Eden"-type paradise; the wicked will die and cease to exist.

- Reject the existence of eternal punishment and torment in hell, teaching instead that the wicked will be annihilated.

> *"I take great pride in and highly appreciate the fact that our people have overcome the ordeals of history and displayed to the full the heroic mettle of the revolutionary people and the indomitable spirit of chuch'e Korea, firmly united behind the party. . . . No difficulty is insurmountable nor is any fortress impregnable for us when our party leads the people with the ever-victorious chuch'e-oriented strategy and tactics and when all the people turn out as one under the party's leadership."*
> —Kim Il Sung

Major Differences from Christianity

Belief	Juche
Sacred Text(s)	No "holy books" specified; official state documents are authoritative
Nature of God	Atheistic; the state is supreme, especially the president of the country
Jesus Christ	Not acknowledged or worshipped
Human nature	Human beings are the masters of the world and control their own destiny
About human need	To live independently, freely, patriotically, and sacrificially
Salvation	Any thoughts of salvation would be material, not spiritual (that is, deliverance from the need to rely on others)
Afterlife	No expressed doctrines or beliefs about heaven or hell; emphasis is on this life

Number of Followers

Juche (pronounced "choo-CHAY"), or *chuch'e* in Korean, is North Korea's government-authorized state religion. Based on population estimates, Juche has between nineteen million and twenty-three million official adherents, making it the tenth largest religion in the world. A very small number of followers may be found in other countries.

Major Figures/Prophets

- **Kim Il Sung** (1912–1994)—the "Great Leader" or "Eternal Leader" of North Korea, and founder of Juche
- **Kim Jong Il** (1942–present day)—the son of Kim Il Sung, who assumed power over the military in 1992, and became "president for eternity" in the new Constitution of 1998

Short History

Juche was established in the mid-1950s by the North Korean government of President Kim Il Sung as a reaction against the outside influences of Moscow and Beijing. It began to be taught in the schools as a secular, ethical philosophy. Nationally, it was an effort to silence opposition to the Kim regime and to create a national, ideological consensus. Internationally, it represented an attempt to develop North Korea's own unique national identity, an independent foreign policy, and a self-sustaining economy.

It took some years for the ideas of Juche to gain a wide foothold in North Korean culture. Pro-Soviet and pro-Chinese elements had to be purged from positions of power and influence. Sharp drops in foreign money from these communist regimes created economic difficulty. Even so, references to Marxism and Leninism were gradually eliminated from all official documents, most notably the revised Constitution (1998).

Juche Tower in Pyongyang, North Korea

The official claim is: "Pyongyang and today's North Korea is a socialist paradise, where all the people have a life with dignity, without poverty and more than ever demonstrate the invincibility and union of the masses around the Leader."

The real facts are that in recent years, North Korea has been increasingly linked with radical regimes worldwide, even selling missile technology. Human rights groups have also documented horrific torture against dissidents.

Basic Beliefs and Values

Juche (which means "self-reliance" or "self-dependence" in Korean) is a political ideology with roots in Marxist-Leninism and Maoism. In a national context, Juche is seen as the capacity to act autonomously and without outside interference. It is a secular religion, with the State standing in the place of God as the authority.

Observations about this little-known "religion":

- Despite the official stand of "self-reliance," North Korea has long relied on foreign aid.

- All citizens of North Korea are considered members of this religion, yet many so-called adherents do not deeply embrace the philosophy of Juche.

- Under Juche, no other ideologies or religious ideas are permitted.

- Juche adherents are expected to demonstrate unblinking allegiance to the State, which involves personal sacrifice, patriotism, austerity and national unity.

View of God

With roots in atheistic communism, Juche does not embrace or promote the idea of God as a spiritual Creator, Lord, and Judge. The first leader, Kim Il Sung, and his son, Kim Jong Il, are revered as Supreme Leaders.

Worldview

Juche is humanistic and materialistic in its suppositions. It is also officially isolationist (causing North Korea to gain the nickname the "hermit kingdom"); though critics point out the country's ongoing reliance on international aid, its vast expenditures on building a large military establishment (while many North Koreans go without food and basic necessities), and growing evidence of sponsoring various terrorist groups and "rogue nations" worldwide.

View of the Afterlife

No evidence exists that the average follower of Juche has any belief in a heaven or hell, or any kind of afterlife.

Sacred Texts

No books are considered inspired or divine. Official government documents (that is, the Constitution) are regarded with deference and honor.

Worship Services

As a secular, state-authorized ideology, Juche has no regular worship services.

Important Dates

Since 1998, the nation of North Korea has had its own calendar, with year one beginning in 1912 (the year of Kim Il Sung's birth). Holidays include:

New Year's Day (January 1)
Kim Il Sung's birthday (April 15)
Kim Jong Il's birthday (February 16)
Founding of the Democratic People's Republic of Korea (September 9)

"Leave your country, your people and your father's household and go to the land I will show you. I will make you into a great nation and I will bless you; I will make your name great, and you will be a blessing. I will bless those who bless you, and whoever curses you I will curse; and all peoples on earth will be blessed through you."
—God's call of Abraham (found in Genesis 12:1–3 NIV)

Major Differences from Christianity

Belief	Judaism
Sacred Text(s)	The Old Testament (the Tanakh), and especially the first five books, the Torah; the Talmud (commentary by various rabbis and interpretations) is also respected by many Jews
Nature of God	God is Spirit; One (not triune), eternal, holy, all-knowing, all-powerful, omnipresent, merciful, and just
Jesus Christ	Not the Messiah promised in the Old Testament, but either a misguided but well-meaning rabbi, or a dangerous revolutionary
Human nature	All are God's children, created in God's image, with a moral conscience, the capacity to make ethical choices, and certain inclinations toward evil
About human need	Need to repent of (that is, turn away from) selfishness and wrong behavior and live morally and ethically
Salvation	Keeping God's law to the best of one's ability; salvation viewed more in a national sense than a personal one
Afterlife	For some: a physical resurrection for all—the God-fearing to eternal life, the unrighteous to suffering; for others: no conscious life after death

Number of Followers

Judaism is the oldest of the religious faiths that trace their roots back to Abraham (the others are Christianity and Islam). It has around twelve million to fourteen million followers worldwide, of which an estimated six million live in the United States.

Major Figures/Prophets

- **Abraham**—the first great patriarch of the Jewish people, to whom the one true God revealed Himself and His plan to establish a redemptive nation on earth

- **Sarah**—the infertile wife of Abraham, who through divine intervention became the mother of the Jewish people

- **Ishmael**—the son of Abraham and his wife's servant Hagar, who became the father of the Arab peoples, and the connection between Abraham and Islam.

- **Isaac**—the biological son of Abraham and Sarah, who fulfilled God's promise to Abraham of offspring who would become a great nation

- **Jacob**—the younger of the twin sons of Isaac (Esau was the older brother), whose name God changed to Israel; his twelve sons ultimately became the heads of the twelve tribes of Israel

- **Joseph**—the favored son of Jacob, betrayed by his jealous brothers, who rose to power in Egypt and provided safe refuge for his family when they fled Canaan's drought and famine

- **Moses**—the great liberator called by God to lead the Jews out of slavery in Egypt; the great lawgiver who formed the people of Israel into a theocratic nation at Mount Sinai; regarded by the Jews as the greatest of the prophets

- **Joshua**—the military successor to Moses, who led Israel's successful invasion and settlement of Canaan ("the Promised Land"), including the famous battle of Jericho

- **Saul**—the first king of Israel, whose forty-year reign was marked by disobedience and disgrace

- **David**—the shepherd boy who became the second and greatest king of Israel, presiding over a period of expansion and prosperity

- **Solomon**—King David's son via an adulterous liaison with Bathsheba; builder of Israel's first great temple; the third and final king of Israel's "United Kingdom" history

Short History

Judaism's roots go back some four thousand years to Abraham of Ur. The Old Testament of the Bible claims that Abraham was chosen by God at around 2000 BC to father a new nation through which God would bring salvation to the world (see Genesis 12). The remainder of the book of Genesis details the sacred history of Abraham's growing family and ends with the children of Israel (named after the patriarch Jacob, who was renamed Israel) in Egypt.

Jewish religious implements, including a Torah

Exodus and Leviticus—the second and third books of the Torah—document God's miraculous deliverance of the Jews from slavery in Egypt, and also record God's explicit charter for His chosen people, given to and through Moses. The book of Numbers tells the story of how God sustained His people during their forty years of "wilderness wandering" before entering Canaan. Deuteronomy, the last book of the Pentateuch, is Moses' final address to the nation, a reteaching of God's laws to the new generation that was poised to go into the Promised Land.

After conquering and settling Canaan (see the book of Joshua), the tribes of Israel experienced seven dreary cycles (almost four hundred years) of apostasy, judgment, and repentance (see Judges). Then came the United Kingdom period (1 Samuel–1 Kings 11), a 120-year span marked by the kingships of Saul, David, and Solomon. After the death of Solomon in 930 BC, the nation split into a northern kingdom (ten tribes that took the name "Israel") and a southern kingdom (two tribes that took the name of the larger tribe, "Judah").

According to the Old Testament, the northern tribes became increasingly godless (see 1 Kings 12–2 Kings 17). Despite repeated warnings from the prophets Hosea and Amos to repent and resume their calling to be a light to the nations, the chosen people of God continued in their rebelliousness and sin. Ultimately, God appointed/allowed Assyria in 722 BC to conquer and scatter the northern kingdom.

In 605 BC, the southern kingdom, having ignored the prophetic warnings of numerous prophets, including Habakkuk, Isaiah, Joel, Jeremiah, Micah, and Zechariah, was similarly judged, this time by the Babylonians, who took the inhabitants of Judah into captivity (see 2 Kings 25). During a seventy-year period of exile, Ezekiel and Daniel prophesied about Israel's future restoration.

The Western Wall in Jerusalem, part of the temple destroyed in AD 70

In 536 BC, King Cyrus began allowing the Jews to return to their homeland. Thanks to the exhortations of the prophets Haggai, Zechariah, and Malachi, the temple at Jerusalem was rebuilt over a period of twenty years. Known as Zerubbabel's temple, this modest structure was dedicated in 516 BC.

Following their Babylonian captivity, the Jewish people never again regained the prominence they enjoyed under King David. Israel ceased to be an independent state and became a minor territory in a series of world empires. Following the Persian period (450–330 BC), the Greeks, Egyptians, and Syrians took turns dominating the Jewish people (330–166 BC). The Hasmoneans (166–163 BC) were followed by the Roman Empire.

During the course of these centuries, the religious freedom of the Jewish people varied. Some foreign governments were especially oppressive and greatly restricted the practice of Judaism. Even so, by the time of Jesus, Herod had greatly enlarged and enhanced the temple at Jerusalem (a project begun in 20 BC), and Jewish daily life was permeated by religious thought and practice. Various religious parties (the Pharisees, Sadducees, the Essenes, and the Zealots) exercised spiritual influence over the people.

In AD 66, a Judean revolt prompted the Romans to devastate Jerusalem and ultimately destroy Herod's temple. This led to the scattering of many Jews and the rise of rabbinical Judaism, an attempt to reinterpret the faith for people living without benefit of a temple sacrificial system and a priesthood. Rabbis or trained teachers took the place of the scribes and priests of old.

The combination of the rise of Christianity with the fall of Rome resulted in a greater dispersion of the Jewish people throughout Europe and Russia. They met with suspicion and persecution in every era. The atrocities of the Crusades were followed by an almost universal anti-Semitism throughout Europe. The Jews were blamed for the plagues in the Middle Ages. They were targeted during the Spanish Inquisition. They were expelled almost everywhere. No previous pogroms, however, compared with the horrific events of the Nazi Holocaust of the 1930s and 1940s, during which some six million Jews were brutally exterminated. This international tragedy has had a lingering and profound affect on the spiritual beliefs of many Jews.

In 1948, the state of Israel was established. Jews from all over the world began returning to their homeland. In 1967, the Six-Day War ended, with the armies of Israel defeating Egypt, Jordan, and Syria, and reclaiming control of the Holy City of Jerusalem.

Basic Beliefs and Values

Modern Judaism is comprised of four "camps."

- *Orthodox Jews*—Follow a strict interpretation of the Torah and the Talmud, still practicing, for example, the dietary (*kosher*) laws of the Old Testament. Hasidic Jews are considered by some to be the "right wing" of this orthodox group. They are ultra-Orthodox, often wearing *phylacteries* (small black boxes containing scripture portions) on their arms and foreheads. Until the 1800s, all Jews fell into this category. Now this is the smallest of the three primary branches.

- *Conservative Jews* (found primarily in America)—Are somewhat more lenient, believing and practicing their faith's basic traditions even if they do not scrupulously study and follow Judaism's holy books. Their desire is to keep their ancient faith, but adapt it to modern times.

- *Reformed Jews* (sometimes referred to as Humanistic, Progressive, or Liberal Jews)—Attempt to participate in modern culture/society while broadly adhering to Jewish principles and ethics. The goal is to live a moral life, but many do so without any kind of active faith in God.

- *Messianic Jews* (a tiny minority)—Are those who have put their faith in Jesus as Messiah. Despite their Jewish heritage, they are not viewed by others within Judaism as followers of the true Jewish faith.

For all Jews, Jerusalem is the holy city of God.

Other basic beliefs and distinctions about Judaism include:

- The conviction that the Jewish people have a national and eternal covenant with God
- The circumcision of newborn males (*Brit Milah*), eight days after birth, as a sign of the covenant
- The practice of the Sabbath, the weekly day of rest prescribed by God
- Some Jewish people are secular and nonreligious, some even considering themselves atheistic
- Some people are Jewish by birth (a racial heritage), and others consider themselves to be Jewish by belief (implying that converts are welcomed)

View of God

Strict monotheism (nontrinitarian), expressed by devout Jews in the constant recitation of the *Shema* ("Hear, O Israel: The LORD our God, the LORD is One . . ." Deuteronomy 6:4 NIV).

God is Spirit, but He is personal, not a mere force or vague essence. He is the eternal Creator of all. He is holy and perfect (and because of this transcendence, God may seem remote or mysterious). He is omnipotent (all-powerful), omniscient (all-knowing), and omnipresent (everywhere). He is merciful and compassionate. He is just and will judge all people—rewarding the faithful, punishing the wicked.

To Orthodox Jews, God is the eternal, personal Creator. To more "liberal" Jews, God is regarded as impersonal and perhaps unknowable.

In Hebrew, God's name is represented by the four letters, *Yod, Hei, Vav, Hei.* (The English transliteration is YHWH.) This is sometimes called the "Unutterable Name," and it is derived from the Hebrew verb "to be" (see Exodus 3). Because devout Jews so revere the Creator's Name, they will not even write it out, choosing instead to spell it G–d.

Sacred Texts

Central to Judaism is the Tanakh (the Old Testament), especially the Torah (the first five books of Moses, also known as the Pentateuch). The Talmud is a collection of rabbinical interpretations about and commentary on the Old Testament.

Worldview

For most Jews, Judaism (like Islam) is viewed as a way of life. It is an identity that involves varying degrees of devotion. Many modern Jews (at least in the West) do not belong to a synagogue and do not claim a deep, abiding faith in God. Though they may practice certain Jewish rituals and observe some of the holidays of Judaism, they do so primarily out of tradition, not spiritual devotion. Many point to the Holocaust as the one great obstacle to faith in a loving, caring God.

View of the Afterlife

Not a highly developed concept within Judaism, as the Old Testament does not speak in detail about the afterlife. Personal salvation and heavenly reward are less emphasized than national revival and restoration. Jews continue to look forward to the coming of a Messiah (that is, "anointed one") who, as a descendant of King David, will reinstitute God's kingdom on earth. Many believe the dead will be resurrected, and there will be some kind of final judgment.

Worship Services

Synagogue services are held each Sabbath day, which begins Friday at sundown and goes till Saturday evening. Rabbis preside over these services (cantors lead the prayers) and over other important Jewish rituals (circumcisions, weddings, funerals, and coming of age ceremonies for boys, called bar mitzvahs, and for girls, called bat mitzvahs). The synagogue is also a kind of community center and research facility for religious study.

Important Dates

Unlike the conventional Western (that is, Gregorian) calendar, Judaism adheres to a lunar/solar calendar, meaning its holidays "move" each year on our Western calendars.

Judaism is a faith that cherishes its long, rich history through regular remembrances. Some of the more important festivals and holy days include:

Rosh Hashanah (September/October)—a festival celebrating the Jewish New Year

Yom Kippur (September/October)—Day of Atonement, the most solemn occasion in Judaism in which Jews pray for forgiveness

Sukkot (five days after Yom Kippur)—a joyous festival for remembering the almost forty years the Jews wandered in the wilderness on their way to the Promised Land (see the Old Testament book of Numbers); also called the Feast of Tabernacles or booths

Hanukkah (December)—the Jewish "Festival of Lights," which commemorates the victory of the Maccabees over the Syrian armies in 175 BC with the lighting of lamp stands called menorahs

Purim (February/March)—a feast commemorating the salvation of the Jewish people living in exile in Persia, due to the heroic efforts of Esther, a beautiful young Jewish woman who had become queen of Persia

Passover (March/April)—an annual commemoration of God's miraculous deliverance of the Jews from Egyptian bondage (see Exodus 12), under the leadership of Moses

Shavuot (May/June)—a commemoration of Moses' receiving the Torah on Mount Sinai; also the end of the barley harvest and beginning of the wheat harvest

Yom Hashoah (usually in April)—a day for remembering the Holocaust

"What is Kabbalah? Nothing short of an answer to the questions of our universe and the ages. More specifically, Kabbalah is the mystical, esoteric side of Judaism that delves into a deeper understanding of the Hebrew Bible (or Old Testament) beyond its literal interpretation to provide us with information about the soul, the nature of God, Creation, the spiritual world, and about our individual relationship to God and each other."
—Kim Zetter

Major Differences from Christianity

Belief	Kabbalah
Sacred Text(s)	The Old Testament and the Kabbalah texts that help interpret the Old Testament
Nature of God	The eternal, infinite Creator who cannot be defined or named or known. God is referred to *Ein Sof* ("without end").
Jesus Christ	Not emphasized
Human nature	Created in God's image, free to ignore God or to pursue God's truth
About human need	To decipher God's secret codes and unlock the Bible's esoteric yet practical wisdom
Salvation	Enlightenment, spiritual elevation, and ultimately, oneness with God through diligent seeking
Afterlife	God's truth and light will be revealed in all its fullness to those who have sought truth and devoted themselves to good; worldly souls and rejecters of truth will be unable to enjoy eternal pleasures

Number of Followers

Kabbalah (pronounced kah-bah-LAH) is a mysterious Jewish spiritual tradition that is increasingly practiced by followers of various religions. Because Kabbalah is not an organized entity and does not require adherents to officially register or "join," there is no way of knowing how many people currently practice this esoteric brand of Jewish mysticism.

Major Figures/Prophets

- **Akiva ben Joseph** (AD 40–135)—a Jewish rabbi and Sanhedrin member, modest and devout; according to one legend, God had a conversation with Moses at Mount Sinai and named ben Joseph as a future Kabbalistic sage
- **Isaac the Blind** (AD 1160–1236)—a rabbi in the Jewish community of Provence, France, who earned his nickname either because he was vision-impaired or due to the blinding spiritual aura he possessed; he is credited with giving this movement the name Kaballah
- **Moshe ben Jacob Cordovero** (1522–1570)—a rabbi in Safed, Israel, who gathered a devoted following of mystics and ascetics, organizing and catego-rizing Kabbalistic thought into a giant commentary on the *Sefer Ha Zohar,* the greatest classic of Jewish mysticism
- **Isaac ben Solomon Luria**, also known as Ari (1534–1572)—a colleague of Cordovero, who innovated and made more accessible the teachings of Kabbalah

Short History

God's secrets have been around since God first revealed Himself and His will to Adam in the Garden of Eden, then to Abraham in Ur, then to Moses on Mount Sinai. However, the origins of Kabbalah, the movement that seeks to help mysti-cal seekers grasp God's cosmic secrets, are murky and disputed. Some scholars and adherents claim to see traces of Kabbalistic thought among the records of certain first-century Jewish communities. For example, Rabbi Akiva (mentioned above), took a Kabbalahesque, esoteric approach to the study of the Torah (though the word "Kabbalah" was not used for another thousand years).

Not until the twelfth century did Kabbalah come into sharper focus as an iden-tifiable movement. In southern France, a rabbi known as Isaac the Blind discovered and championed a book of mystical Bible interpretations called *Sefer Ha Bahir* ("The Book of Brilliance"). He also wrote extensively about the Genesis story of creation, and his teachings ultimately reached Spain. There, in 1280, *Sefer Ha Zohar* ("The Book of Splendor") was published. This three-volume text came to be regarded as the definitive work on Kabbalah.

In recent years the movement has become something of a fad, in large part be-cause celebrities such as Madonna, Demi Moore, Ashton Kutcher, Paris Hilton, and Britney Spears have at one time or another claimed to embrace its teachings.

Basic Beliefs and Values

Adherents of Kabbalah (the Hebrew word means "to receive") claim their doctrines (or divine secrets) were transmitted by God long ago and handed down—not to the masses, but to worthy seekers in each generation.

Some of the distinctive beliefs, claims, and practices of Kabbalah are:

- Kabbalah represents God's "hidden blueprint," a kind of map for understanding the deepest questions about meaning, a key for unlocking the great secrets of life and the universe. As Kim Zetter puts it, "For anyone who would lament that 'life doesn't come with an instruction book,' the Kabbalists would say, 'Look again.' "

- The Hebrew Bible (that is, the Old Testament) contains God's secret code.

- Special attention is given to the books of Genesis and Ezekiel because of the emphases in these books on creation (Genesis) and face-to-face encounters with God (Ezekiel).

- The acknowledgment that discerning the secrets of Kabbalah is highly subjective and difficult. God's truth is multi-layered and complicated, and we must always look for the deeper, hidden truth.

- The conviction that life is not random and haphazard, but ordered at the deepest levels of reality; all things are connected and interwoven. Kabbalah can help discover this synchronicity.

- Creation is not a past event but an ongoing process; biblical faith and evolutionary science are in concert, not competition.

- The "72 Names of God" come from a secret and complicated pattern of letters and words that Kabbalists "discovered" in Exodus 14:19–21. By following a precise pattern (for example, combining the first Hebrew letter of verse 19, the last letter of verse 20, and the first letter of verse 21), followers are able to decode this passage and form 72 words or names for God. Repeating this formula is thought to bring power. Some believe reciting these names is how Moses parted the Red Sea.

- A few insist that Kabbalah is not an independent, stand-alone religion, but rather a spiritual tradition that can be practiced by adherents of many faiths, including Judaism, Christianity, Rosicrucianism, Tibetan Buddhism, Wicca, Theosophy, and practitioners of magic. The majority of Kabbalists, however, believe that a solid grounding in Judaism is a necessity.

Title page of the first edition of the Sefer Ha Zohar

View of God

God is all-encompassing yet indefinable. Kabbalah asks, "How can finite creatures use finite words and concepts to describe the infinite?" Kabbalists resort to listing ten distinguishable attributes of God, called *sefirot*, which are emanations or manifestations of the divine. Though we cannot know God fully, these sefirot offer the best opportunity for us to comprehend His nature.

Worldview

Modern adherents of Kabbalah seem to share a common hunger for a faith that is more than rational and cerebral; they thirst for a spirituality that lives and breathes, nudges and moves the soul. Perhaps this is a function of the postmodern age.

Kabbalah acknowledges humanity's restlessness and desire for beauty and transcendence. It notes that despite our great technological and educational advances, the human soul is starving for a connection with the divine and is permeated with a desire to make an impact. Surely, life is about more than developing faster computers and buying a more elegant home.

Kabbalists seek a faith tradition that accounts for mystical experiences inexplicable by reason alone. They desire to incorporate into this faith any scientific findings that seem to be at odds with religious tradition.

View of the Afterlife

After this life, human souls will be completely revealed. Even more important, God will be revealed in all His fullness. Therefore, it is imperative for people to deal with their transgressions now, in this world. As humbling and difficult as repentance and the purification process is now, it is nothing compared to the suffering that the unrepentant and impure will experience then. Those who don't seek truth or cultivate a holy hunger for the things of God in this life will be miserable in the life to come.

Sacred Texts

Adherents believe that the Jewish Bible (Old Testament) contains God's secret revelation. Various other Kabbalistic texts purport to give codes and keys for understanding God's word and will. These texts include:

Sefer Ha Bahir ("The Book of Brilliance")—came to light among the French Jewish community between 1150 and 1200. It was discovered by Isaac the Blind.

Sefer Ha Zohar ("The Book of Splendor")—published in 1280 in Spain, this is considered the seminal Kabbalah text. Written in Aramaic, it is a thick, multivolume book full of Jewish biblical commentary (called *Midrash*), essays, sermons, visions, and dialogues. It has been attributed to both Shimon bar Yochai (the protagonist in most of its stories), and Moses de Leon, a Spanish mystic from the 1200s.

The Tanya—written by Rabbi Schneur Zalman in the 1700s, is revered by Hasidic practitioners of Kabbalah.

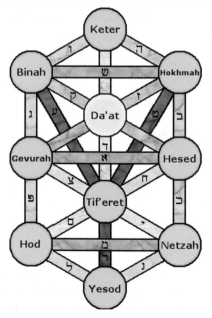

The ten sefirot (attributes) of God

Worship Services

Kabbalah typically emphasizes personal study or classes at a Kabbalah center, not corporate worship in a synagogue or church setting. It primarily involves the individual pursuit of secret spiritual insight. That insight can then be a springboard to richer devotion to God in every part of life.

Important Dates

Kabbalah does not have its own calendar. Devotees (especially those who are part of other faith traditions like Judaism) seek to use the principles of Kabbalah to enhance the manner in which they celebrate other religious holidays or festivals.

Belief	Mormonism
Sacred Text(s)	The Book of Mormon; Doctrine and Covenants; Pearl of Great Price, and the Bible, as far as it has been correctly translated
Nature of God	Many gods; the God who rules our world—called Heavenly Father—is an exalted man who achieved divine status; he is believed to have a physical body
Jesus Christ	A separate being from God the Father, he was created from the sexual union between Elohim and Mary.
Human nature	Preexistent spirit beings (conceived by the physical/spiritual union of Heavenly Father and a Heavenly Mother) that inhabit newborns; sinful, but capable of achieving godhood
About human need	Need to return to God after this life by trusting, obeying, and serving God in this life
Salvation	Eternal life requires faith and works, especially Mormon baptism
Afterlife	Heaven comprised of three kingdoms: celestial, terrestrial, and telestial; all will be resurrected and have immortality; Christ will judge; only the faithful will attain to the highest level

Major Differences from Christianity

"We have come not to take away from you the truth and virtue you possess. We have come not to find fault with you nor to criticize you. We have not come here to berate you. Keep all the good that you have, and let us bring to you more good."
—George Albert Smith, past President of the Mormon Church

Number of Followers

The Church of Jesus Christ of Latter-Day Saints, or as it is commonly known, the Mormon Church, has between eleven million and twelve million followers. (Online sources quote between 10.6 million and 12.2 million.)

Major Figures/Prophets

- **Joseph Smith** (1805–1844)—founder of Mormonism. Smith began the Latter-Day Saints Church in 1830 in Palmyra, New York
- **Brigham Young** (1801–1877)—the successor to Joseph Smith and second president of the Latter-Day Saints Church
- **Ezra Taft Benson** (1899–1994)—former United States Secretary of Agriculture under President Eisenhower and thirteenth president of the Latter-Day Saints Church

Short History

In 1820, Joseph Smith, Jr. was a God-fearing but spiritually confused farm boy living in upstate New York. He lived during a time of great religious fervor, when multiple sects and denominations were each claiming to be the true church with the true gospel.

Conflicted by such religious strife in the face of the Bible's clear, simple claim that there is "one Lord, one faith, one baptism" (Ephesians 4:5 NIV), Joseph prayed earnestly for wisdom and insight as to which of these competing churches was right. Mormons claim that Jesus Christ appeared to Joseph Smith and commanded him not to join any of the existing churches, for they "were all wrong." The Lord went on to say that none had the full, unadulterated gospel, nor did these various churches possess legitimate priesthood authority. Following the deaths of the original twelve apostles, the priesthood had long since disappeared from the earth.

In 1823, Smith claimed that an angel named Moroni appeared to him. Moroni, son of a prophet named Mormon, had recorded previously unknown historical events on some golden plates. These revelations included stories about two migrations of ancient civilizations to the Americas, and Christ's post-resurrection visitation to these "sheep of another fold." Moroni revealed the whereabouts of these buried plates and indicated they contained "the fullness of the everlasting gospel." When Smith unearthed them, he claimed they were written in a curious kind of hieroglyphic writing, which he termed "reformed Egyptian." Smith said he was able to translate them by using two special stones he called "Urim" and "Thummim." In 1830, *The Book of Mormon* was published.

Joseph Smith receiving his first vision

Almost immediately, this new faith with its different views and practices (including polygamy) was viewed with suspicion and met with persecution. Smith and his followers began a gradual migration west, moving from New York to Ohio to Missouri, then to Illinois. During this time (the early 1830s to the early 1840s), Smith claimed more divine revelations,

In short, the Latter-Day Saints church believes that God restored this long-lost priesthood authority to and through Joseph Smith. Hence, Mormons regard only their Latter-Day Saints church as the continuation of the legitimate church of Jesus Christ that we read about in the New Testament book of Acts.

which, when compiled, became the Mormon holy book *Doctrines and Covenants*. This text adds certain beliefs not found in *The Book of Mormon*.

At Nauvoo, Illinois, Smith was arrested, then shot and killed in a gunfight. Brigham Young became the new leader of the group in 1844, and he is credited with relocating the faithful to the valley of the Great Salt Lake in Utah in 1847. Since that time, Salt Lake City has served as the international headquarters of the Church of Jesus Christ of Latter-Day Saints.

- *History*—The so-called "Lost Tribes of Israel" migrated to the Americas around 600 BC. After his burial and resurrection (AD 34), Christ appeared to these inhabitants of the Americas and tried to revive Heavenly Father's plan (that is, His sacraments, kingdom purposes, and so forth) through them. These events and truths were recorded on golden plates, but never enacted. They had failed as their Hebrew ancestors had done, thus setting the stage for the renewal of God's perfect plan through Joseph Smith.

- *Jesus and Satan*—The Latter-Day Saints church claims that Jesus and Lucifer were brothers, the first two spirit children of the Father-God of our universe. When Jesus was selected to be the Savior of the world, Satan rebelled, initiating a great holy war in heaven. As punishment, Heavenly Father decreed that he would never have a human body.

- *Human Nature*—Mormonism teaches that we are all preexistent spirit beings—the result of spiritual/sexual union of Heavenly Father and Heavenly Mother. We became embodied at the moment of our birth, the immaterial spirit child indwelling the newborn infant body. In addition, Mormons teach that because we are the literal children of God, we are gods in the making: "As man is, God once was: as God is, man may be" (James Talmadge in *A Study of the Articles of Faith*). Live as a devout Mormon, and you can literally one day be the god of your own universe.

- *Jesus*—The Mormon church declares that Jesus was not conceived by the Holy Spirit as the Bible teaches, but rather is the result of sexual union between Father God and Mary. This makes Jesus the "elder brother" of all mankind.

• *Salvation*—In short, to the Mormon way of thinking, salvation is by faith and good works (Mormon baptism, tithing, temple marriage, and participation in secret rituals). They believe that a person must be baptized to become a member of the restored Church—The Church of Jesus Christ of Latter-day Saints—and to eventually enter the kingdom of heaven.

Basic Beliefs and Values

Mormonism teaches a number of historical and theological ideas that most uninformed non-Mormons find surprising:

Because Mormon baptism is essential for salvation, Mormons engage in the little-known practice of proxy baptism, or "baptism for the dead." Relying on vast genealogical research and records, devout members of the Latter-Day Saints church attempt to help nonchurch members make it into heaven by serving as "stand-ins" at continuous baptismal ceremonies held in Mormon temples.

• *Other Churches*—The current official Latter-Day Saints church view is that orthodox Christian churches are incomplete rather than corrupt. The so-called "Great Apostasy" means that historic Christianity lost the "fullness" of the gospel, not the entire message and teaching of Christ. Through the revelations given to Joseph Smith, Mormons believe God restored the true gospel. Mormons do not dismiss other people's religious experiences, and believe that anyone who accepts Jesus Christ as the Son of God is a Christian and can have divine guidance.

• *Practices*—Mormons do not have paid clergy. All church work is voluntary. All services are led by the laity. While women are eligible to serve in various capacities, the priesthood is open only to faithful, worthy men. Each authorized, ordained successor of Joseph Smith—there have been fourteen Mormon "presidents" since Joseph Smith's death—is regarded as a modern-day, God-appointed prophet. Each president has the assistance of a group of contemporary apostles.

View of God

Faithful and devout adherents to Mormon doctrine call God "Heavenly Father." In Mormon theology, "Heavenly Father" (also known as *Elohim*) was once a man ("As man now is, God once was"). This is known as "theosis"—the notion that divinity is the result of an eternal progression. Through this process, Mormons are also taught that they, too, can eventually achieve the status of deity. One Web site source states,

"Having a divine nature as a child of God, you can with the assistance and power of Christ, progress to become one day even as He is." Thus Mormonism is technically polytheistic.

In Mormon thought, God is physical. Joseph Smith claimed, "The Father has a body of flesh and bones as tangible as man's," (from *Gospel Doctrine*, Joseph Smith). God is also married. Heavenly Father is not Triune. The Father, Son, and Holy Spirit are actually three separate Gods.

Regarding the Holy Spirit (Mormons prefer to call Him the Holy Ghost), Latter-Day Saints doctrine says, "All good people can feel the influence of the Holy Ghost, but only those who are baptized and who receive the gift of the Holy Ghost by priesthood authority have the right to His constant companionship throughout life."

Other Practices

All devout Mormons participate in a full-time mission (lasting eighteen to twenty-four months). Their missionary service, usually done while in their late teens or early twenties, primarily involves door-to-door evangelism. Committed members of the church tithe faithfully (that is, giving 10 percent of their income to the work of the church). In addition, Mormons have strict prohibitions against the use of alcohol or tobacco. Caffeinated drinks are taboo also.

Worldview

Mormons regard themselves as Christians (in fact, as stated above, they see the Latter-Day Saints church as the only true and pure church of Jesus Christ). They claim belief in the Bible and faith in Jesus Christ. And yet many Christian scholars and denominations see Mormonism as an aberrant belief system that uses orthodox terms even while giving those words new, unorthodox theological meanings.

What is not disputed are these realities: the warm, profamily emphasis within the church (Monday nights are typically reserved for family activities); the commendable work ethic of Latter-Day Saints members; the fierce commitment to healthy living; the rigorous generosity of most Mormon families; and the zealous devotion of the faithful for missionary activity.

Polygamy (the practice of marrying more than one wife) was formerly an accepted practice within the Latter-Day Saints Church. Though still practiced among some remote Mormon groups and sects, the official Mormon stance adheres to civil laws forbidding such domestic arrangements.

View of the Afterlife

Latter-Day Saints church doctrine says that after death comes the resurrection. After the resurrection come judgment and/or reward. Mormons teach three levels of heaven, or three kingdoms. The highest, where God dwells and for which devout Latter-Day Saints church members are eligible, is the celestial. In this state, according to the teachings of Joseph Smith, "The same sociality which exists among us here will exist among us there, only it will be coupled with eternal glory" (Doctrine and Covenants 130:2).

Next is the middle or terrestrial kingdom, which will be the eternal address for those "who refuse to accept the gospel of Christ" (those who do not fully embrace the teachings of Mormonism), but who mostly "live honorable lives."

The lowest level of heaven is called the telestial kingdom. This is the ultimate destination for those "who continue in their sins and do not repent until after they have died." Truly wicked, unrepentant sinners are banished to the "outer darkness."

The Salt Lake Temple in Salt Lake City, Utah

Sacred Texts

The Book of Mormon, Doctrine and Covenants, and *Pearl of Great Price* (all composed, compiled, and written primarily by Joseph Smith) are viewed by Mormons as the most recent and most trustworthy of divinely-inspired texts. Latter-Day Saints church members also study and revere the Bible, considering it authoritative, "as far as it is correctly translated."

Mormons teach that from 1823 to 1827, an angel named Moroni revealed gold plates to Joseph Smith, written in a kind of ancient hieroglyphic. (Moroni was the son of a prophet named Mormon.) Using a special pair of divinely supplied stones, called Urim and Thummim, Joseph Smith was able to translate these ancient writings into English. The finished result, published in 1830, is *The Book of Mormon: Another Testament of Jesus Christ*, the never-before-revealed account of what happened when Jesus Christ lived in the Americas from approximately 590 BC to AD 421. Books in *The Book of Mormon* are named after the prophets who kept the records, such as Nephi, Mosiah, Alma, and Mormon.

Worship Services

Local Latter-Day Saints congregations (called wards or branches) are found in most small cities and larger towns. Wards assemble each Sunday and typically meet in modest "chapel" buildings. Visitors are always welcome at these sixty to seventy-five minute services, called "sacrament meetings." There is no firm and fixed liturgy, but typically these gatherings include congregational hymns and prayer, the partaking of the sacrament (communion), and two or three short messages from assigned speakers (laymen in positions of leadership, as there are no paid clergy). Various Sunday school classes are also commonly offered either before or after the sacrament meeting.

Mormons emphasize the building of temples. Currently there are more than 100 temples in the world. In these holy places, Latter-Day Saints church members learn Mormon doctrine and engage in Mormon ordinances (marriage, baptism, proxy baptism). Only Latter-Day Saints church members in good standing may participate in temple rituals.

Easter (date varies)—commemorating the suffering, death, and resurrection of Jesus Christ	**Anniversary of the Founding of the Mormon Church** (April 6)
Christmas (December 25)—celebrating the birth of Jesus Christ.	**John the Baptist's visitation to Joseph Smith** (May 15)
Pioneer Day (July 24)—commemorates the 1847 arrival of the first group of Latter-Day Saints settlers into Salt Lake Valley after their westward migration.	**General Conference** (first weekends in April and October)—not technically "holidays" but considered important days in the church year.

"We want our people in America whose parents or grandparents were descendants from slaves to be allowed to establish a separate state or territory of their own— either on this continent or elsewhere. We believe that our former slave-masters are obligated to provide such land and that the area must be fertile and minerally rich. We believe that our former slave-masters are obligated to maintain and supply our needs in this separate territory for the next 20 or 25 years, until we are able to produce and supply our own needs. Since we cannot get along with them in peace and equality after giving them 400 years of our sweat and blood and receiving in return some of the worst treatment human beings have ever experienced, we believe our contributions to this land and the suffering forced upon us by white America justifies our demand for complete separation in a state or territory of our own."
—Elijah Muhammad

Major Differences from Christianity	
Belief	**Nation of Islam**
Sacred Text(s)	The Qur'an
Nature of God	One God whose proper name is Allah, who appeared in the person of Master W. Farad Muhammad in 1930
Jesus Christ	A moral but dead prophet who "cannot do us any good or harm"; His teachings are used by white Christians to exploit blacks
Human nature	Blacks are direct descendants of the Creator; the white race is a race of devils that cannot be righteous
About human need	Blacks need to throw off the subjugating influence of the white race
Salvation	Less emphasis on spiritual reconciliation with God; more emphasis on social advancement, cultural separation, economic prosperity, and political empowerment
Afterlife	Nation of Islam members, as God's chosen people, will be resurrected mentally

Number of Followers

The Nation of Islam, sometimes called the "Nation of Peace" or the "American Muslim Mission," is thought to have between ten thousand to one hundred thousand followers. Original members of the group referred to themselves as Black Muslims, a term that was later disavowed by Nation of Islam leader Louis Farrakhan.

Major Figures/Prophets

- **Noble Drew Ali**, formerly Timothy Drew (1886–1929)—founder of the Moorish Temple of Science Organization, a group that advocated the idea that the African peoples were originally Islamic; this notion later became one of the central tenets of the Nation of Islam

- **Wali Farad Muhammad**, formerly Wallace Dodd Fard (c.1891–1934?)—the Detroit salesman and disciple of Drew; he founded the Nation of Islam in 1930, and mysteriously disappeared in 1934

- **Elijah Muhammad**, formerly Robert Poole (1897–1975)—the successor to Wali Farad, who moved the Nation of Islam headquarters to Chicago and declared that Farad was Allah in the flesh

- **Warith Deen Muhammad**, formerly Wallace Muhammad (1933–present day)—the son of Elijah Muhammad who succeeded his father as leader; moved the Nation of Islam away from its radical "black racial superiority" teachings toward pure, traditional Sunni Islam, changed name to the American Muslim Mission

- **Malcolm X, formerly Malcolm Little** (1925–1965)—the ex-convict who became a leading spokesman for the Nation of Islam under Elijah Muhammad (and later, Muhammad's most vocal critic); assassinated in 1965 by fellow Black Muslims

- **Louis Farrakhan**, formerly Louis Eugene Walcott (1933–present day)—a defector from Wallace Muhammad's American Muslim Mission in 1977, who reorganized the Nation of Islam and restored its original doctrines of black racial supremacy and black nationalism, as espoused by Elijah Muhammad

Short History

The Nation of Islam began as a socio-politico-economic movement as well as a religious ideology. At the end of World War I and at the beginning of the Great Depression, tens of millions of Americans faced poverty and uncertainty. No group was more imperiled or disillusioned than inner-city African-Americans.

In this dire sociological context a message of black freedom, equal justice and opportunity, and empowerment was extremely appealing. Enter Wallace Dodd Fard,

A Nation of Islam speaker in London

a door-to-door salesman in Detroit, Michigan. Fard had been deeply influenced by the teachings of Timothy Drew (known as Noble Drew Ali), founder of the Moorish Temple of Science Organization. In 1930, seizing upon black discontent and anxiety, Fard established the Lost-Found Nation of Islam, and came to be known as Wali Farad Muhammad. This early Nation of Islam was a very Americanized version of Islam with a belief in Allah, but with an added insistence that whites were evil, and that blacks should separate and form their own state. (Christianity was viewed as a white man's religion used to subordinate poor, trusting blacks.)

When Fard suddenly and mysteriously disappeared in 1934, Robert Poole assumed leadership of the group. He changed his name to Elijah Muhammad, and declared that Fard (Farad Muhammad) had been Allah in the flesh. He moved the organization from Detroit to Chicago. Even when convicted and imprisoned for draft evasion, Elijah Muhammad continued to exert absolute control of the Nation of Islam.

In the early 1960s, Muhammad came under fire from Malcolm X, one of his disciples and the close friend of Muhammad's own son, Wallace. Specifically, Malcolm was disillusioned by the discovery that Elijah Muhammad had fathered children with several women who worked in Nation of Islam. Malcolm X left Nation of Islam, and made these facts public. In 1965, he was shot and killed.

Upon Elijah Muhammad's own death in 1975, his son, Wallace Muhammad, assumed control of the movement.

A reformer, Wallace Muhammad immediately took steps to move the Nation of Islam away from its notions of black supremacy and back toward the doctrines of mainstream, orthodox Islam. He even changed the name of the group to the World Community of Al-Islam in the West (1976), and later to the American Muslim Mission (1980). All these changes prompted large-scale defections.

The most prominent defector during these years was Louis Farrakhan, who reorganized the more militant Nation of Islam in 1978. In 1997, Farrakhan sought to move the Nation of Islam closer to traditional Islam. In 2000, he held reconciliation meetings with Wallace Muhammad of the American Muslim Mission. These efforts, while not resulting in a reunification, did much to minimize the hostility between the two groups.

Basic Beliefs and Values

To clarify the beliefs and values of the Nation of Islam, this chart compares the beliefs of traditional Islam with the Nation of Islam.

	Traditional Islam	Nation of Islam
Beliefs about Allah	Never incarnate	Incarnated as Wallace Fard
Prophets	Muhammad was Allah's final prophet	Elijah Muhammad is another prophet
Equality of Peoples	All are equal	The black race is superior
Practices	Five Pillars of Faith	Five Pillars of Faith
Christianity	An error-filled faith	A tool used by whites to oppress blacks
Primary Emphasis	Spiritual	Racial and cultural
Seeks to reach	All mankind	Blacks who are descendants of slaves

Other beliefs and practices:

- Nation of Islam members pray five times daily, facing Mecca.
- Women adherents must never be alone with any man other than their husbands.
- Interracial marriage is strictly off-limits.
- The white race is evil, inferior, and the enemy.

View of God

As mainstream Muslims, members of the Nation of Islam believe in one God, whose name is Allah. Allah is described as beneficent, merciful, and the final judge of all.

However, in a serious doctrinal departure from historic, orthodox Islam, adherents of the Nation of Islam believe that Allah was incarnated in 1930 in the person of Wallace Dodd Fard (Farad Muhammad).

Worldview

One of the central tenets of historic Islam is the complex, highly-debated notion of *jihad* ("struggle"). Most Muslims regard this as a call to personal struggle—the individual effort to resist sin and revere Allah. A radical minority interpret jihad to mean war against non-Muslims. The Nation of Islam—existing as a minority faith in an affluent American culture with a history of oppression—sees jihad as the struggle to overcome what it sees as a long-term, systemic racism that results in civil, educational, economic, and political mistreatment of blacks. Thus, there is a subtle but significant difference between mainstream Islam and the Americanized Nation of Islam.

Historic Islam points first to its all-encompassing devotion to Allah, and second, to the broad and deep cultural impact of Islamic belief. The Nation of Islam seems to point primarily to needed cultural change, then secondarily, to its Islamic religious beliefs and principles.

This much is true: the Nation of Islam is marked by an extreme mistrust of the United States government, and bitterness over historic oppression and unjust treatment of blacks, especially slavery and its lingering effects. It is also dominated by a desire to create a separate black civilization built by hard work and self-reliance and marked by purity, morality, and brotherhood.

View of the Afterlife

The Nation of Islam believes in a coming judgment by Allah, happening first in America. "We believe in the resurrection of the dead—not in physical resurrection—but in mental resurrection. We believe that the so-called Negroes are most in need of mental resurrection; therefore they will be resurrected first. Furthermore, we believe we are the people of God's choice, as it has been written, that God would choose the rejected and the despised. We can find no other persons fitting this description in these last days more than the so-called Negroes in America. We believe in the resurrection of the righteous."

Sacred Texts

The Nation of Islam believes in the Qur'an. Regarding the Bible, the Nation of Islam states, "It has been tampered with and must be reinterpreted so that mankind will not be snared by the falsehoods that have been added to it."

Worship Services

Members of the Nation of Islam are expected to participate in a minimum of two temple services per week.

Important Dates

The Nation of Islam celebrates the holidays of traditional Islam (page 109). In addition, it recognizes:

Savior's Day (February 26)—a celebration of the birthdate of Wallace Fard Muhammad, whom Black Muslims regard as Allah incarnate
The Birthday of Elijah Muhammad (October 7)

"Most adherents to traditional American Indian ways characteristically deny that their people ever engaged in any religion at all. Rather, these spokespeople insist, their whole culture and social structure was and still is infused with a spirituality that cannot be separated from the rest of the community's life at any point. . . . Whereas outsiders may identify a single ritual as the 'religion' of a particular people, the people themselves will likely see that ceremony as merely an extension of their day-to-day existence, all parts of which are experienced within ceremonial parameters and should be seen as 'religious.' "
—George E. Tinker

Major Differences from Christianity	
Belief	**Native American Spirituality**
Sacred Text(s)	No written Scripture but many oral traditions and ancient stories are continually being collected and preserved
Nature of God	The eternal, all-powerful, impersonal Great Spirit who permeates all creation
Jesus Christ	Not emphasized
Human nature	"There is no tree in the forest that is straight, though all are reaching up for the light, and trying to grow straight"
About human need	To win the Great Spirit's favor by reverence, honesty, and a life of courage and service
Salvation	Not liberation from sin and its consequences but achieving harmony with the Great Spirit and with creation
Afterlife	One's spirit departs this world and enters the world to come

Number of Followers

The best estimates of ethnic Native Americans range from one million to three million, mostly living in North America. (These numbers include one million Native Americans living on three hundred Indian reservations in the United States.) It is unknown how many of these people still practice traditional Native American spirituality.

Major Figures/Prophets

- **The Great Peacemaker** (c.AD 1570)—a spiritual leader and prophet who founded the Iroquois Confederation and influenced Hiawatha
- **Powhatan** (1547–1618)—father of Pocahontas
- **Wabasha** (c. 1718–?)—a Santee Sioux chief and philosopher
- **Tecumseh** (1768–1813)—legendary Shawnee chief and statesman
- **Crazy Horse** (c. 1840–1877)—chief and ethical leader of the Lakota Sioux
- **Sitting Bull** (1831–1890)—revered mystical chief of the Hunkpapa Sioux
- **Geronimo** (1834–1909)—chief of the Chiricahua Apaches

Short History

Are Native Americans actually native to America? Despite the insistence by some that their people have always been here, many scholars say no and believe that they were the migratory descendants of ancient Northern European/Asian peoples, who hunted and gathered their way eastward across the Bering Strait and south into North, Central, and South America.

With them, these newcomers brought an eclectic, religious belief system that included nature worship (mountain and sky gods), goddess worship, and animistic beliefs (the notion that all creatures and things—even inanimate objects—are permeated by spirits.)

For centuries these tribes flourished, each with its own oral spiritual tradition, unique legends, myths, and folklore. However, the arrival of Christian Europeans in North America in the 1500s began the gradual suppression and/or elimination of much Native American spirituality, and at times, its syncretism with Christian theology.

In 1978, the U. S. Congress passed the Freedom of Religion Act, in large part to help protect and restore Native American spirituality. Since that time, a revival movement has flourished as many Native Americans seek to return to the spiritual roots of their ancestors.

In recent years it has become common for some New Age followers, self-proclaimed shamans, and enterprising capitalists to coopt certain Native American spiritual practices and sacred symbols for profit. This kind of religious and commercial exploitation has angered many tribal leaders. One representative stated, "Being spiritually bankrupt themselves, they want our spirituality as well."

Basic Beliefs and Values

One could spend a lifetime reading and researching, and still not fully comprehend the complex array of unique spiritual beliefs of Native Americans. With so many tribes, so much history and diversity, and so many fascinating sacred traditions, we must settle for a few oversimplified generalizations.

Native American spirituality typically is marked by the following understandings and habits:

- No division of life into the sacred and secular; all of life is spiritual.

- Commonplace, daily events and routines (for example, hunting, harvesting corn, getting dressed, and so forth) are accompanied by simple prayer and ceremonial actions.

- A community orientation rather than an individualistic mindset; every act must benefit the tribe.

- One doesn't choose which religious ideas and practices to embrace; as a member of a certain community and tradition, one inherits an all-encompassing spirituality.

- The unity and duality of all existence.

- The importance of place and space in spirituality (versus the Euro-American religious emphasis on time)

- An all-encompassing reverence for creation; a connection or sense of brotherhood with the natural world.

- Certain members/leaders in the tribe possess a mystic wisdom and occult-like clairvoyance cultivated through trances and visions.

View of God

Native Americans view God as the eternal Great Spirit or Great Mystery. Various tribes call the Great Spirit by different names. The Pawnee, for example, call the Great Spirit *Tirawa*, and describe Him as "omnipotent and beneficent. He pervades the universe, and is a Supreme Ruler. Upon His will depends everything that happens. He can bring good or bad; can give success or failure" (from Earnest Thompson Seton, *The Gospel of the Redman*).

Worldview

Traditional Native Americans view all of life as being fundamentally spiritual. The goal of existence is not to accumulate material wealth but to live with reverence and to serve one's people. Life is not a personal, private, individual pursuit, but a community affair.

Orrin Lewis of the Cherokee Nation observes, "American Indian spirituality is not evangelistic. It is private and entirely cultural. You cannot convert to 'Native American' any more than you can convert to African-American or Korean or any other cultural identity you would need to be raised in to understand."

A man performing a sunset blessing

View of the Afterlife

Native Americans believe in a world to come. However, it's not clear exactly what that future existence will look like. Charles Eastman wrote that Native Americans are "content to believe that the spirit which the 'Great Mystery' breathed into man returns to Him who gave it, and that after it is freed from the body, it is everywhere and pervades all nature, yet often lingers near the grave or 'spirit bundle' for the consolation of friends, and is able to hear prayers."

Sacred Texts

There is no Native American scripture. Rather, each Native American tribe has its own sacred stories and spiritual legends—mostly passed down in oral form and preserved through distinctive songs and dances. Increasing interest in American Indian history, together with a growing concern for the preservation of Native American culture, has resulted in a vigorous effort to put these assorted myths and fables into written form.

In Native American Spiritualituy, acts of reverence are simple. Daily prayer at daybreak acknowledges the Unseen Spirit by quietly facing the dawn with awe and gratitude. A type of grace or invocation is offered before meals and at the conclusion of a successful hunt.

Worship Services

When worshipping according to traditional custom, Native Americans do not gather in groups for a liturgical service. On the contrary, they worship in silence (wordless adoration) and solitude. There is no church or temple, no preaching, and no clergy. It would seem sacrilegious to build a house for the Great Spirit, "who may be met face to face in the mysterious, shadowy aisles of the primeval forest, . . . and yonder in the jeweled vault of the night sky! He who enrobes Himself in filmy veils of cloud . . . needs no lesser cathedral!" (Charles Eastman).

Important Dates

While individual tribes commemorate special events (for example, the Lakota Sioux's "Seven Sacred Rites"), the general rule among Native Americans is that no days are regarded as holy or set apart for special observances, because every day is permeated with the sacred.

"I think the new spirituality will be a spirituality that's not based on a particular dogma. And that steps away from the old spiritual paradigm that we have created on this planet, which comes from a thought that there is such a thing as being better."
—Neale Donald Walsch

"In every community, there is work to be done. In every nation, there are wounds to heal. In every heart, there is the power to do it."
—Marianne Williamson

Major Differences from Christianity

Belief	New Age Spirituality
Sacred Text(s)	No holy book, though many ancient writings (especially Eastern texts) are useful for gaining wisdom
Nature of God	Most view God as impersonal—a cosmic force that permeates all things and indwells all people
Jesus Christ	Not a focal point, though some regard him as a wise teacher, guru, enlightened master (one more expression of the divine)
Human nature	Basically good, essentially divine, capable of anything if one believes and works with others
About human need	Enlightenment—realization that we are divine and have unlimited potential
Salvation	From awareness of one's true divine nature
Afterlife	Most believe in some form of reincarnation

Number of Followers

Precise figures are difficult to ascertain because many practitioners of other faith traditions (including some Christians) embrace various New Age beliefs. Based on surveys, it is accurate to state the number of those who hold to some New Age beliefs (for example, beliefs in astrology and reincarnation), or who participate in some New Age practices (for example, relying on crystals to heal, seeking contacts with angels, and so forth) as being in the tens of millions.

Major Figures/Prophets

Being the amorphous movement that it is, New Age Spirituality has no real founder. Many contemporary spiritual leaders have borrowed Eastern ideas and dabbled in novel spiritual beliefs. However, a few individuals (who may or may not describe themselves as "New Agers") have been instrumental in popularizing various New Age ideas. These include:

- **Alice Bailey** (1980–1949)—British writer and teacher, who meshed together Christian doctrines and tenets from Theosophy and the occult; credited with being one of the first to use the phrases, "Age of Aquarius" and "New Age"

- **Maharishi Mahesh Yogi** (1917–present)—Hindu guru who popularized Transcendental Meditation in the West

- **Shirley MacLaine** (1934–present)—Oscar-winning actress who wrote about her New Age beliefs and experiences in the books, *Out on a Limb* and *Dancing in the Light*

Shirley MacLaine

- **David Spangler** (1945–present)—self-described "popular mystic" and pioneer of the modern New Age movement via his work with both the Scottish Findhorn Foundation and the Lindisfarne Association, a New Age think tank

- **Dr. Larry Dossey** (unknown–present)—Texas-born internist, author of *Reinventing Medicine, Healing Words*, and *Recovering the Soul*; former editor of the journal *Alternative Therapies in Health and Medicine*; advocate for role of the mind and spirituality in healthcare

- **James Redfield** (1950–present)—psychologist and novelist whose book *The Celestine Prophecy* has sold in excess of twenty million copies; proponent of the idea of synchronicity, the notion that everything in the universe is connected

- **Marianne Williamson** (1952–present)—author of *A Return to Love* and lecturer; developed a self-study system called "A Course in Miracles," which she claimed was dictated to her by Jesus; former head pastor of the Unity Church's Renaissance Unity Interfaith Spiritual Fellowship

Short History

New Age Spirituality is the catch-all term used to describe the vast but loosely-connected network of individuals and groups who share a hodgepodge of Eastern beliefs and a common desire to usher in a "new age" of nonreligious spirituality. Also called the New Age Movement, it is made up of mystics, self-styled gurus, channelers, hypnotists, alternative healers, astrologers, and assorted seekers.

The turbulent decade of the 1960s is usually cited by historians as the era in which New Age Spirituality became a recognizable entity. The historical context is important. Western societies were disenchanted with organized religion (especially Christianity) and frustrated with secularism's inability to answer personal questions of meaning and address serious cultural problems.

In England many people began turning to "new" and exotic non-Western, nontraditional belief systems such as Wicca, Gnosticism, Hinduism,

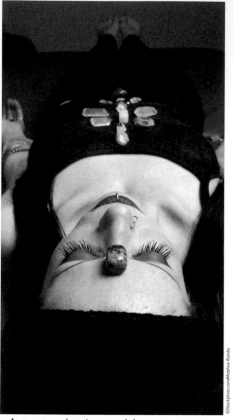

A woman undergoing crystal therapy

Neopaganism, Taoism, Spiritism, and so forth, as well as esoteric practices like astrology, astral projection, meditation, and channeling. Quickly, this growing fascination with Eastern thought spread west across the Atlantic to North America.

Beginning in 1971, groups like Edgar Cayce's Association for Research and Enlightenment began holding workshops and New Age seminars. This pick-and-choose, nondogmatic spirituality, with its promise of personal enlightenment and goal of social change, found a receptive audience in America, making inroads in science, politics, medicine, and education. Popularity of the movement peaked in the late 1970s and 1980s, boosted by celebrity books such as Shirley MacLaine's *Out on a Limb*. Many former adherents have since gravitated to other spiritual belief systems.

Basic Beliefs and Values

In contrast to recently founded religions such as Scientology or Christian Science, the New Age Movement is not an organized, clearly definable religious institution or church. New Age Spirituality has no established hierarchy, creed, official Web site, or international headquarters. There is no membership process; anyone can "join" by embracing some of the ideas or practices.

New Age Spirituality is a curious and highly individualized mix of monism (everything is one), pantheism (God is everything and everything is God), Hinduism, Taoism, Gnosticism, and/or Buddhism.

Not every New Ager holds all the following beliefs nor engages in all the listed practices, but some of the most commonly held ideas and popular activities are:

- *Unlimited human potential*—The belief that God, the cosmic life force and the creative spark, is everywhere and in all people.

- *Ecological sensitivity*—Often including the belief that the planet is a living organism, called Gaia, or Mother Earth.

- *Emphasis on holistic health*—Practices include a plethora of alternative healing techniques—everything from acupuncture to psychic healing to crystal therapy. Homeopathy, massage, and reflexology, touch therapy (harnessing the divine current that flows through the universe and focusing it to parts of the body that need healing), and music therapy (using New Age music) are also common.

- *Meditation*—Clearing the mind of negative thoughts and energy; a means of relaxing and also opening oneself up to the divine; may involve some kind of mantra. This can involve spending time at a New Age retreat center, often in beautiful, natural settings.

- *Divination*—Using tarot cards, astrology, or psychic readings to predict the future.

- *Communication beyond this world*—Consulting with psychics, channelers, teachers of astral projection, and so on.

- *Attending New Age gatherings and workshops*—Some "symposiums" and conventions resemble spiritual "shopping malls," offering all sorts of New Age goods and services.

View of God

When it comes to defining God, New Agers have various views. Most are pantheistic, believing that God is everything and everything is God, including humans. Others are panentheistic, believing that God is everything and also beyond everything.

In most cases, God is viewed as impersonal and powerful, a life force that can be appropriated and harnessed for personal enrichment and cultural change.

Worldview

New Age Spirituality is eclectic, antiauthoritarian, and tolerant of other spiritual ideas. Some of the underlying suppositions that provide its basic structure are:

- *Relativism*—Truth is not absolute but is relative; that is, it is personal, individualized, and subjective. You have your truth; I have my truth. And even though we believe contradictory things, we are both right.

- *Universalism*—Reality is like a single giant mountain with God at the top. Divergent religions and belief systems are really just different paths up the same mountain. One day, we will all meet at the top and become one with God. In short, there are many, many different ways to God; all are valid.

- *Environmentalism*—Because the earth is a living organism (called Gaia or Mother Earth), and because all is God, the earth is divine and deserves our reverence, worship, and care.

- *Mysticism*—Too much thinking stifles our ability to encounter the divine. To be truly spiritual we need to jettison our Western rational mind-set and embrace Eastern ways of emptying the mind and opening it up to new spiritual experiences. This can be accomplished through meditation, hypnosis, guided imagery, dreaming, and sometimes through the use of hallucinogenic drugs.

View of the Afterlife

The majority of New Age Spirituality adherents seem to embrace some kind of belief in reincarnation. Borrowing from Hinduism, the prevailing view among New Agers is that they have lived many previous lives, and after this life, they will again return in some form.

Sacred Texts

There is no official New Age scripture or text. Truth for New Age Spirituality practitioners is found not in a holy book (though they believe that many revered writings contain wisdom and make for worthwhile reading and study). Truth is found within the self (because the divine lives within all); truth is also found in nature/creation.

This is considered necessary because of the law of karma—wrongs done in the past must be "undone" or "canceled out" by good deeds in the future. One's future existence will be positive (full of reward) or negative (full of punishment and pain), depending on how one lives in the present.

Worship Services

Worship in New Age Spirituality is as diverse as the individuals who practice it. With no official creed, church, or clergy, there is no set place or time to worship, and no liturgy.

Important Dates

There are no holidays distinct to New Age Spirituality, though many New Agers choose to celebrate Earth Day, summer and winter solstices, as well as special days commemorated in other (often Eastern) spiritual traditions.

"Up to now, nobody has said that there is anything beyond enlightenment. That's why I say, I am a milestone. With me, a new chapter in the history of consciousness begins. Enlightenment will be now the beginning, not the end. The beginning of a nonending process in all dimensions of richness."

—Osho

Major Differences from Christianity

Belief	Osho
Sacred Text(s)	No scriptures, per se—primarily the teachings of Rajneesh
Nature of God	Not a person but a presence that is in everything; all is one and all is God (monism)
Jesus Christ	Jesus became Christ on the cross; he died at age 112 in Kashmir
Human nature	Spiritual and part of the divine essence, but unaware. Sin means forgetting that one is a seeker.
About human need	Need enlightenment
Salvation	Understanding who one is, finding the truth of your own being, and becoming joyful
Afterlife	Believes that life is eternal, there is no death, no beginning, no end; we will always exist in different forms.

Number of Followers

At the height of its popularity in the 1970s and 1980s, Osho operated about six hundred centers around the world and claimed some two hundred thousand followers. Currently the group is thought to have fewer than ten thousand devotees.

Major Figures/Prophets

- **Bhagwan Shree Rajneesh** (1931–1990)—founder of Osho, formerly called *Rajneeshism*, in 1964. *Bhagwan* means either "God" or "the Blessed One"; *Shree* means "Master."

Short History

Rajneesh was born and grew up in Kuchwada in central India. One of twelve children, his parents were devotees of Jainism (page 110). Rajneesh was a well-read, religious-minded youth. He studied philosophy, eventually earning a master's degree and becoming a professor. During his young adult years, he experimented with a hodgepodge of religious concepts, philosophical notions, and controversial ideas. At age twenty-one, he claimed to have reached enlightenment. He left the university and hit the guru lecture circuit, gaining notoriety for, among other things, advocating sexual freedom as a means of reaching spiritual enlightenment.

In the mid 1970s, Rajneesh opened an *ashram* (a religious retreat) in Poona, India, which attracted large numbers of followers from around the world—including many Westerners. There he developed and popularized unique meditation techniques. Contrary to the quieter Hindu style, Rajneesh's "dynamic meditation" was active and often accompanied by dancing or jumping, shouting, and loud music.

In 1981, Rajneesh and his followers ventured west, relocating to the United States, in part, so that Rajneesh could pursue medical treatment for unknown health problems. The Osho adherents purchased Big Muddy Ranch, a sixty thousand-plus acre spread near Antelope, Oregon. The goal was a self-sustaining commune called *Rajneeshpuram* ("city of Rajneesh").

These new neighbors sparked immediate and heated controversy in rural Oregon. They ran for and won political offices. They renamed the town of Antelope the City of Rajneesh. Criminal activity by the group, including building a stockpile of automatic weapons, was alleged. A long-running series of legal battles began.

As public opposition mounted, Bhagwan Rajneesh and his followers began to fear that federal law enforcement agencies

Big Muddy Ranch, formerly Rajneeshpuram, an international community led by Osho

were on the verge of invading their compound. His top associate, Sheela Silverman, fled, and Rajneesh began to try to make her the scapegoat of all the negative allegations. When Rajneesh tried to flee the country, he was apprehended in Charlotte, North Carolina, and charged with violating U.S. immigration laws. He was eventually fined and deported. Returning to India in 1987, he was met with suspicion and occasional hostility.

Relocating yet again—this time to Uruguay—Rajneesh changed his name to *Osho*. (Rajneesh claimed the word was derived from the expression "oceanic experience" by William James, adding, "It is a healing sound.") Since that time, the followers of Rajneesh have been known as Osho. The name/word *Osho*® was registered as a trademark in order to be able to license and sell certain products.

In 1990, Rajneesh/Osho died from unknown causes. Though his death certificate listed "heart failure" as the official cause of death, some devotees maintain he was poisoned by the CIA; critics contend he died from the complications of a sexually transmitted disease.

Before his death, Osho created a board/organization to oversee the affairs of the group. Offices in India and New York administer the worldwide affairs of the group.

Basic Beliefs and Values

Osho's essential theological beliefs come right out of the Hindu-Buddhist tradition—that God is in all things and all persons, a living current of the energy flowing through the illusory world of forms.

Bhagwan Rajneesh claimed that all religions were one—though he was often critical of other faiths. He seemed to derive special pleasure in saying and doing shocking, provocative things. (He has been called "a spiritually incorrect mystic.") Consider this example from one of his discourses in which he described an exchange of letters with Mother Teresa:

> *Because I criticized her a few years ago, she wrote a letter to me: "I cannot understand your criticism. Service to humanity is the true religion. Don't you agree with it?"*
>
> *I wrote to her, "Yes, I agree. Tell all six hundred million Catholics to commit suicide. That will be a service to humanity." The world is suffering from overpopulation—Christians should start committing suicide and serve humanity. But they go on doing just the opposite; they go on opening hospitals, they go on saving orphans. They are against birth control, they are against abortion. This is service to humanity? Nothing can be more poisonous to humanity than what Mother Teresa is doing.*

For the most part, Bhagwan borrowed and combined elements from major religious traditions such as Zen (he delighted in the "illogic" of it), Taoism, Hinduism, Jainism, and Christianity. He also incorporated ancient Greek philosophy, humanistic psychology, modern forms of therapy, and meditation techniques.

He had no belief in sin: "To forget that you are a seeker is dangerous. It is falling into sin. This is the only sin I accept as sin."

Bhagwan considered Jesus Christ, Lao-Tzu, and the Buddha, among others, to be enlightened beings. In his teaching/lecture sessions, multiple holy books from various faith traditions were quoted and discussed. He would reference the Upanishads, the New Testament, and the Tantra. If his teachings seemed contradictory, all the better:

> *This is not a teaching, a doctrine, a creed. That's why I can say anything. I am the most free person who has ever existed as far as saying anything is concerned. I can contradict myself in the same evening a hundred times. Because it is not a speech, it has not to be consistent.*

One of his most eyebrow-raising teachings was the notion that sexual energy was the fundamental source of all human energy. He created even more controversy by insisting that repressing this energy was the source of most personal problems. Cult-watch organizations and many parents of Rajneesh devotees claimed a rampant sexual immorality within the group.

Though Bhagwan demanded that his followers live ascetic, frugal lifestyles, he was known for his extravagant and luxurious lifestyle, maintaining—for example—a fleet of Rolls-Royce automobiles. There were credible claims that he developed addictions to alcohol and nitrous oxide ("laughing gas"), and that he gave no attention to personal hygiene.

Osho majors on the individual "inner science" of meditation. Meditation is seen as the key to a fulfilled life. By it you can access your "inner powerhouse of consciousness," and know who you really are. As you become more aware of your identity and potential, you gradually eliminate the need for any kind of external authority, ideology, or institution.

> When cobbled together, Bhagwan's various "pursuits of truth" and theories of wholeness offered a fundamental message: no creed. No need to worship an external higher power. Look within your own soul. Discover your true divine self. Spend your existence knowing yourself. The kingdom of heaven and the path to fulfillment are within.

In contrast to quieter and more contemplative traditions, Osho offers a variety of "active meditations" lasting about an hour, that often involve dancing, humming, speaking gibberish, and whirling. Adherents claim these assorted exercises can reduce stress, enable one to "let go," ultimately bringing about a condition of inner stillness. Indicative of the group's belief in the importance of "freeing the mind," the Osho.com Web site includes not a "Thought for the Day" but a "No-thought for the Day."

Worldview

In comparison to many other religions that speak of selfless service to the world and helping others, Osho is clearly self-oriented. The goal is personal fulfillment—achieving bliss, finding one's own way, one's own joy and happiness, and realizing one's divine potential. There is little emphasis on compassion and ministry. A better world is the by-product of this personal journey. Bhagwan shrewdly wed the metaphor of a "Buddha" mentality (serious, deep, contemplative, wise) with the notion of a "Zorba" lifestyle (wild, carefree, celebratory).

View of the Afterlife

Osho believed that death "is the greatest joke there is. Death has never happened, cannot happen in the very nature of things, because life is eternal. Life cannot end; it is not a thing, it is a process. It is not something that begins and ends; it has no beginning and no end. You have always been here in different forms, and you will always be here."

Perhaps Osho's own grave marker best sums up the guru's (and the group's) view of human existence:

Never Born
Never Died
Only Visited this
Planet Earth between
Dec. 11, 1931—Jan. 19, 1990

View of God

God is in everything and everyone. All is divine. The divine essence flows through the universe.

Sacred Texts

A booklet was published in 1983 by the commune, in which "Rajneeshism" was described as a lifestyle of meditation, a lifelong process of learning to maintain a meditative attitude in work and play. One could grasp the philosophy and techniques by listening to the lectures of the guru. This official booklet contained chants, named religious holidays, and outlined religious rituals to be used on the occasions of birth, marriage, caring for the sick, and death. It further spelled out the loose organization of the group.

Adherents of Osho do not follow a "holy book." Rather, as indicated above, they read and follow a hodgepodge of religious and philosophical writings, including teachings from the Upanishads, the Bible, and mostly the lectures and writings of Rajneesh himself.

Worship Services

With the dismantling of the Oregon compound and the subsequent death of Osho, the group no longer has the high profile it had in the 1980s. It is not now and never was highly organized.

The group's publishing headquarters are in New York. It also operates a forty-acre International Meditation Resort near Poona, India. Other Osho centers and institutes are found around the world, operating more like franchises. In 2007, official Osho centers were located in only nineteen of the fifty United States.

Adherents attend various meditation training workshops and conferences. Individuals still read Osho's writings, buy instructional tapes and CDs, listen to his teachings online (paid subscriptions are available), and privately practice his meditative techniques.

Important Dates

Unlike most faiths that set aside certain days as "holy," there is little emphasis in the Osho online community on such things. Various meditation centers offer regular meditation camps, but few special observances.

Osho's birthday (December 11)

April Fool's Day (April 1)—due to Osho's emphasis on joy and celebration (he often cracked jokes in his discourses), the Osho World Foundation in 2007 held a big event on this day with guest comedians.

Sannyas Day (late September)—the day Osho initiated his first group of disciples as *sannyas,* who had committed to his vision of a rich, robust, joy-filled life.

"We are looking to Haile Selassie for the spiritual deliverance of the world, not only among coloured races but whites as well. We are working towards a closer unity among mankind. The principles of the organization are based on Bible prophecies borne out by the coronation of Haile Selassie in 1930 when he was proclaimed King of Kings and Lion of Judah. We claim him to be the Messiah."
—Altamount Reid, Rasta leader

"Rastafari means to live in nature, to see the Creator in the wind, sea and storm. Other religions pointed to the sky, and while we were looking in the sky, they dug up all the gold and diamonds and went away with them"
—Jimmy Cliff, Jamaican reggae musician and Rastafarian follower

Major Differences from Christianity

Belief	Rastafarianism
Sacred Text(s)	The Holy Piby ("Black Man's Bible"), and to lesser degree the *Kebra Negast*, a history of Ethiopia
Nature of God	Similar to the Judeo-Christian God, but called Jah, and believed to be manifested in Ethiopian Emperor Haile Selassie
Jesus Christ	An incarnation of Jah, who was black, not white
Human nature	Rastas believe they are "everliving" (both physically and spiritually immortal)
About human need	Blacks need liberation from white oppression, and reunification
Salvation	Being one with Jah and with fellow Rastas
Afterlife	Africa (called "Zion") is viewed as heaven on earth; no beliefs in traditional heaven or hell

Number of Followers

The total number of adherents worldwide is estimated at seven hundred thousand to one million. Followers are mostly male and mostly of African descent. It is reported that around three thousand to five thousand Rastafarians live in the United States.

Major Figures/Prophets

- **Marcus Garvey** (1887–1940)—Jamaican-born opponent of black oppression and attempts at integration, leader of the Universal Negro Improvement Association, and a proponent of black nationalism (that is, reunifying and returning blacks to their African homeland); for Rastafarians, a kind of "John the Baptist" figure

- **Emperor Haile Selassie** (1892–1975)—ruler of Ethiopia; regarded by Rastafarians as the messiah and founder of their faith, though he himself denied all attributions of divinity; was an Ethiopian Orthodox Christian

- **Leonard Howell** (1898–1981)—an early leader of the Jamaican Rastafari movement, arrested and jailed in 1933

- **Bob Marley** (1945–1981)—Jamaican reggae artist who popularized Rastafarian beliefs through his music

Short History

The seeds of Rastafarianism (Rastas prefer the phrase "the Rastafari movement") were sown in the early 1900s by Marcus Garvey, later known as "Black Moses." Garvey was a powerful promoter of the idea of black repatriation to Africa. He believed Africans were the true Israelites, scattered throughout the world (including Jamaica) as a result of divine punishment. He wanted blacks worldwide to separate from white culture, reunite, return to the so-called Dark Continent, and restore its ancient glory. Speaking of Africa's eventual redemption, Garvey declared, "It is in the wind. It is coming." He further urged blacks to "look to Africa for the crowning of a king to know that your redemption is near."

When Prince Ras Tafari Makonnen became Emperor of Ethiopia in 1930, taking the name *Haile Selassie* (HI-lee suh-LASS-ee, meaning "power of the Trinity"), many blacks were euphoric. Several Rastafarian groups sprang up in Jamaica and began claiming Selassie as divine. They saw

The late Emperor Haile Selassie

A Rastafari in Jamaica

in these events the fulfillment of Garvey's prophecies. However, Garvey, an orthodox Christian, was never enamored with Selassie, and Selassie himself refused to endorse the Rastafarian movement that revered him, denying claims of deity.

From the 1930s through the 1950s, conditions for Jamaican blacks worsened. Rastafarians were impoverished, disillusioned, angry, and viewed with increasing suspicion as a cult of dreadlocked drug users by Jamaica's ruling elite. The movement became increasingly politicized and less religious in nature.

A visit by Haile Selassie to Jamaica in April 1966, altered the trajectory of Rastafarianism. Selassie successfully urged the Jamaican Rastas to focus less on returning to Africa and more on raising the conditions of Jamaican blacks.

In the 1970s, Rastafarianism managed to reinvent itself as a positive cultural movement. Reggae music (especially the music of Bob Marley) became a popular vehicle for introducing Rasta ideals to the world. Jamaican art also flourished.

In 1975, the death of Emperor Selassie sent shock waves through the Rastafarian community. Some viewed the reports skeptically as a hoax, a deceptive attempt by "Babylon," the white power structure, to shatter the hopes of blacks. Others envisioned Selassie as spiritually enthroned on Mount Zion. Still others responded to his death by concluding that their God/Savior was no longer physically present on the earth, but living on in the hearts of individual Rastas.

Basic Beliefs and Values

Rastafarianism has never had a firm set of official doctrines or a widely-held creedal belief system. In keeping with its Jamaican roots, it is very individualized and "laid-back, Mon!" Some of its most distinctive features include:

- *"I and I"*—A phrase that attempts to express the oneness of two persons; the implication is that God is within all, and we are all one people.

- *God*—Revealed Himself first through Moses, then Elijah, then Jesus, and finally through Ras Tafari (Emperor Haile Selassie of Ethiopia).

- *Dreadlocks*—Symbolize Rasta's roots and serve as a contrast with the straighter, often blonde hair of whites; they are not to be cut (see Leviticus 21:5).

- *Ganja* (marijuana)—Considered a holy herb, a "wisdom weed"; smoking it is regarded as a holy sacrament by Rastafarians. (Bible verses cited to justify this practice are Genesis 3:18; Exodus 10:12; and Psalm 104:14 in the King James Version). Author Leonard Barrett writes, "The herb is the key to new understanding of the self, the universe, and God. It is the vehicle to cosmic consciousness."

- *Vegetarianism*—Many devout Rastafarians practice vegetarianism, eating only natural "I-tal" food.

- *Leadership*—Within contemporary Rastafarianism, there is no clear leader; the group is very unstructured and unorganized.

Worldview

Rastafarians see themselves (and all Africans) as the legitimate people of God, and Emperor Haile Selassie as a physical descendant of King Solomon and the Queen of Sheba, and a spiritual messiah and incarnation of God. Thus, the Rastafari movement is Afrocentric and built in large part on a few facts from biblical history.

Rastas see the world as being under the control of an oppressively evil white power structure called "Babylon." Spiritually and culturally, the goal is the restoration of true Zion by a worldwide repatriation of blacks to Africa. Until that day, most Rastafarians work quietly through social and political channels for the advancement of impoverished blacks.

View of God

Called Jah by Rastafarians, God is present in His children. He is regarded as all-knowing and all-loving. He binds all together. Jah manifested Himself fully and finally in Ras Tafari Makonnen, who was crowned Ethiopian Emperor Haile Selassie in 1930.

View of the Afterlife

Rastafarians do not believe in heaven or hell as commonly understood in the Christian tradition, but rather see Africa in general and Ethiopia in particular as a kind of heaven on earth.

Sacred Texts

Rastafarians read the Bible and revere portions of it, but view it as largely corrupted by the white establishment called "Babylon."

Holy Piby, the so-called black man's Bible is the sacred text of choice. Another text called *Kebra Negast* is highly regarded. It purports to tell the history of how God and the Hebrew ark of the covenant made its way from Jerusalem to Ethiopia, thus establishing the true faith and the Solomonic kingship in Africa.

Worship Services

Rastafarian rituals and gatherings tend to be very informal and unstructured. Many Rastas see their own bodies as the temple of God, and thus see no need for physical buildings or "brick and mortar" church.

Reasonings are small groups of Rastas who smoke the holy weed and discuss assorted issues. *Binghis* (see below) are special occasions marked by festive celebrations.

Important Dates

Rastafarians perform a special dance (called *nyabinghi* or *binghi*) on special occasions. These holidays include:

January 6—the ceremonial birthday of Emperor Selassie

April 21—a commemoration of the 1966 occasion of Haile Selassie's visit to Jamaica

July 23—the Emperor's actual birthday

August 1—emancipation from slavery

August 17—Marcus Garvey's birthday

November 2—a celebration of His Imperial Majesty's coronation

"I have come to light the lamp of Love in your hearts, to see that it shines day by day with added luster. I have not come on behalf of any exclusive religion. I have not come on a mission of publicity for a sect or creed or cause, nor have I come to collect followers for a doctrine. I have no plan to attract disciples or devotees into my fold or any fold. I have come to tell you of this unitary faith, this spiritual principle, this path of Love, this virtue of Love, this duty of Love, this obligation of Love."
—Sri Sai Baba

Major Differences from Christianity

Belief	Sai Baba
Sacred Text(s)	The Hindu Vedas
Nature of God	One God called by many names (Allah, Krishna, Lord, and so forth)
Jesus Christ	Not emphasized; Sathya Sai Baba casts himself as a Christ figure, an incarnation of God and Savior of the world
Human nature	Eternal spirits that temporarily occupy these bodies and minds
About human need	Enlightenment; need to recognize the divinity inherent within and become who we really are; follow our conscience
Salvation	Achieve union with God; turn inward and yearn to know God.
Afterlife	Reincarnation based on karma

Number of Followers

Researchers estimate there are perhaps six million devotees of Sai Baba in India, Europe, and North America combined. According to the various Sai Baba Web sites, the Sai Baba movement includes more than twelve hundred Sathya Sai Baba Centers in nearly 130 countries around the world.

Major Figures/Prophets

- **Shirdi Sai Baba** (1838–1918)—the human embodiment of the god Shiva (according to Sathya Sai Baba), who lived as a penniless guru and was the first of three Sai Baba incarnations

- **Sathya Sai Baba** (1926–present)—a self-proclaimed avatar (embodiment) of God, the alleged incarnation of the gods Shiva and Shakti
- **Prema Sai Baba** (to come)—the third (future and final) Sai Baba incarnation, first mentioned by Sathya Sai Baba in 1963, destined to embody Shakti and appear on the earth eight years after the passing of Sathya Sai Baba

Short History

Sathya Sai Baba was born in South India in 1926. As a boy he exhibited unusual character traits: compassion, wisdom, and generosity. At the age of fourteen, he announced his mission was to bring about the spiritual regeneration of humanity by modeling and teaching love for God, service to mankind, inner peace, truth, and righteousness of life.

Baba's followers claim that he has miraculous powers—that he can levitate, perform healings, transform substances instantly, and make items materialize out of thin air.

In 1950, devoted followers built an *ashram* (a spiritual compound) near the village of Sathya Sai Baba's birth. Named *Prasanthi Nilayam* ("Abode of Divine Peace"), this "holy headquarters" has been visited

Tapestry depicting Sai Baba of Shirdi (the "first" Sai Baba)

by millions of seekers and pilgrims from all over the world. It is reported that more than one million people attended Sai Baba's eightieth birthday celebration in 2006, including representatives from 180 nations.

Basic Beliefs and Values

According to Sai Baba, it is not necessary to know or study the details of all religions nor to read multiple holy books. The teachings of Sathya Sai Baba (a kind of simplified Hinduism) are said to be the essence of all religions. These teachings can be distilled as follows:

- *Belief in one God*—Called many names by different religions.

- *Practice devotion to God*—*Bhakti*, repeating his name using a mantra, reading holy texts, clearing the mind, and singing hymns.

- *Follow one's own religion sincerely*—Sai Baba claimed, "I have come not to disturb or destroy any faith, but to confirm each in his own faith—so that the Christian becomes a better Christian, the Muslim a better Muslim, and the Hindu a better Hindu."

- *Respect for all religions*—All religions should be unified and syncretized.

- *Service*—Serve others selflessly (*dharma*) and with no thought of rewards.

- *Cultivation of inner character*—Traits includes truth, love, righteousness, peace, and nonviolence (*himsa*).

- *Live by simple mantras*—"Help ever, hurt never!" and "Love all, serve all!"

- *High view of women and mothers*

In short, Sai Baba teaches one caste (the caste of humanity), one religion (the religion of love), one language (the language of the heart), and one God, who is omnipresent.

View of God

Sathya Sai Baba claims that he is the embodiment of God. To be fair, he further claims that everyone else is, too. The difference? Sai Baba says that he is enlightened and is aware of his divinity, while few others realize their godhood.

Worldview

Sai Baba's mission is to serve mankind selflessly, gladly, and generously. It seeks to do this through a network of free schools, hospitals, and drinking water projects.

In a departure from traditional Hinduism, the spirituality of Sai Baba rejects the caste system and treats all people as equals. It further insists that loving God involves more than sitting and praying. Sai Baba is an active and compassionate spirituality with a goal of helping others. Out of internal devotion comes the external and tangible service that can better the lives of the unfortunate. In Baba's own words:

If there is righteousness in the heart, there will be beauty in the character.
If there is beauty in the character, there will be harmony in the home.
If there is harmony in the home, there will be order in the nation.
When there is order in the nation, there will be peace in the world.

View of the Afterlife

As with Hinduism, Sai Baba teaches that our souls are continuously reincarnated, and future incarnations depend on past and present moral choices. *Moksha* (liberation from the endless cycle of rebirth) is the ultimate goal. For traditional Hindus, the emphasis in achieving moksha seems to be through knowledge and devotion; for followers of Sai Baba, the emphasis is on *dharma* (spiritual service to others).

Sacred Texts

Sai Baba relies mostly on the Hindu Vedas and the teachings of Sai Baba, many of which are on the Internet.

Worship Services

At the Sathya Sai Centers, followers can study the teachings of Sathya Sai Baba and the literature of other religions. Activities include singing devotional songs called *bhajans*, meditating, yoga, and engaging in collective service, or *seva*.

There is no charge to join one of these centers, and members are not required to make donations or purchase materials.

Important Dates

Sai Baba followers celebrate the festivals of India. They are encouraged to see them as not only external feasts, but also as opportunities for worshipping the Divine and experiencing joy as a worshipper. The holidays can assist one in cultivating higher wisdom and cosmic consciousness. Among the special occasions that followers of Sai Baba are encouraged to observe are:

New Year (January 1)
Sankranthi (January 14)—a celebration of the glory of the Sun God
Maha Shivarathri (February 16)—a night dedicated to chanting Shiva's name
Sri Rama Navami (March 27)—a celebration of the birthday of the Hindu god Rama
Buddha Poornima (May 2)—a celebration of the birthday of Lord Buddha

Easwaramma Day (May 6)—a celebration
of the birthday of Sai Baba's mother

Krishna Janmashtami (September 4)—a celebration of Krishna's birthday

Ganesh Chaturthi (September 15)—a festival in honor of
the birthday of Lord Ganesh, the Hindu elephant god

Dasara/Vijayadashami (October 21)

Deepavali (November 9)—a Hindu
festival of lights to express thanksgiving

Akhanda Bhajans (November 10–11)—
a twenty-four-hour devotional singing session

Ladies Day (November 19)—a day honoring
Indian women of exceptional character

Bhagawan's Birthday (November 23)—the birthday of Baba

Christmas (December 25)

"I have lived no cloistered life and hold in contempt the wise man who has not lived and the scholar who will not share. There have been many wiser men than I, but few have traveled as much road. I have seen life from the top down and the bottom up. I know how it looks both ways. And I know there is wisdom and that there is hope."
—L. Ron Hubbard

Major Differences from Christianity

Belief	Scientology
Sacred Text(s)	*Dianetics: The Modern Science of Mental Health*; other writings by L. Ron Hubbard
Nature of God	Does not define God; does not acknowledge the God of the Bible
Jesus Christ	Not acknowledged nor revered within Scientology
Human nature	Man is basically good; all humans are made up of a body, mind, and "thetan," that is, their essential immortal spirit
About human need	No mention of sin or repentance; humans need to be "clear" of engrams (destructive thoughts)
Salvation	Deliverance from the endless cycle of lives through "auditing" (ridding the mind of negative mental thoughts) by reaching a state of "clear" and becoming an Operating Thetan
Afterlife	Continuing up the Operating Thetan Bridge until one is free from the cycle of birth and death and from the restraints of matter, energy, space, and time; this "eighth dynamic" is the urge toward existence as infinity, or the Supreme Being.

Number of Followers

Because Scientology has multiple membership "levels" (attending a lecture, going for an "auditing session," and so forth), it is difficult to know exactly how many adherents the church has. One online source lists 4,200 groups, missions, and churches worldwide, serving some ten million Scientologists (www.ReligiousTolerance.org).

Major Figures/Prophets

The founder of Scientology was

- **Lafayette Ronald (L. Ron) Hubbard** (1911–1986)—Founder of Scientology. A Nebraska native, Hubbard was exposed to Sigmund Freud's theory of psychoanalysis at age twelve. He became fascinated with the human mind and went on to study mathematics, engineering, and nuclear physics at George Washington University. In his twenties and thirties, he enjoyed success as a science fiction writer. He traveled extensively and developed an interest in Eastern philosophy, especially Hinduism, Buddhism, and Taoism. Blinded and crippled in World War II, Hubbard developed a unique religious/scientific/philosophical belief system that would later be called *Dianetics*. This "modern science of mental health" was proposed by Hubbard as an alternative to expensive sessions of psychotherapy. By showing readers the dangers of a "reactive mind" (wrong thinking), Dianetics purports to be able to eliminate negative and painful emotions, stress, unhappiness, and psychosomatic illness.

Short History

Scientology (which literally means "the study of truth" or, in Hubbard's words, "knowing in the fullest sense") began with the publishing of *Dianetics* in 1950. The first Scientology church was established in California in 1954, but this launched a vigorous forty-year battle with the Internal Revenue Service (IRS), the agency denying that Scientology was a legitimate church worthy of religious tax exemption. During this time, Hubbard became very reclusive. In 1993, the IRS finally granted the Scientology church its long-sought tax-exempt status.

Following the death of Hubbard in 1986, David Miscavige became Scientology's leader in 1987. The church's headquarters are in Clearwater, Florida.

Basic Beliefs and Values

What are the basic underlying ideas? Every person is a *thetan* (pronounced "thay-ton"), an immortal spirit being with multiple births and lives, and with infinite potential. The soul has enormous power. We have the potential to solve our own problems, accomplish our goals, and gain lasting happiness. We can achieve new, higher states of awareness and ability;

> Scientology is a unique combination of ideas from Eastern religion and modern philosophy, mixed with a dose of American individualism. "In Scientology no one is asked to accept anything as belief or on faith. That which is true for you is what you have observed to be true," says one online source.

however, negative experiences in our many lives have produced *engrams* (negative mental images) that prevent the soul from using its vital force.

These negative mental thoughts and images (stemming from negative experiences in life) cloud our ability to think analytically and solve our problems rationally. As a result, we go through life reacting negatively and foolishly. Until we trace a reactive choice/action back to the negative thoughts that prompted it, we cannot get to the root of the problem.

Thus Scientologist "auditors" (the religion's version of clergy) guide adherents through a process called *clearing*. By using E-meters (electropsychometers, a machine comparable to a lie detector that measures pulse rate and body temperature as counselees discuss their lives), auditors are able to pinpoint areas of wrong thinking (or engrams). Then through drills, certain disciplines, and further counseling, one is believed to be able to erase engrams from the mind. Only by this process is the soul able to achieve its full potential. Through these practices Scientologists attempt to gain more knowledge and insight and ultimately grasp the divine force that is their true, essential nature.

By most standards, the Church of Scientology is controversial. Critics say that the church charges excessive amounts of money for its auditing and other services. Others accuse the church of brainwashing or mind control. Even so, the public is, by and large, fascinated in knowing more about Scientology because some of Hollywood's biggest celebrities (such as Tom Cruise and John Travolta) are devoted adherents.

Scientology adamantly insists that it respects all religions and that it "shares with other religions the dreams of peace and salvation." The second article of the Scientology Creed, written by L. Ron Hubbard in 1954, states that, "All men have inalienable rights to their own religious practices and their performance."

Tom Cruise, possibly the most well known practitioner of Scientology today

View of God

Scientology speaks frequently of "God" (or the "Supreme Being" or "infinity"). However, upon closer review, this theological belief is quite vague and undefined. The official church Web site says that as one develops deeper spiritual awareness, he or she is allowed to reach an individual conclusion about the nature of God. "Unlike religions with Judeo-Christian origins, the Church of Scientology has no set dogma concerning God that it imposes on its members. As with all its beliefs, Scientology does not ask individuals to believe anything on faith."

View of the Afterlife

Scientology seems uncomfortable with the concept of reincarnation as it is typically understood (that is, being reborn as a different life form). However, the Church does teach that one can be born again into the flesh of another body. In other words, we have had past lives. They state that our experience extends beyond a single lifetime. The Christian idea of heaven is foreign to Scientology.

Worldview
The official aims of Scientology are:
A civilization without insanity, without criminals and without war, where the able can prosper and honest beings can have rights, and where man is free to rise to greater heights.

Sacred Texts

L. Ron Hubbard's *Dianetics* is the bible of Scientology. The word comes from the Greek word *nous* (meaning "soul") and the prefix *dia* ("through"). Thus, Dianetics attempts to describe what the soul is doing to the body through the mind. It claims to be "a thoroughly validated method that increases sanity, intelligence, confidence, and well-being." With diligent application it promises to deal decisively with the subconscious root causes of unpleasant emotions and psychosomatic illnesses that are keeping a person from a happy and productive life. "Dianetics rests on basic principles that can be easily learned and applied by any reasonably intelligent person—as millions have. It is the route to a well, happy, high IQ human being."

Other writings (reportedly five hundred thousand pages total) and lectures by L. Ron Hubbard on Dianetics and human potential (sometimes called "Operating Thetan" materials or doctrines) are also regarded with great reverence by members of the church. The church has gone to court to prevent the dissemination of these materials, especially on the Internet.

Worship Services

Scientology churches are open daily, and they hold weekly services. These meetings do not include prayer and do not make reference to God. Clergy perform christenings, baptismal rites, weddings, and funerals.

Important Dates

National Founding Day (February 8)—to recognize the 1954 establishment of the first Scientology church in the United States

L. Ron Hubbard's birthday (March 13)

Anniversary of the publication of *Dianetics* in 1950 (May 9)

Sea Org Day (August 12)— a celebration of the Sea Organization, a group of devout Scientology recruits

Clear Day (September 4)—to commemorate the 1965 inauguration of the Clearing Course

Auditor's Day (second Sunday in September)—to honor those dedicated to "bringing man up the Bridge to Total Freedom"

Freedom Day (December 30)—to celebrate the official recognition of the Church of Scientology in the United States.

"As Humanists we remain among the few who both challenge religious authoritarian propaganda and who offer people other ways of organizing their lives apart from traditional religious assumptions. Our methods of setting aside traditional religious assumptions, focusing on things in this world, valuing people, and emphasizing reason offer the best hope people have for reaching consensus on problems facing the world today."
—Larry Reyka

Belief	Secular Humanism
Sacred Text(s)	No holy books, but guided by *Humanist Manifestos I, II, and III*
Nature of God	Most are atheistic or agnostic (a few are deistic)
Jesus Christ	If He existed, He was a religious/moral teacher, but not a divine being or savior who performed supernatural acts
Human nature	Material beings; no evidence of a "soul"; people not inherently sinful, but conditioned to engage in negative, hurtful behavior
About human need	Knowledge/rationalism (liberation from the superstitions of religion)
Salvation	Consists of reaching one's potential and trying to better the world through altruism
Afterlife	Most have no belief in spiritual existence after death, this life is all we can know for certain

Major Differences from Christianity

Number of Followers

There is no way to accurately quantify how many people are proponents of secular humanism. It is a philosophical approach to life that rejects all supernatural and authoritarian beliefs and embraces the notion that through reason and science, humanity can solve its own problems. One online source estimates there may be over one billion secular and nonreligious agnostic/atheists worldwide. Yet in more detailed surveys, almost half of those who say they are nonreligious do admit to some sort of belief in a Higher Power.

Major Figures/Prophets

Secular humanism, as a modern philosophical system, could be described as the gradual, collaborative effort of a number of prominent thinkers, scientists, and authors through the centuries. Contemporary humanists stand on the shoulders of:

- **Confucius** (551 BC–479 BC)—Chinese philosopher who promoted a non-religious system of morals and ethics

- **Aristotle** (384 BC–322 BC)—Greek philosopher who advocated a secular world view, eliminating the need for religious faith

- **Epicurus** (341 BC–270 BC)—Greek philosopher who argued for an eternal universe and rejected the concept of an afterlife

- **Voltaire** (1694–1778)—French philosopher and avowed enemy of Christianity

- **David Hume** (1711–1776)—Scottish philosopher and religious skeptic

- **Thomas Paine** (1737–1809)—Revolutionary-era deist and opponent of formal religion

- **Ludwig Feuerbach** (1804–1872)—German atheistic philosopher who advocated the idea that "God" is a manmade invention, based on human needs and desires

- **Auguste Comte** (1798–1857)—French thinker who pushed for a non-theistic "religion of science"

- **Charles Darwin** (1809–1882)—English naturalist who is the father of modern evolutionary theory

- **Robert Ingersoll** (1833–1899)—renowned American orator, lawyer, and agnostic

- **Corliss Lamont** (1902–present)—author of the influential *Humanism as a Philosophy* (1949)

- **Paul Kurtz** (1925–present)—Founder, Chairman of the Council for Secular Humanism, principal author of *Humanist Manifesto I* and *II*

Short History

The modern movement known as secular humanism has roots that go back to the primitive naturalism and materialism of ancient Greek and Chinese philosophers.

Humanists say that during the Dark Ages (roughly AD 500–1000), the Church utterly dominated all aspects of European society, effectively stifling scientific advancement and stagnating cultural progress. Then came the Renaissance (AD 1300–1700) and the Scientific Revolution (beginning in the 1540s). Intellectual inquiry exploded. Artistic expression flourished. The humanism of this era was not irreligious—far from it. Most artists and scientists were theists, some quite devout. The Church benefited greatly from the achievements of these humanists. But complex questions were being raised about the nature of man and the role of the church. Tension developed between faith and science.

For several centuries, assorted thinkers advanced various irreligious theories, but it was Charles Darwin, with his *The Origin of Species* (1859), who did the most to pave the way for modern secular humanism. If accurate, Darwin's painstaking research demonstrated humanity's ability to answer the deepest mysteries of existence through science and reason, quite apart from faith. Even more significant, if Darwin's evolutionary model was true, it eliminated the need for a Creator.

Agnostics and atheists were emboldened. Skepticism came out of the closet. *Humanist Manifesto I* (1933) was largely the work of Unitarian ministers who used the term "religious humanism" to refer to their progressive emphasis on humanity rather than deity. The writers attempted to expand the meaning of the word "religious" to include their own nontheistic view.

David Hume, an Enlightenment philosopher and atheist

Humanist Manifesto II (1973) represented an effort to update secular humanism's ideals and agenda after the horrors of Nazism and World War II, the nuclear arms race, and the bitter civil rights era. Signers included science fiction writer Isaac Asimov, Alan Guttmacher of Planned Parenthood, and psychologist B. F. Skinner.

Humanist Manifesto III (2003) represented a further update of modern humanist ideas. Signers included Oxford professor/author Richard Dawkins (*The God Delusion*, 2006), filmmaker Oliver Stone, novelist Kurt Vonnegut, and DNA pioneer Francis Crick.

Basic Beliefs and Values

Most secular humanists would either shake their heads in disgust or chuckle at being discussed and dissected in a *Handbook of World Religions*. Humanists—as they are quick to tell anyone who will listen—are irreligious, even antireligious.

Although some humanists attend the Unitarian-Universalist church or participate in other similar free-thinking groups, secular humanism is neither a church nor a religion in the normal sense of those terms. Adherents do share a set of consensus beliefs as well as objectives to which they are fiercely committed. In short, secular humanists:

- *Champion tolerance and freedom*—Tyranny over the mind of man must be abolished; free inquiry must be allowed; all points of view must be heard;

morals must not be imposed (this requires the absolute separation of church and state).

- *Embrace reason, not revelation*—"The universe or nature is all that exists or is real" (Steven Schafersman); "Trust in human intelligence rather than in divine guidance; we believe the scientific method, though imperfect, is still the most reliable way of understanding the world. Hence, we look to the natural, biological, social, and behavioral sciences for knowledge of the universe and man's place within it" (Paul Kurtz).

- *Are ethical*—One can be honest and moral and committed to justice and freedom without being religious; moral (but irreligious) development should be cultivated in children, but religious indoctrination of the young is immoral.

- *Seek knowledge, trust reason, value/celebrate art, literature, and music*—Rather than seeking and valuing a deity who does not even exist.

- *Take responsibility*—Don't wait for an imaginary deity to save you or transform the world; take action to decide your own destiny. Reason and knowledge enable us to solve problems.

- *Are altruistic*—Always seek the greater good of humanity; be socially and globally responsible and compassionate.

Worldview

Humanists look with a critical eye at the problems of the world, but they insist that solutions to these problems lie in the robust, concerted efforts of knowledgeable and dedicated people. In their view, religion is largely an obstacle to progress. They might concede that religions have helped humanity in some ways, have built hospitals and schools, but they claim that religions have also caused tremendous suffering and fear through intolerance and dread of punishment in the afterlife.

View of God

No belief in deities, transcendental entities, a supposed "God" or "gods." The *Humanist Manifesto II* states, "As nontheists, we begin with humans not God, nature not deity."

Secular humanists use the following words and phrases to describe themselves and their movement: progressive, thoughtful, without supernaturalism, rational, "inspired by art, and motivated by compassion," democratic, taking planetary responsibility, a "joyous alternative to religions that believe in a supernatural god and life in a hereafter."

Worship Services

There are no formal worship services since there is nothing to worship. For major life events such as marriage and death, humanists do engage in nonreligious celebra-

View of the Afterlife

Secular humanists do not believe in the afterlife. "We have found no convincing evidence that there is a separable 'soul' or that it exists before birth or survives death.... Life can be lived without the illusions of immortality or reincarnation" (Paul Kurtz).

Sacred Texts

Humanists are rationalists, and do not accept any so-called sacred religious books as true. They do not have any guiding holy books or dogmatic creeds. They do express a consensus of goals and ideals as set forth in various *Humanist Manifestos*.

tions and memorials. Groups like the Council for Secular Humanism also sponsor summer camps and courses for children to educate them in critical thinking and ethical values.

Important Dates

No special dates are specified.

36 SHINTO

"The origins of Shinto are lost in the hazy mists enshrouding the ancient period of Japanese history, but from the time the Japanese people became conscious of their own cultural character and traditions, the practices, attitudes, and ideology that eventually developed into the Shinto of today were already included within them."
—Clark B. Offner, *The World's Religions*

Major Differences from Christianity

Belief	Shinto
Sacred Text(s)	Kojiki, Nihongi or Nihon Shoki, Engishiki or Yengishiki
Nature of God	Many gods (*kami*). Many impersonal gods rather than one personal God
Jesus Christ	Not emphasized or recognized
Human nature	As children of the kami, people are sacred and essentially good (though Shinto purification rites are necessary)
About human need	To acknowledge the kami, and live pure lives of peace, respect, and kindness
Salvation	Human effort required: followers enjoy the favor of the kami by living honorably and following purification rites
Afterlife	Not emphasized

Number of Followers

Sources that cite the number of Shinto followers in the one hundred million-range should be viewed with suspicion because they regard much of the Japanese general population as being adherents of Shinto. (This is a bit like assuming there are two hundred million American Christians, due to their Judeo-Christian heritage.) Though the average Japanese person almost surely subscribes to at least some of the ideals taught in Shinto, some polls indicate that as little as three to four percent of the Japanese people faithfully practice this faith. A more likely figure of adherents is 2.8 million to 4 million worldwide, with most of these being found in Asia.

Major Figures/Prophets

- **Kamo Mabuchi** (1697–1769 — a reformer who sought to revive Shinto to its pre-Buddhist and pre-Confucian roots.

- **Motoori Norinaga** (1730–1801)—a Mabuchi disciple who called for devotion to the Kojiki (see below) and who advocated the divinity of Japan's royal family

- **Hirata Atsutane** (1776–1843)—a Norinaga disciple who pushed for emperor-centered nationalism

Short History

Shinto means "the way of the gods." It is the most ancient religion of Japan, rooted in primitive history and mythology. The religion does not have a founder, and it is difficult to pinpoint a firm beginning date.

Mix ancestor worship with reverence for nature, add a touch of shamanism and divination to the beliefs of eastern fertility cults, and the result is this experiential "faith." Shinto has never been a highly doctrinal religious system with firmly established beliefs. Instead, it focuses on nature, believing in numerous gods that reside in trees, boulders, mountains, plants, animals, birds, seas, and even departed ancestors. Shinto calls these supernatural spirits *kami.*

In the sixth century (AD 552), Emperor Kimmei Tenno welcomed Buddhist teachings as a way, he believed, of enriching the practice of Shinto. In this blending and merging, known as *Shin-Butsu Shugo*, the kami were regarded as local manifestations of the buddhas and bodhisattvas. The two religions often shared temples. Buddhist art became common, and Buddhist monks often participated in Shinto festivals. Confucianism was also introduced during this period, but its influence extended mostly to matters of moral conduct and social order.

Over the centuries, the distinctively Japanese facets of Shinto were gradually obscured by Buddhist theology and principles of Confucianism. A revival of Shinto began in the 1700s, and by 1868, under the rule of Emperor Meiji, Shintoism was recognized as the official state religion. Buddhist elements were purged from Shinto shrines, and Shinto traditions were taught in Japanese schools. During this era, Shinto took two very different courses. Sectarian Shinto (*Kyoha*), practiced by various sects, maintained its distinct religious flavor. Meanwhile, Shrine Shinto (*Jinja*) morphed into a political ideology. It was this religion-tinged nationalism that helped Japan's ruler unify the nation. Devotion to both the emperor and the empire combined to make the nation a fearsome military power. Increasing allegiance to Japanese Shinto led to increasing hostility toward non-Japanese religions and cultures (such as the Buddhism of China and the Christianity of the West). Following the Japanese defeat in World War II, religious freedom was reestablished, and in 1946 Emperor Hirohito renounced the Shinto belief in the divinity of the imperial family.

Basic Beliefs and Values

At the heart of Shinto is an animistic belief in the kami. These spirits or gods can embody natural objects, such as rocks, mountains, rivers, trees, and so forth; natural forces, including the processes of creativity, healing, growth; as well as deceased ancestors or heroes and rulers.

While devout Jews revere the Ten Commandments and faithful Muslims practice the Five Pillars, adherents to Shinto seek to follow Four Affirmations: 1) loyal devotion to family; 2) love of nature; 3) personal cleanliness (purification rites with frequent washings); and 4) worship of the kami (commonly through festivals called *matsuri*).

Due in part to the influence of Confucianism, Shinto also advocates virtues such as honesty, kindness, respect for elders and superiors, and since World War II, peace.

Shinto is a tolerant religion and accepts the validity of other religions. The historical connection and interaction between ancient Shinto and Buddhism and the teachings of Confucius mean that many followers of Shinto practice elements of all three religions.

View of God

Shinto is a polytheistic religion and its adherents believe in many gods. While not personal, these gods are generally regarded as watchful and helpful beings. In Shinto, there are no concepts of the wrath of the gods, their omnipotence, or of separation from gods due to sin. Some Shinto gods worshipped by adherents:

- *Amaterasu Omikami*—the Sun Goddess, the supreme god in Shinto
- *The Seven Gods*—of fortune/good luck (originally Buddhist deities)
- *Daikoku*—the god of wealth and the patron of farmers
- *Ebisu*—son of Daikoku, the god of honest labor

Worldview

Without a highly developed set of doctrines or code of conduct, Shinto advocates a very general morality, doing what is helpful to others. "Shinto emphasizes right practice, sensibility, and attitude over conceptual understanding of the universe and holiness" (N. Alice Yamada).

View of the Afterlife

Shinto does not emphasize life after death.

Sacred Texts

Shinto does not boast any "inspired" books (like the Bible for Christians or the Qur'an for Muslims). However, it does depend on a few ancient texts that shed light on Japan's history and ancient mythology.

- Kojiki, about AD 712 (Records of Ancient Matters)

- Nihongi or Nihon Shoki, about AD 720 (Chronicles of Japan)

- Engishiki or Yengishiki, about AD 925 (regulations concerning shrine rituals, liturgies, prayers, instructions for religious leaders)

Worship Services

In Shinto, there are no set weekly meetings, but many adherents visit shrines on the first and fifteenth of each month. Shinto shrines are typically situated in beautiful natural settings. Features generally include rocks and trees and pools. In this

Shinto prayer gates (torii)

peaceful settings the kami are believed to dwell. Many Shinto homes feature a small shrine called a *kami dana* (which literally means "a shelf of gods").

Each public shrine is marked by a sacred entrance called a *torii*. A torii is thought to be a kind of gate between the finite world of men and the infinite world of the gods. Before entering a torii, Shinto adherents will wash their hands and rinse their mouths at an ablution basin. This physical act symbolizes removing mental and moral impurities. Inside the shrine, the worshipper will recite prayers (first bowing to show respect, then clapping, presumably to get the gods' attention) and offer gifts to the kami—money, flowers, small cakes.

Important Dates

Seasonal festivals (*matsuri*) are held each spring and fall. Special anniversaries focusing on the history of a shrine or of a local patron spirit are also held. These celebrations feature any or all of the following: purification rites, prayers, offerings, colorful costumes, sacred music and joyous dance, a sermon or speech, occasional sumo wrestling matches, and feasting.

"I am with thee. I have made thee happy, and also those who shall take thy name. Go, and repeat Mine, and cause others to do likewise. Abide uncontaminated by the world. Practice the repetition of my Name, charity, ablutions, worship, and meditation. . . . My Name is God, the primal Brahma. And thou are the divine Guru."
—The call of Guru Nanak Dev, founder of Sikhism

Major Differences from Christianity

Belief	Sikhism
Sacred Text(s)	The Adi Granth
Nature of God	One supreme, impersonal, true God, who is just and gracious, but beyond knowing or comprehending, though He dwells everywhere, including within our own being
Jesus Christ	Not a relevant, mentioned part of the Sikh faith
Human nature	Spiritual beings/souls in a "shell"; flawed but capable of merging with God by becoming "saint soldiers" and striving for good
About human need	Need to overcome self-centeredness and worldly illusion (*maya*), align one's life with the will of God
Salvation	*Mukhti* (salvation) is more enlightenment than deliverance from sin; it is becoming God-centered by realizing—through meditation and good works—His presence within
Afterlife	A merging of the self into the infinite; reminiscent of Buddhism and Hinduism; no literal heaven or hell

Number of Followers

Estimates range from eighteen million to twenty-six million followers. Most are found in and around Punjab, India. An estimated half-million Sikhs live in North America. Sikhism is universally regarded as the fifth largest religion in the world.

Major Figures/Prophets

- **Guru Nanak Dev** (1469–1538/39?)—the founder of Sikhism, and the first of its ten *gurus* ("venerable teacher")

- **Guru Angad Dev** (1504–1552)—the second guru of Sikhism and the developer of Gurmukhi, the script used for the Punjab language. He wrote some of the hymns in Guru Granth Sahib

- **Guru Ram Das** (1534–1581)—the fourth guru of Sikhism and founder of the holy city of Amritsar

- **Guru Hargobind** (1595–1644)—Sikhism's sixth guru, who declared himself a military leader as well as a spiritual leader

- **Guru Gobind Singh** (1666–1708)—the tenth and final guru of Sikhism, who founded the Khalsa and announced that the Sikh holy book Granth would be the ultimate and eternal Guru of the faith

Short History

Guru Nanak Dev, founder of Sikhism, was born into a Hindu family in India in 1469. Some biographers state that his father worked for a Muslim. Whatever the case, Nanak grew up curious about religion in a culture that was permeated by conflict between these two competing faiths. Disillusioned by this religious division, Nanak left his family as a young man and traveled in search of truth.

Around the beginning of the sixteenth century, Nanak claimed to have had a vision in which God revealed himself and declared Nanak his chosen guru. Nanak emerged from this experience proclaiming, "There is no Hindu, there is no Muslim, so whose path shall I follow? I shall follow the path of God." With the help of a musically gifted Muslim named Mardana, Nanak set out on an ambitious evangelistic mission of seeking *Sikhs* (devoted disciples).

The Golden Temple in Amritsar, India

During this period, Guru Nanak wrote *Granth* ("book"), the sacred scriptures of Sikhism. This new faith attempted to syncretize elements of Hinduism (for example, the belief in karma and the doctrine of reincarnation) with tenets of Islam (such as the emphasis on monotheism). At the same time, Nanak's new religion eliminated certain aspects of each faith. For example, he did away with Islam's requirement that women wear veils, and replaced Hinduism's caste system with a faith in which both rich and poor partook in a kind of communal meal. Nanak died in 1538, and was succeeded by the Guru Angad. By 1600, devout Sikhs had deified Nanak: "Guru Nanak is God, the Supreme Brahma" (Gurdas 13:25).

By 1708, Sikhism shifted its emphasis away from living, breathing gurus. The tenth and final human guru, Gobind Singh, declared the Sikh scripture to be the very embodiment of God. With this pronouncement, the Granth began to be regarded as Guru Granth Sahib, "The Lord's Book." It was enthroned under a jeweled canopy at Amritsar, India, the "Mecca" of the Sikh faith.

In recent years, Sikhism has become a defensive, militant movement. In June of 1984, Indian troops stormed the Golden Temple, killing several hundred Sikhs. The Sikhs retaliated later that year by assassinating Prime Minister Indira Gandhi.

Basic Beliefs and Values

As mentioned, Sikhism seems to be a melding of various Hindu and Islamic beliefs. And yet, it also breaks new ground, embracing certain ideas found in neither religion. Here are the basic beliefs of Sikh thought and practice:

- *Sin*—The forgetting the true name (and nature) of God. "They who forget the Name, go astray."

- *Four stages of spirituality*—*Manmukh* (total self-absorption and worldliness); *Sikh* (becoming a new follower of the faith); *Khalsa* (total dedication to Sikhism—see below); and *Gurmukh* (becoming God-centered).

- *Salvation*—Consists in reaching *Gurmukh,* knowing God and being absorbed into Him by yielding fully to his kindness and grace and requirements for living.

- *Fully devoted Sikh*—One becomes a fully devoted follower through the Amrit ceremony, which designates one as a *Khalsa* (literally "pure"). This sacred baptism ceremony consists of multiple vows: no use of tobacco or any intoxicants, no cutting or removal of hair, the wearing of a turban, no eating animals sacrificed in the Muslim way, no illicit sex (outside of marriage).

- *Lifestyle*—One demonstrates his/her pure devotion through displaying the five symbols of identification: *Kesh*—uncut hair on the body, combined with the wearing of a turban; *Kangha*—a wooden comb inserted in the hair to symbolize personal cleanliness; *Kara*—wearing a steel bracelet to symbolize allegiance to God and bondage to truth; *Kachh*—white cotton undershorts, symbolizing moral purity; and *Kirpan*—a short ceremonial sword or dagger to symbolize the resistance against injustice and evil.

- *No religious, sexual, or spiritual hierarchy*—All are equal in God's sight.
- *A tithe*—10 percent of one's income, called *Dasvandh*, is mandatory.
- *The name Singh*—Every Sikh male adds *Singh* (which means "lion" or "lion-hearted") after his given name; females add *Kaur* ("princess") after their names.

As Christians use a cross to symbolize the essence of their faith, Sikhs utilize a *Khanda* (a double edged sword). This symbol suggests divine knowledge, which is able to separate truth from falsehood.

Worldview

Taking into account its varied beliefs and practices, Sikhism can be described as a highly moral religion that emphasizes a contented life of strict devotion to God and compassionate service to others. Its devotees are hard-working, serious-minded people who are called to live in the world but still remain pure. Devout Sikhs see themselves as soldiers, scholars, and saints. Interestingly, this serious-minded faith rejects many of the restrictive and ritualistic aspects often associated with religion. It is egalitarian, treating rich and poor, male and female the same. It is more a celebratory faith than an ascetic religion. It requires no dietary restrictions like vegetarianism or fasting. Because of its high regard for God as the giver and taker of life, Sikhs are opposed to abortion, euthanasia, and suicide.

View of the Afterlife

There is no literal heaven or hell in Sikh thought. Though Sikhs speak much of God's grace, they simultaneously emphasize the idea that salvation (defined as breaking the cycle of birth and death and merging ultimately with God) is realized through "following the teachings of the Guru, meditation on the Holy Name, and performance of acts of service and charity." Sikhs are also charged with overcoming the five cardinal vices (lust, anger, greed, worldly attachment, and pride) in order to achieve this ultimate union with God.

View of God
Sikhs practice a strict monotheism, declaring that God is Creator, Sustainer, and Destroyer, and that He cannot take human form. The God of Sikhism, while regarded as great beyond comprehension and ultimately unknowable, is yet viewed as essentially kind and gracious.

Sacred Texts

The Sikh Bible is called Granth. It was primarily written by Guru Nanak. Following the reigns of the ten gurus, Granth, or, as it then become known, Granth Sahib ("the Book of the Lord"), was declared to be the final guru of Sikhs. The original text is found in Amritsar, the holy city of Sikhism. At night it is literally "tucked into bed," guarded until morning, then "awakened and enthroned again under its jeweled canopy." Copies of Granth Sahib are displayed in all other Sikh temples.

Worship Services

Sikhs are devoted to prayer and typically gather three times a day. They are careful not to use any kinds of images, statues, or icons. In the morning, they read two long prayers from the Granth Sahib. In the evening, after the work day, more prayers are said. At bedtime, a brief hymn prayer is offered.

A number of special events are held at the *gurdwara* (temple). These include the naming of a newborn child, baptism into the Khalsa brotherhood, funeral ceremonies, and Sikh weddings (called *anand karaj*).

Akhand Path is the cover-to-cover reading of Sri Guru Granth Sahib. This uninterrupted event (which takes about forty-eight hours!) requires the attendance of the entire family, and is done in both joyous times and during periods of hardship.

Important Dates

Important anniversaries from the lives of the ten gurus are celebrated annually. These include birthdays, death days, or the days upon which an individual became a guru. Other significant days in the Sikh calendar are:

> **Baisakhi**, also known as **Vaisakhi** (on or around April 13)—a spring festival commemorating the founding of the Khalsa; this event features fairs and parades and signals the beginning of the Sikh New Year
>
> **Diwali** (around October 25)—the Indian festival of lights, which Sikhs use to cover the Golden Temple with lights
>
> **Maghi** (around January 14)—a commemoration of the martyrdom of forty followers of Guru Gobind Singh
>
> **Hola Mohalla** (around March 17)—this festival features mock military exercises

"The Spiritism religion is an act of devotion that is performed within each heart. It is the elevation of one's sentiments, of love for one's fellow beings, and of constant work in favor of one's neighbor. Only thought that is well balanced in goodness can link us to God, and it is only the practice of good actions that make us truly blessed."
—Internet quote

Major Differences from Christianity

Belief	Spiritism
Sacred Text(s)	The works of Allan Kardec: *The Spirits' Book*, *The Mediums' Book*, *The Gospel According to Spiritism*, *Heaven and Hell*, *The Genesis*
Nature of God	The Supreme Intelligence, First Cause of all things
Jesus Christ	The perfect moral example and guide and model for mankind
Human nature	Immortal, pre-existent "spirits who are God's children" that inhabit earthly bodies and are given free will to choose between good and evil
About human need	Spiritual evolution into pure spirits through the pursuit of true knowledge and practice of moral living
Salvation	Reaching perfection through diligent effort that results in moral transformation
Afterlife	No literal heaven or hell; disincarnation, a continued existence after death as bodiless spirits that live and move in the spiritual world, our true homeland; and periodic reincarnation until reaching "unalterable bliss"

Number of Followers

A variety of sources estimate the number of American practitioners of Spiritism (also called Spiritualism) at somewhere between 150,000–700,000. The worldwide total is equally uncertain, with numbers ranging between seven million and fifty million. Precise figures are difficult to come by since those who officially join Spiritualist churches are thought to be only a fraction of those who believe Spiritism's claims and participate occasionally in certain of its practices.

Major Figures/Prophets

- **Emanuel Swedenborg** (1688–1772)—a Swedish inventor, writer, and mystic who claimed the ability to talk with angels, demons, and others in the spirit realm

- **Allan Kardec** (1804–1869)—a French educator who investigated and codified Spiritist Doctrine

- **Léon Denis** (1846–1927)—a French salesman who promoted Spiritism

Short History

Spiritism is the broad name given to the belief that people can communicate with the spirits of the dead through the help of psychics and/or mediums. Communication with the dead is an ancient practice, part of the animistic and shamanistic religions of Africa and Asia. It is even mentioned and condemned in the Old Testament of the Bible (see Leviticus 19:31; 20:6; 1 Samuel 28:3; 2 Kings 21:6; 23:24; Isaiah 8:19).

In the 1700s, Emanuel Swedenborg and Franz Mesmer pioneered and popularized the practice of trying to contact the spirits of the deceased. Mesmer dabbled in hypnotism and clairvoyance, and his ability to put people in a trance-like state resulted in the coining of the verb "to mesmerize."

Modern Spiritism got its start in 1848. Three sisters—Leah, Margaret, and Catherine (Kate) Fox—reportedly began hearing unexplained thumping or rapping sounds in their Hydesville, New York home. The two younger girls, Kate and Margaret, concluded that a spirit was the source of the sounds. After a makeshift séance, they claimed to have made contact with the spirit of a murdered peddler (a skeleton unearthed in the family basement seemed to give credence to their story).

Franz Mesmer pioneered the practice of contacting the dead

The girls were immediately famous and began demonstrating their spirit-contacting abilities (via automatic writing and channeling) to fascinated audiences. This created a wave of interest and involvement in practices such as table-spinning and talking boards (early versions of Ouija boards). When the frenzy hit Europe, Frenchman Allan Kardec began to investigate the craze.

In the United States, the movement reached its peak in the 1860s. No doubt the mass casualties of the Civil War fueled the desire of millions to contact their departed family members. Even Mary Todd Lincoln, wife of President Abraham Lincoln, held séances at the White House in her grief over the death of her young son Willie.

Basic Beliefs and Values

Spiritism claims to be a scientific, philosophical, and spiritual belief system that seeks to answer fundamental questions about life, such as: Who am I? Why am I here? Where did I come from? Why is there so much suffering in the world? Why do some enjoy blessing and others seem to be cursed?

Some of its essential doctrines and practices include:

- God is spirit, we are spirit, departed loved ones are spirit, enemies are spirit; and that is how we are all connected.

- Disembodied (or "discarnated") spirits are everywhere. They have the same personalities they had while embodied on earth. They can see us and know our thoughts. They can contact us through mediums.

- Watch for deceptive spirits and false mediums; all supposed contacts with the spirit world must be analyzed rationally and carefully.

- Good spirits spur us toward good and help us in trials, and imperfect spirits encourage us toward error and evil.

- Reincarnation is simply the consequence of our own actions and choices. Yet it gives us the opportunity to face and address past mistakes and make amends, often by having to endure difficulties and pain. Reincarnation may sometimes be to other planets, as suggested by the words of Jesus, "In my Father's house are many mansions" (John 14:2 NKJV).

- Prayer is how we adore God and withstand temptations; God answers prayer by sending us help in the form of good spirits.

View of God

In Spiritism, God is viewed as the supremely perfect, immaterial Creator, the beginning and end of all things. God is eternal, unchangeable, all-powerful, and just. Because God is infinite and we are finite, we can know God only in a limited way.

Worldview

Spiritists are, not surprisingly, obsessed with spirits. They see themselves essentially as eternal spirits, in need of evolving or being perfected. They see the world

View of the Afterlife

According to Spiritism, there is no literal heaven or hell; there are only "soul states" that can be described as either heavenly or hellish. One's experience depends on one's choices, that is, how well one has respected God's laws. There is no eternal punishment. Through various reincarnations each spirit can acquire more learning and knowledge, eventually evolving to perfection.

as permeated by spirits. Thus, the emphasis is not on the material world but on the spiritual. The way to make spiritual progress is to serve others, to learn, to promote the love and brotherhood of mankind, and to take responsibility for one's own actions.

Sacred Texts

The five highly influential books of Allan Kardec are *The Spirits' Book, The Mediums' Book, The Gospel according to Spiritism, Heaven and Hell,* and *The Genesis.*

Worship Services

Spiritism for many individuals is practiced informally and may include visits to "Spirit Centers" and mediums, séances with friends, study in parapsychology, exploration of paranormal activity, use of Ouija boards and self-proclaimed psychics.

In areas where larger numbers of Spiritists live, adherents may attend a Sunday worship gathering at an actual Spiritualist church. One example is the First Spiritual Temple in Brookline, Massachusetts, that claims to be the "oldest Christian Spiritualist Church in the world." Services include hymns, an offering, Scripture readings, and sermons. Once a month there is a "trance address" delivered by spirit Syrsha through the mediumship of the pastor, as well as a healing service with spirit John.

Important Dates

There are no holidays unique to those who practice Spiritism.

"Taoism is . . . a 'Way' of life. It is a River. The Tao is the natural order of things. It is a force that flows through every living and sentient object, as well as through the entire universe. When the Tao is in balance, it is possible to find perfect happiness."
—Online source

Number of Followers

Researchers estimate there are some twenty million devotees to Taoism (pronounced DOW-ISM, and sometimes spelled "Daoism") worldwide. Most live in China, Taiwan, or Southeast Asia.

Major Figures/Prophets

- **Lao Tzu**, literally "the old philosopher" (sixth century BC)—contemporary of Confucius; some scholars doubt his existence. Late in life, saddened by the corruption of his culture and seeking solitude in his final years, Lao Tzu headed westward toward what is now Tibet. Taoist tradition says that he was detained at the border by a truth-seeking guard who would not allow him to cross until he first wrote down all his teachings and wisdom for the people he was forsaking. The resulting poems, written in a matter of days, became the Tao Te Ching, the Bible of Taoism
- **Chuang Tzu** (399–295 BC)—influential teacher who developed Lao Tzu's teachings and recorded his interpretations in various books, including one that bears his name

Belief	Taoism
Sacred Text(s)	Tao Te Ching and Chuang Tzu
Nature of God	The supreme being/ultimate truth is the impersonal Tao, beyond concepts and words
Jesus Christ	Not emphasized
Human nature	Humans are basically good and able to seek the Tao and do good
About human need	To learn how to be spontaneously in harmony with the natural order of things; "go with the flow" (*wu wei*)
Salvation	There is nothing that one needs to be saved from
Afterlife	Death means the end of individual consciousness, but not of one's life force

Major Differences from Christianity

Short History

By the time of Confucius (551–479 BC), China's long history of social harmony and propriety was no more. The famous philosopher unsuccessfully pushed

A statue of Lao Tzu in China

for a return to cultural civility by stressing civic responsibility and social obligation.

As the story goes, Confucius met with Lao Tzu to discuss these matters. Lao Tzu roundly rejected such a heavy-handed governmental solution to what he believed was an internal, individual problem. Rather than resort to moral authoritarianism, Lao Tzu proposed encouraging people to gently align themselves with the Tao, that underlying controlling principle or force he saw running through the natural world. Rather than forcing people to comply with legislative rules and societal expectations, people should be encouraged to surrender to the force of the Tao, as explained in Lao Tzu's Tao Te Ching.

Over a century later, in writings that bear his name, Chuang Tzu further developed these tenets of what is now called philosophical Taoism.

Basic Beliefs and Values

The word *Tao* means "way," "road," or "path." The Tao is ultimate, uncreated reality. It cannot be grasped or understood. One source describes it this way: "It has no characteristics, yet it is not nothingness. In fact, it is better understood as 'everythingness,' as it contains within itself all potential characteristics." To follow the Tao is to follow the way of nature, the way of the universe.

Within the "river" of Taoism are two streams. One version, already mentioned, is referred to as "philosophical Taoism" (*tao-chia*); the other stream is called "religious Taoism" (*tao-chiao*). It is probably fair to say that the modern-day Western adherents of Taoism typically belong to the philosophical school. Eastern followers of Taoism are more likely to belong to the religious school.

Yin and *yang* are the two opposite but complementary halves of the Tao. Yin is the dark, female, passive, soft force. Yang is the light, male, active force. Together these forces interact and balance the universe.	*Ch'i* (which means "air" or "breath") is the animating life energy that flows through the universe, including the human body. One's health and longevity depend upon one's ability to tap into and regulate this energy. Ch'i empowers one to follow the Tao.

[200]

The goal of life is to live in harmony and unity with the Tao. Doing so involves *wu-wei* ("nondoing"—not inaction or "do-nothingness," but rather a serene, non-striving, effective approach to life) and *wu* ("emptiness"). Only this balanced, easy-going, thoughtful, intentional way of life frees the soul from the desires of this world and leads to immortality.

Taoists cherish the so-called Three Jewels: showing compassion (without the need for recognition), moderation, and humility. In addition, it is important to be deliberate, peaceful, and flexible. Striving, struggling, fighting—these are not the ways of a follower of Taoism. Techniques used to achieve harmony and balance include pursuing simplicity and inner peace through breath control, meditation, yoga, chanting, and the ancient exercise form known as *t'ai ch'i*.

The *te* is Taoism's term for the unique pattern of each thing. Only by knowing and embracing our te— our individuality—and the te of all other objects and creatures can we achieve harmony with the universe. Judging or resisting the te is counterproductive and violates the Tao.

> Water is the natural element that most clearly demonstrates Taoism. It is supple and strong. It adapts and is unobtrusive. It flows and fills, shapes and submits. It "works without working," subdues and supports without straining.

View of God

Philosophical Taoism operates with the belief that what many call "God" is actually an impersonal force or reality that flows through everything and is the underlying cause of everything. The Tao is mysterious, unknowable, and inexplicable. As soon as we think we have grasped the essence of the Tao, it is proof that we have oversimplified it. If we start talking about the Tao, it is a sure sign we are not talking about it.

Religious or popular Taoism, rooted in ancient Chinese folklore and superstition, sees the universe as populated by a complicated hierarchy of forces and deities, demons and ghosts. At the top of this "divine organizational chart" is the Jade Emperor. Lesser gods or powers rule over villages; mightier deities reign over larger domains. The Eight Immortals are perfect spiritual beings worshipped and/or revered by religious Taoists. Each has a special power. All are associated with good luck.

Worldview

Taoism shares the same ancient, Eastern worldview as Confucianism and Chinese folk religion. According to one source, this worldview includes "an awareness of man's close relationship with nature and the universe, a cyclical view of time and the universe, veneration or worship of ancestors, the idea of 'Heaven,' and belief in the divinity of the sovereign."

Philosophical Taoism may have arisen largely as a backlash against the rigorous civic expectations of Confucius. Rather than devote themselves to social duty and public mores, Lao Tzu and his followers sought to follow a private, mystical path of quiet simplicity and meditation in harmony with nature.

Religious Taoism grew out of primitive, polytheistic Chinese folk religion. It involves a mixture of some aspects of philosophical Taoism (especially the theory of yin-yang), magic, alchemy, fortune-telling, exorcism, ancestor worship, special diets, and the recitation of scriptures—all in the attempt to find immortality.

The influence of Taoism in the West is seen in the increasing acceptance of holistic medical practices (acupuncture, herbalism, and so forth), participation in certain martial art forms (like t'ai ch'i), and the popularity of feng-shui (which is thought to enhance the flow of ch'i in one's living space).

View of the Afterlife

Death is viewed by philosophical Taoists as part of the natural order of things and the way one returns to the Tao. It is not to be resisted. Religious Taoism uses alchemy and magic to attempt to resist death.

Sacred Texts

Tao Te Ching (meaning "The Book of the Way" or "The Way of Power") is the supposed collected poems and writings of Lao Tzu. This short text (eighty-one chapters) teaches the way to peace and discusses the nature of life.

The collected writings of Chuang Tzu contain more Taoist teaching and techniques of meditation and breathing, as well as advice about diet and sexual activity.

Worship Services

In religious Taoism, priests preside over various ceremonies: thanksgiving services, healing rituals, exorcisms, ordinations, and birthdays of deities. Regular services are not scheduled. Rather, public temples remain open and worshippers are free to come and go to light incense and pray to the gods. Deities who do not seem to respond to the sacrificial offerings and faithful prayers of worshippers may become unpopular and be replaced by other gods.

Important Dates

Chinese New Year (in February)
Birthdays of the gods—celebrated throughout the year

On October 23, 1838, through the mouth of our foundress, Miki Nakayama, God the Parent spoke to human beings for the first time, declaring, "I am God of Origin, God in Truth. There is causality in this Residence. At this time, I have descended here to save all humankind. I wish to receive Miki as the Shrine of God." The third day after this revelation, October 26, marks the beginning of Tenrikyo.
—Tenrikyo.com

Major Differences from Christianity

Belief	Tenrikyo
Sacred Text(s)	Three scriptures: the *Ofudesaki*, the *Mikagura-uta*, and the *Osashizu*
Nature of God	Creator of all, referred to as "God the Parent"
Jesus Christ	No emphasis on Christ; Oyasama takes on a Christ-like role within Tenrikyo—revealing the truth of God the Parent, healing, living after death
Human nature	No inherent sin, people are simply plagued by wrong ways of thinking; the body is on loan from God the Parent; the individual controls his/her own mind
About human need	Achieving *yoki yusan* (the "Joyous Life") by overcoming self-centered thinking and using one's body to help others
Salvation	Attained via a long healthy life (115 years) filled with joy and service
Afterlife	Limited discussion of the afterlife; some hints of reincarnation

Number of Followers

Current sources cite about two million adherents worldwide, with most of those in Japan. Among world religions, Tenrikyo ranks eighteenth.

Major Figures/Prophets

- **Miki Nakayama** (also known as *Oyasama*)—Revered as the originator or "foundress" of Tenrikyo. In 1838, at the age of forty-one, Oyasama's mind was replaced by the mind of God the Parent. From this moment, she became regarded as the Shrine of Tsukihi, or the revealer of God the Parent and the ultimate model to the path to the Joyous Life. Oyasama spent the next fifty years teaching the intention of God the Parent, writing down God's will, speaking it to others, and demonstrating how to lead the Joyous Life. Though no longer present physically on the earth, Oyasama is believed to live on as the mother of all humanity, lavishing her boundless love on all people everywhere. Her residence is called the Foundress' Sanctuary. Followers of Tenrikyo believe that Oyasama, though hidden from sight, continues to give truth through the *Shinbashira* (which means literally, "Main Pillar," that is, the current spiritual and administrative leader of the faith). It is said that adherents continue to prepare meals and draw baths for Oyasama daily in the Sanctuary, even as guards stand post by her door.

Short History

On April 18, 1798, Miki Nakayama was born in Sanmaiden Village, Japan. Married at thirteen years of age, Miki was by all accounts a virtuous wife, daughter-in-law, and neighbor.

On October 23, 1838, it is claimed that God the Parent settled within Miki's body and mind and began revealing to

The emblem of Tenrikyo

her and through her the divine words and will. Over the ensuing years, Oyasama gave away all her possessions. Her willingness to endure abject poverty was seen as a picture of God the Parent's single-minded desire to save the world. However, it was her purported power to deliver the sick from illness and her ability to enable women to enjoy pain-free childbirth that both attracted followers and aroused the jealousy of priests, exorcists, and other religious practitioners.

In 1864, Oyasama's followers began constructing the Place for the Service (a kind of temple or shrine where religious meetings would take place). Five years later, Oyasama began writing the Ofudesaki, the core of the teachings of Tenrikyo. In 1875 she identified the *jiba*, the place of humankind's origin. She was frequently detained by the political authorities, but she resolutely continued her work with joy.

Tenrikyo is derived from three words: *ten*, which means "heavens," *ri,* which means "truth," and *kyo,* which means "teach." Put together, Tenrikyo means: "Teaching of Divine Wisdom."

In 1887, Oyasama died at the age of ninety while listening to the music of the service. Interestingly, Tenrikyo practitioners do not speak of her death.

Basic Beliefs and Values

According to Tenrikyo, the purpose of our existence (and the goal of Tenrikyo) is to find and lead the "Joyous

Life." We experience and enjoy such a life by obeying God the Parent's instructions about living selflessly, helping others, and living in harmony with people and nature. We become unhappy when our minds are dominated by "dust" (that is, self-serving thoughts and attitudes). The eight "dusty" attitudes specifically warned against in Tenrikyo are: miserliness, covetousness, hatred, self love, grudge bearing, anger, greed, and arrogance. Tenrikyo seeks to teach its followers to sweep or blow away this dust. We are to pursue a life that makes others happy. We are to live with grateful minds and bodies given over to serving others.

View of God

In Tenrikyo teaching, there is one deity called "God the Parent," also referred to as "God of Origin," or "God in Truth." All of creation and humanity emanates from God the Parent, who sustains and nurtures us. The word "Parent" reminds us that God's love for us is analogous to the tender care and concern that human parents show to their children. As adherents of this religion grow in their comprehension of Tenrikyo, they will move from a general belief in God as Creator to a more intimate belief in God as Parent.

Tenrikyo actually shares some similarities with Buddhist and Shinto thought. However, the official Tenrikyo Web site does not specifically address other religions. Because many adherents view Tenrikyo as less of a religion and more of a "way of life," many hold other religious beliefs while also seeking to follow Tenrikyo principles.

Worldview

The Tenrikyo creation story states, "In the beginning, the world was a muddy ocean." Finding that condition unacceptable, God the Parent decided to create the human race. God wanted to see our Joyous Life and share in that joy. The whole creation originated from this thought. Ever since creation, humans have been nurtured by God the Parent while undergoing many rebirths over an extremely long time.

This story reflects God the Parent's love and providential care for all, the idea that we are all brothers and sisters, and that the purpose of human existence is to lead the Joyous Life, living selflessly and thankfully (*hinokishin*). Nature is not to be conquered by humankind, but people and nature should coexist peacefully.

View of the Afterlife

Tenrikyo mostly focuses on this life, living the Joyous Life for 115 years (considered by Oyasama as the ideal lifespan). There are some hints of reincarnation in Tenrikyo teachings, but this is not a central teaching or highly developed doctrine.

Sacred Texts

Tenrikyo has three scriptures:
1) the *Ofudesaki*, The Tip of the Writing Brush, which contains metaphorical teachings from God the Parent;
2) the *Mikagura-uta,* songs for accompanying the service, which teach how to live the Joyous Life;
3) the *Osashizu,* directions about using the mind and conduct in life.

Worship Services

The *kagura service* is seen as the ultimate way to focus the mind and return to one's original state. It is an elaborate and mystical ceremony involving ten mask-wearing dancers, five male and five female. These dancers use movements and hand motions to symbolize the ten aspects of God the Parent's complete providence. The dance is intended to reflect harmony, beauty, unity, and joy. As the performers dance, the gathered worshippers attempt to focus their minds in a unified way on God the Parent's desire to bring about the Joyous Life in the world. This is the purpose of the kagura service.

Following the kagura, three men and three women line up and perform the *teodori* ("Dance with Hand Movements"). This ritual also is thought to bring about mental cleansing and healing as worshippers watch the tenets of Tenrikyo acted out.

Local Tenrikyo congregations conduct a monthly service in which their church members are able to receive the truth of the kagura service performed at the *jiba*. The jiba is the "holy of holies" in Tenrikyo. It is the most sacred place in the sanctuary of the main Tenrikyo temple in Tenri city, the site where adherents believe the creation of the world took place.

Shuyoka is a kind of communal training program or extended retreat for adherents seventeen years old and up, who wish to learn the ins and outs of Tenrikyo. This intensive immersion into Oyasama's teaching lasts three months.

Besseki is the name for the crucial lecture that helps one attain spiritual rebirth:

> *Rebirth here refers to transformation from a point of view that desires one's own salvation to the point of view that desires the salvation of others. Happiness as enjoyed without caring about others is, in fact, like an illusion, which is devoid of reality. Only when one's happiness brings happiness to others, can it be true happiness* (quoted from online source).

The *amulet* is a patch of red cloth that was part of Oyasama's attire. Only those who make the pilgrimage to the jiba may receive this protective clothing that is thought to guard one's mind against straying from the teachings of Tenrikyo.

The *grant of safe childbirth* is another blessing bestowed at the jiba. Women who are at least six months pregnant can get three packets of sacred rice. Consumed with gratitude and trust, this rice-eating ritual insures a no-stress pregnancy.

Important Dates

New Year's Day Service (January 1)—for giving
thanks and praying for God's blessings

Spring Grand Service (January 26)—commemorating the day
when Oyasama withdrew from physical life (her death)

Oyasama Birth Celebration Service (April 18)—
a celebration of Oyasama's birthday

Autumn Grand Service (October 26)—a remembrance of the
day the Teaching was founded (the beginning of Tenrikyo)

Monthly Service (the 26th of each month, except January
and October)—at this gathering, the kagura service,
Tenrikyo's most important rite, is performed

"The Cosmic Masters are highly evolved extraterrestrial beings. As far as we on Earth are concerned, the Cosmic Masters come mainly from the other Planets in this Solar System. They reside on the higher realms of their respective planets making them undetectable by any instruments yet devised on Earth. They are, however, capable of vibrating themselves onto any level of existence and can make themselves visible at will. They are beings of colossal advancement, millions of years our senior scientifically and spiritually."
—The Aetherius Society Web site

Major Differences from Christianity

Belief	The Aetherius Society
Sacred Text(s)	The writings of Dr. George King (actually ancient and previously secret wisdom received via extraterrestrials/cosmic masters)
Nature of God	Pantheistic: All of life is divine, all comes from and is connected with the Absolute and is evolving toward a reunion with the Absolute
Jesus Christ	A cosmic master, sent to earth to offer help, a great moral, wise teacher in the line of Krishna and Buddha; he returned in 1958 in undisguised splendor
Human nature	Selfish, violent, ignorant, and focused on the wrong things, but a divine spark of the Creator, capable of tapping into the energy being offered by evolved beings
About human need	Mankind is out of karmic balance and needs to evolve quickly to save itself and the earth from a host of problems
Salvation	Accepting the spiritual energy, wisdom, and methods being offered by spiritual masters from other worlds until one ultimately becomes one with the Absolute
Afterlife	Reincarnation—the lengthy and necessary process for mastering essential lessons, with brief interludes in the spiritual realm—until one passes through the portal of ascension and becomes a Cosmic Master

Number of Followers

Estimates of the number of members of The Aetherius Society range from two thousand to three thousand people (with some ten thousand others on various mailing lists). In the United States, chapters are located in California, Michigan, Florida, Virginia, and New Jersey.

Major Figures/Prophets

- **Dr. George King** (1919–1997)—founder of The Aetherius Society

Short History

As a boy, George King became disillusioned with his traditional Christian up-bringing. He dabbled in psychic phenomena and then found yoga in his early twenties. For the next ten years, he allegedly spent eight to twelve hours a day practicing yoga, eventually mastering the ability to reach *samadhi*, an elevated state of consciousness. Because of this diligent training, King was chosen for a unique mission. In May of 1954, he claimed to have heard an audible voice that said, "Prepare yourself! You are to become the voice of Interplanetary Parliament."

A few days later King was visited by a world-renowned yoga master, who materialized in his apartment despite the fact that the dwelling's door was closed and locked. When this guru vanished, King discovered he possessed the skill of being able to establish mental rapport with advanced spiritual masters from other planets. He could tune into the messages being directed to earth by advanced extrater-restrials, and discern the difference between these spiritual encounters and "contacts with [lesser] discarnate entities living on the astral planes of Earth."

King believed and taught that these evolved spiritual beings populate the cosmos and are interested in helping mankind. They visit the earth in technologically advanced spacecraft (what many people term "UFOs"). They offer en-ergy and techniques that can assist in the spiritual evolution of the human race.

The Aetherius Society believes their teachings come from extraterrestrial beings

In 1955, King established The Aetherius Society in England and began publishing a journal titled *Cosmic Voice*. In 1959, he incorporated The Aetherius Society in the United States. Until his death in 1997, Dr. King acted as a human, cosmic transmission channel, recording more than six hundred com-muniqués from the Cosmic Masters. He also oversaw a number of cosmic missions, aimed at focusing healing energy toward needy places in the world and toward the earth itself, seeking to restore the karmic balance of the human race.

Two other "UFO religions" are worth mentioning. The Raelian Church was es-tablished in 1973 by Frenchman Claude Vorilhon, after he claimed to have had an encounter with an alien being. Vorilhon was renamed "Rael" and was told that the common word for "God" in the Old Testament is the Hebrew *Elohim*, which really means "those who come from the sky." In other words, the Raelians believe the human race was created by advanced creatures from other planets. The Raelian group anticipates the arrival of these extraterrestrials before the year 2035. This church made news in 1997 by its close ties to Clonaid and Dr. Brigitte Boisselier, who claimed to have cloned a human child.

Heaven's Gate was the doomsday, UFO group in California that committed mass suicide in 1997. Founded and led by Marshall Applewhite, the group of thirty-nine people believed that their disconnected souls, freed at death from their earthly bodies, would be transported by UFOs (identified as the Hale-Bopp comet) to a level beyond normal humanhood.

Basic Beliefs and Values

A quick review of the teachings and practices of The Aetherius Society:

- The world faces a host of monumental problems including terrorism, hedonism, pollution, starvation, poverty, economic disparity, dwindling resources, and so forth.

- Advanced cosmic masters, highly evolved beings, have come to earth from other worlds to help, but our leaders have spurned their advances. The planetary need is desperate as human technology has far outpaced mankind's spiritual progress. The Earth is at a crossroads: either disaster or a wonderful new age.

- These highly evolved species travel to Earth in flying saucers. Living on higher planes of existence, "mainly within our own Solar System," these extraterrestrials are undetectable because of their advanced technologies.

- The human race has destroyed itself previously. Once, eons ago when mankind inhabited a planet named Maldek (between Mars and Jupiter), a global war annihilated people and the planet itself. (The asteroid belt between the two planets is actually the remnants of Maldek.) The destruction of Atlantis was a second instance.

- The Aetherius Society advocates the law of *karma* (that is, reaping what one has sown): "Put out selfishness and negativity and one gets this back, until such a time that one learns to act otherwise. Put out love and healing, and one gets these energies back." The Aetherius Society says that karma is not so much a reward system as a pressure or force that can be manipulated. The cosmic masters, exhibiting amazing grace and compassion, are trying to "speed up mankind's journey through karma" toward true freedom and enlightenment.

- We humans live in a "sea" of spiritual energy (*prana*) and can help others by learning to harness and manipulate and direct this subtle spiritual energy toward those in need of healing and help. Dr. King taught that much of this energy was deposited by the cosmic masters in nineteen holy mountains around the earth during a three-year mission (1958–61) called *Operation Starlight.* Ever since, in "Operation Sunbeam" The Aetherius Society members have used the science of radionics to transmit these mountainous energy stores into Mother Earth herself to replenish her and build positive karma for mankind.

- The goal of existence is the evolution of the self—indeed, of the whole human race—beyond nirvana, back to oneness with the Absolute, "amalgamation with the Godhead" and beyond. This journey involves nine steps.

- The twelve blessings are exercises by which The Aetherius Society members give thanks to the Cosmic Masters who assist us lesser evolved "earthlings" and through which members are able to direct healing streams of light and energy to the imperiled world (including the world of animals and plants).

- Service is the greatest value and most important human activity: "One person who is rendering true Spiritual SERVICE, not self delusion, but true spiritual SERVICE to those who need it, is worth ten who retreat from the suffering of others in order to bring about a state of joy and peace within themselves."

- Four times a year, spiritually evolved extraterrestrials orbit the earth in a huge but undetectable UFO called "Satellite No. 3." The purpose of this quarterly mission is to transmit a helpful magnetic energy to all who are engaged in active spirituality, regardless of their religious affiliation.

View of God

The homepage of The Aetherius Society says: "Blessed is the Great Being known as the Galaxy." Aetherians embrace a pantheistic/monistic theology. God is the Absolute. Everything is connected. All is one. We are all divine sparks.

Thus, the God of The Aetherius Society is not personal. And yet the Cosmic Masters (of whom Jesus was one), those enlightened extraterrestrials who seek to help the human race evolve toward union with God, are kind, benevolent, gracious, and compassionate.

Worldview

The Aetherius Society believes the future of the earth and the human race hangs in the balance. Adherents further believe that we are not alone in the universe. Advanced, intelligent life exists, and these friendly beings visit the earth regularly in UFOs. Either we will heed the extraterrestrial wisdom of these Cosmic Masters who want to bring salvation from space, or we will perish.

> Those who are enlightened must see this life as a classroom for human and spiritual evolution and must engage in unselfish service—learning to channel and direct the healing energy that has been deposited on earth for humanity's metaphysical deliverance. Personally, members are expected to evolve spiritually through yoga, meditative prayer, and healing exercises.

View of the Afterlife

The Aetherius Society teaches that at death, one's consciousness (or soul) leaves the physical body and inhabits what is called "a subtle body." This new "body" can experience other spiritual realms and dimensions ("ghostly realms," contacts with the dead via séances, the world of the psychic). After a time, this individual is reborn into another physical body on earth to continue the learning process. The length and timing of all these transitions is directly linked to karma.

When one finally passes through the portal of Ascension, he or she has a choice: a graduation of sorts as a bona fide Cosmic Master to a "higher classroom in a more evolved civilization," or sticking around as a member of the "Spiritual Hierarchy of Earth" to help lesser evolved humans. These advanced beings are believed to live underneath sacred mountains such as the Tetons, Himalayas, and Mount Kilimanjaro.

Sacred Texts

Members of the Aetherius Society consider The Nine Freedoms, ancient enhanced wisdom delivered to George King in 1961, to be the authoritative, metaphysical text. This revered scripture includes drawings of UFOs/spacecrafts and accounts of interplanetary travel. King compiled a number of other books that the group claims are messages and wisdom from the cosmic masters.

Worship Services

The Aetherius Society chapters have weekly services, typically on Sundays and Thursday evenings. These meetings involve readings and teachings. The group offers an array of membership levels with varying privileges and responsibilities.

Full membership involves whole-hearted involvement in the The Aetherius

Society mission: observing the annual July 8 holiday and other important dates in The Aetherius Society calendar; participation in special services, lectures, seminars, and workshops, as well as home services. Filling out an annual questionnaire regarding activities for the group and for mankind and paying an annual fee are required. For this amount, one receives the group's newsletter and journals. After three years, members are eligible to apply for temple degree initiation. Passing this exam gives one the right to wear a robe of initiation (the color reflects one's level), vote at general meetings of The Aetherius Society, and receive special assistance upon death from "entities of a high caliber who will help . . . during the transition period."

Associate members are those who cannot commit to the same level of participation and service. They pay the same fee, but do not enjoy voting rights, the opportunity for temple degree initiation, or the extra help and service upon their demise.

Important Dates

For adherents of The Aetherius Society, important dates are as follows:

Primary Initiation of Earth —the most significant event for adherents of The Aetherius Society took place on July 8, 1964, between 10:00 and 10:57 p.m. (PDT). On this day, during these fifty-seven minutes, Mother Earth (a living organism) received an infusion of "colossal spiritual energy" that now lies dormant in the inner core of the planet. This monumental moment was foretold by the Mayans and by Nostradamus. The Aetherius Society members consider this the first day of the spiritual New Year.

Magnetization Periods, providing uplifting energy to those interested and engaged in spiritual efforts to better the world (via a giant, invisible UFO), are as follows:

April 18–May 23
July 5–August 5
September 3–October 9
November 4–December 10

"If the evil forces led by the Jews are victorious, future humanity is doomed to tens of thousands of years of slavery, misery, and bestiality, a situation from which there is no reversal and from which it can never recover. If, on the other hand, the White Race wins, led by the program and vision of Creativity, a bright and beautiful new world will emerge. It will be a world of grandeur and beauty, a world of continuing advancement, of cultural, economic, and genetic well-being. The outcome, my dear White Racial Comrades, depends completely on how hard you struggle to bring about victory."
—Ben Klassen, Founder of The Creativity Movement

Major Differences from Christianity

Belief	The Creativity Movement
Sacred Text(s)	The writings of founder Ben Klassen
Nature of God	No belief in God or the spiritual realm
Jesus Christ	The only "evidence" for Christ's existence is from Jewish sources, and is, therefore, not to be trusted
Human nature	The white race is superior to all other "mud races" (which are subspecies)
About human need	Concerned only about the needs of the white race; it must be preserved, advanced, and exalted
Salvation	Being fruitful and multiplying the white race so as to create "a whiter and brighter world"
Afterlife	No life after death; no heaven or hell

Number of Followers

The Creativity Movement is believed to have had as many as three thousand adherents (called "Creators") during the height of its popularity in 2000–2001.

Major Figures/Prophets

- **Ben Klassen** (1918–1993)—founder and First Pontifex Maximus of The Church of the Creator (later known as The Creativity Movement)

- **Matthew Hale** (1971–present)—Southern Illinois University law school graduate who took over the group in 1996

Short History

In 1973, Ukrainian-born Ben Klassen began the Church of the Creator, a white supremacist group that managed to attract hundreds of followers from the United States, Canada, Europe, and South Africa.

In the 1990s, the church faced a barrage of problems. One of its members, George Loeb, was convicted in the 1991 first-degree murder of Harold Mansfield, Jr., an African-American man in Florida.

The Mansfield family filed and won a one million dollar civil judgment against the group. In 1993, a despondent Klassen committed suicide.

Three years later, Matthew Hale, a young law school graduate, began to lead the Church of the Creator. An effective recruiter and promoter, Hale often appeared on talk shows. He changed the name of the group to the World Church of the Creator in order to suggest the ultimate goal of worldwide white supremacy. Hale eventually gained notoriety and support from other white supremacists for being denied a license to practice law in Illinois, despite having passed the bar exam.

Matthew Hale rose to national prominence in the mid 90s

Perhaps in response to this legal setback, another member of the group, Benjamin Smith, went on a shooting rampage, targeting minorities before turning the gun on himself.

In 2000, an Oregon church, which had legally registered the name "Church of the Creator," filed suit against Hale's group for trademark infringement. In 2002, U.S. District Court Judge Joan Lefkow barred the white supremacist group from using the name "Church of the Creator" or any name containing the words "church" and "creator." Hale changed the name of the group to *The Creativity Movement*.

In early 2003, Hale was arrested and indicted for soliciting the murder of Judge Lefkow. The man serving as his security chief was actually an FBI informant. Hale was convicted, and in April 2005, he was sentenced to forty years in a maximum security Colorado prison.

Since that time, The Creativity Movement has splintered into multiple smaller groups, and members have kept a low profile.

Basic Beliefs and Values

- The Creativity Movement is dedicated to the survival, expansion, and advancement of the white race. Its goal is to build a "whiter and brighter world," by encouraging whites to "be fruitful and multiply and fill the earth."

- Membership is restricted to those wholly or mostly of European descent; they are called "creators."

- The Creativity Movement's logo is circular, featuring a halo above a crown, sitting over a large *W*. The *W* stands for the white race. The crown is the white race's elite, aristocratic position. The halo signifies the unique sacredness of the white race. Circling it are the phrases: "White People Awake" and "Save the White Race."

- Hate is considered a necessary and even constructive emotion—one needs to exercise both love and hate to survive. According to Hale, "If you love something, you must be willing to hate that which threatens it."

The Creativity Movement advocates five fundamental beliefs: (1) racial survival and advancement is their religion; (2) the white race is "nature's finest"; (3) racial loyalty is the greatest of all honors, and racial disloyalty is the worst of all crimes; (4) what is good for the white race is the highest virtue and what is bad for whites is the ultimate sin; and (5) Creativity—the white race religion—is the only salvation for the white race.

View of God

The Creativity Movement is a racial movement not a spiritual one. It regards the white race as "nature's finest" (not "*God's* finest"). Followers are called to be protectors of the white race. So in a sense, adherents "worship" (that is, they value and devote themselves to above all else) the white race. The official Web site states: "A Creator is not superstitious and disdains belief in the supernatural. He will waste no time giving any credence to, or playing silly games with imaginary spooks, spirits, gods, and demons."

Worldview

The Creativity Movement teaches that the white race is under attack and must fight back in order to survive and to resume its rightful place as the controlling race in the world. The Creativity Movement sees the problems of the world as the fault of nonwhites. Members are vehemently opposed to any kind of racial interaction.

View of the Afterlife

The Creativity Movement does not believe in heaven or hell, or any existence after this life.

Sacred Texts

The writings of founder Ben Klassen are the "holy books" for members of The Creativity Movement. These include the foundational book *Nature's Eternal Religion*, which sets forth the ideology of The Creativity Movement. The sequel is called *The White Man's Bible*.

Additional writings by Klassen include: *Expanding Creativity, Building a Whiter and Brighter World, Rahowa! This Planet Is All Ours, The Klassen Letters, Volumes 1 and 2,*

A Revolution of Values Through Religion, The Little White Book, Salubrious Living, an autobiography titled *Against the Evil Tide,* and *On the Brink of a Bloody Social War.*

Worship Services

There are no organized services or congregations. Creators are asked to recite the five fundamental beliefs of The Creativity Movement five times per day.

They perform a version of a baby dedication ceremony, in which both parents pledge to raise the newborn child to become a loyal member of the white race. When the child turns thirteen, followers of The Creativity Movement hold a kind of "confirmation ceremony" that solicits a promise of loyalty to the white race.

Important Dates

The Creativity Movement abandoned the Gregorian calendar for its own system of dating. Since the group was founded in 1973, it declared that 1974 was 1 A.C. ("Anno de Creativitat"). The year 1972 was called 1 P.C. ("Prius Creativitat").

Holidays of The Creativity Movement include:

Klassen Day (February 20)—a commemoration of the founder's birth
Founding Day (February 21)—the anniversary of the publication of Klassen's book, *Nature's Eternal Religion*
Martyr's Day (September 15)—an observance of the death of Creator minister, Ben Smith
West Victory Day (December 29)—a celebration of the white race's final defeat of Native Americans in 1890
Festum Album (December 26–January 1)—a week-long celebration of white pride and unity

"The so-called Christian Church today is built essentially on man-made doctrine, tradition, confusion, bondage trips, and contradiction to the word as it was originally God-breathed."
—The Way Magazine

Major Differences from Christianity

Belief	The Way International
Sacred Text(s)	The Bible in original Aramaic; writings and teachings of V. P. Wierwille
Nature of God	No Trinity; God is one person
Jesus Christ	Not eternal but created, not God; a perfect human who died to make salvation possible; Christ rose from the dead, ascended to heaven, sits at the right hand of God, and will return one day
Human nature	Consists of a body and soul (the spiritual aspect of humanity was lost in the Fall—Genesis 3); man's spiritual essence is restored at salvation
About human need	Spiritual rebirth and growth (according to the true teachings of The Way)
Salvation	The basis for forgiveness is belief in Christ's death and resurrection
Afterlife	Annihilation of the wicked (no hell); soul sleep for the faithful, meaning that there is no conscious existence after death until Christ returns

Number of Followers

In the 1970s, the nondenominational Bible study fellowship known as The Way International had up to a hundred thousand adherents in more than sixty countries. In the turbulent years following the death of its founder in 1985, membership levels dropped dramatically. Best current membership estimates range from five thousand to twenty thousand people in thirty countries.

Major Figures/Prophets

- **Victor Paul Wierwille** (1916–1985)—the Ohio-born, Princeton Seminary-trained, minister who claimed a miraculous visitation from God in 1942, which led to the founding of The Way International.

- **L. Craig Martindale** (1948–present)—successor to V. P. Wierwille as leader of The Way International ministry, who resigned amidst scandalous accusations in 2000

- **Rosalie F. Rivenbark**—president of The Way International since 2000

Short History

In 1942, Victor Paul Wierwille was in his mid-twenties and a new pastor at the Evangelical and Reformed Church in Payne, Ohio. Feeling overwhelmed by the daunting challenge of shepherding a congregation, Wierwille contended that he heard the audible voice of God while praying one fall day. Wierwille alleged that God essentially offered him this deal: *I will teach you the Word as it was originally revealed and taught in the first century, if you will promise to pass on the truth to others.*

Wierwille asked for a sign—instant snow. When he opened his eyes from praying, he claimed he found himself in near blizzard conditions. Assured that he had God's blessing, Wierwille intensified his scripture studies, launched a radio program called "Vesper Chimes," and began developing and teaching the Bible training classes that would ultimately become the official "curriculum" for his new ministry.

In 1955, The Way, Inc. was officially chartered. Between 1959 and 1961, Wierwille renovated his three hundred-acre family farm in New Knoxville, Ohio, into the current headquarters of his ministry. In the 1960s, the Jesus People movement exploded onto the national scene. Wierwille traveled to San Francisco in search of truth seekers and found many hungry disciples who readily submitted to his teachings.

The Way International reached its zenith in the mid- to late-1970s, but allegations of cult-like behavior (including excessive authoritarian control and brainwashing) caused a growing public backlash. With the death of founder Wierwille due to cancer in 1985, the group encountered major upheaval. Many members left, some reporting serious power struggles for control of the organization. Wierwille's successor, L. Craig Martindale, eventually resigned in 2000, facing multiple lawsuits, including allegations of sexual harassment and rape. Rosalie Rivenbark, a long-term leader in the group, became The Way International's third president.

Basic Beliefs and Values

The Way International is fiercely committed to studying and teaching the Bible and applying it to life. It maintains that deep scripture research is for every believer, not just professional clergy. All members are passionate about the Bible (especially their understanding of it), and most are warm and friendly to any who are earnestly seeking the truth.

Though it is clearly a Bible-centered organization, The Way International does differ from mainstream, evangelical Christianity in some very significant ways, particularly its teaching regarding the Trinity. For more information read the View of God section below.

Other observations about the organization, beliefs, and practices of The Way International include:

- The group derives its name from John 14:6 (KJV): "Jesus saith unto him, I am the way, the truth, and the life: no man cometh unto the Father, but by me."

- Much emphasis is given to helping followers understand the historical context (including ancient customs) and the literary genres in which the Bible was written. The interpretations of The Way International leaders are taught as the correct ones.

- The Way International is a proponent of what is sometimes called ultra-dispensationalism. Dispensationalism is the belief that though God Himself never changes, the way He administers His eternal plan in different eras does change. Each of these periods in God's plan is called a "dispensation." For example, the specific commands given to Adam and Eve in Eden represent a different dispensation from the laws God gave Moses and the people of Israel at Mt. Sinai. The Way International goes even further, claiming that the commands and practices described in the earliest New Testament books (such as the Gospels, Acts, and even Hebrews and James) are not relevant to believers living today in the current age. Thus, The Way International puts primary emphasis on the writings of Paul—especially his "church epistles."

- Followers of The Way International are trained in special classes called "The Way of Abundance and Power." V. P. Wierwille originally titled this course "Power for Abundant Living." Three levels are offered: foundational, intermediate, and advanced. Involvement in a home fellowship is a prerequisite.

- Members who have completed all three levels of the classes are eligible to be trained to spread their faith to others outside the group in the "Disciples of the Way Outreach Program."

- Members believe speaking in tongues is the normal manifestation of having God's power and presence in one's life.

View of God

Strictly monotheistic and anti-Trinitarian, adherents of The Way International believe that God is a single person who has revealed Himself in various modes or forms throughout biblical history.

Jesus Christ is not God, nor is he coeternal or coequal with God. Jesus is a created being, the perfect Son of God, and the Savior, but not the same essence as God.

The Holy Spirit is not a distinct personage within the Godhead but a manifestation of God's power. The Spirit's presence in a believer's life is confirmed by the ability to speak in tongues.

Worldview

Devout followers of The Way International see the world and especially those in mainline churches as being deceived or ignorant of the truth about God. They believe The Way International leaders are God-appointed purveyors of the little-known truth of the lost gospel.

View of the Afterlife	Sacred Texts
Various sources report that The Way International teaches that true believers do not go immediately into the presence of the Lord at death. Rather they enter into a state of soul sleep, while they await the return of Christ. Unbelievers experience annihilation at death. Thus there is no such thing as a literal hell.	The Lamsa Bible, an Aramaic (also known as Syriac) version of the Old and New Testaments, is regarded as the most accurate revelation from God. Writings by V. P. Wierwille, especially *Jesus Christ Is Not God*, and certain Bible scholars like E. W. Bullinger are very influential.

Worship Services

Home fellowships are the lifeblood of The Way International's ministry. The main church is viewed as the Tree, home fellowships are known as Twigs, and clusters of home groups are called Branches. The home fellowship gatherings are led by trained laymen and feature upbeat Bible teachings, prayer, singing, accountability, and encouragement. Also, each Sunday afternoon, a large service with prayer, singing, and Bible teaching is held at the Ohio headquarters of The Way International. These services are made available on video and CDs.

Important Dates

No special dates are specified.

"Once you are accustomed to this basic pattern of life, then you don't have to pray so much because everything you do is prayer. Once you pray, God will just reply, 'Go ahead and do it.' Now and then you would pray to make sure that what you are doing is what God wants and the universe wants; then you can pray for power if you are worn out.

"In your case, you can tell me that since I know so much more about prayer than you that I should do the praying and you will just follow what I say. That attitude and action are as meaningful as your individual prayer."
—Sun Myung Moon

Major Differences from Christianity

Belief	Unification Church
Sacred Text(s)	*The Divine Principle*, a book by Rev. Sun Myung Moon; also his transcribed speeches that explain the true meaning of the Bible
Nature of God	God is the Creator with a dual masculine-feminine nature; not a Trinity
Jesus Christ	Lord and Savior who brought salvation through His sacrifice, but whose messianic mission was left unfinished when the people of His day rejected God's kingdom
Human nature	Created with bodies to rule the physical world and spirits to dominate the spiritual realm, but fallen and in need of salvation
About human need	Forgiveness of sin (redemption) and reunion with God's purposes (restoration)
Salvation	Trusting in Christ for spiritual salvation, and following the teachings of Rev. Moon (which means becoming part of the "True Family") for physical salvation
Afterlife	No physical resurrection, but a spiritual one to a realm called paradise, to await the revealing of the kingdom of heaven

Number of Followers

The Unification Church has between a quarter of a million and one million followers, according to some sources. The Church itself claims three million members (often referred to as "Moonies").

Major Figures/Prophets

- **Reverend Sun Myung Moon** (1920–present day)—the Korean founder and leader of the Unification Church
- **Hyun Jin Moon** (1969–present day)—the third son of Sun Myung Moon, a Columbia University graduate, who is viewed as the likely successor to his aging father

Short History

The Holy Spirit Association for the Unification of World Christianity, or the Unification Church as it is more commonly known, began in 1954 under the leadership of Reverend Sun Myung Moon.

Born in 1920, Moon grew up as a Presbyterian in Japanese-controlled, Shinto-dominated Korea. In 1935, he claimed to have experienced a heavenly vision in which Jesus appeared to Moon, asking him to complete Jesus' unfinished messianic mission. Moon said he was given the specific task of bringing about Christ's kingdom on earth. In 1946, Moon began to preach his new theological beliefs and gather followers. This resulted in his excommunication from the Presbyterian Church of Korea. On a missionary trip to communist North Korea, Moon was imprisoned, tortured, and according to his testimony, then miraculously healed. Surviving the brutal North Korean gulag, Moon made his way back to South Korea and, in 1954, officially began the Unification Church.

> To discover all that his calling entailed, the Korean teen began an intense study of scripture. From this study he developed the Divine Principle, a set of novel doctrines that would eventually comprise the tenets of the Unification Church.

Despite run-ins with the religious and political establishment, the church grew and the message of Moon's Divine Principle spread. An able missionary named Sang Ik Choi brought the Unification Church's beliefs to Japan in 1958. Another missionary named Young Oon Kim came to the United States in 1959.

In 1960, Moon married Hak Ja Han, an event he described as the "marriage of the Lamb," a reference to Revelation 19:9. The official church Web site states: "This marked the beginning of the restoration of humankind back into God's lineage. By the power of God and sacrificial love, Sun Myung Moon and Hak Ja Han established the position of True Parents. They are the first couple to have the complete blessing of God, and to be able to bring forth children with no original sin."

By the early 1970s, Moon presided over a growing church and a prosperous global business enterprise. He relocated to the United States and embarked on an upbeat program that advocated patriotism and Judeo-Christian values. He moved in

Rev. Moon meeting with President Nixon. Moon was staunchly opposed to communism.

elite political circles and enjoyed favor in Washington and with the media. However, with the Watergate scandal in 1973–74, his diehard support of President Richard Nixon created a backlash.

Critics began to look harder at Moon's beliefs, his far-flung business ventures (including his founding of the ultraconservative *Washington Times* newspaper in 1982), and the various activities of the Unification Church. Watchdog groups accused Moon of being a cult leader who brainwashed his followers. This prompted many concerned parents to "kidnap" their own adult children away from the group in order to subject them to controversial deprogramming techniques.

Following a five-year IRS investigation, Moon was indicted and convicted of tax evasion. He served thirteen months at Danbury Federal Prison, Connecticut, and was released in 1985.

After a triumphant return to North Korea in 1991, Moon declared himself the Messiah. The official church biography of Sun Myung Moon concludes with these words: "True love has now triumphed over evil. All the satanic barriers have been broken down. The Completed Testament Age has dawned. God's true love, which was lost at the fall of man, has made its triumphant reappearance in the world. This love is the power of new life for all individuals, marriages and families the world over."

Basic Beliefs and Values

Some of the major tenets of Sun Myung Moon's Divine Principle are:

- God's original intent and plan for the world was for a perfect man, Adam, and perfect woman, Eve, to perfectly express God's male-female, loving nature, and while living in a perfect environment, to have perfect children who would help build a perfect kingdom of God.

- The great original sin in Eden was not simple disobedience to God, but was (1) Eve's sexual seduction by and union with Lucifer, which resulted in mankind's spiritual fall (all people being born with a sinful nature); and (2) Eve's illicit premarital sexual liaison with Adam, causing the physical fall of the human race.

- Jesus Christ's atoning death resulted in spiritual salvation for the human race; however, His death prevented Him from bringing about mankind's physical salvation (since Jesus was unable to marry and father children without a sinful nature, and thus bring about God's kingdom on earth).

- Rev. Moon is the third Adam, the Lord of the second advent, a kind of "new" Messiah, that is "anointed one," appointed by God to finish Christ's incomplete mission.

- The Unification Church seeks to bring together all faiths, all factions, all things into one entity. World unity and peace is achieved when followers form "true families."

- Moon and his wife are the "true parents." Those who follow Moon's teachings and couples who seek a "true blessing" (by participating in personal or mass Unification Church wedding ceremonies) become part of the "true family" of God.

- The paying of *indemnities*; that is, trying to do penance for personal failures in the hopes of loosening Satan's grip and/or renewing one's relationship with God.

Worldview

The Unification Church places enormous emphasis on marriage. Theologically, it views marriage as pointing to God's very nature. It is essential for bringing about God's plan for a renewed, restored humanity. Early on, many Unification Church marriages were arranged by Moon himself—often between people of different racial and cultural backgrounds. It is expected that Unificationists are to remain celibate before marriage and to practice sexual fidelity within marriage.

Unificationists also spend much effort in seeking to bring together disparate groups, to reconcile various religious and political factions.

Perhaps due to Rev. Moon's torturous treatment at the hands of the North Korean Communist regime in the late 1940s, the Unification Church has always had staunch views against communism.

View of God
Divine Principle 2.1 states: "God, the Creator of all things, is the absolute reality, eternal, self-existent and transcendent of time and space." Unificationists are anti-Trinitarian, and believe that God is all-wise and all-powerful. They believe that God possesses a dual nature, and is both masculine and feminine. His ultimate purpose is said to be the establishment of the perfect, true family.

[225]

View of the Afterlife

The teachings of Moon on resurrection and the life to come are rather complicated. Essentially those who believed in Christ during the New Testament era (that is, the time from the first coming of Christ to the arrival of Rev. Moon, the Lord of the second advent) became life spirits at death and entered paradise, to await the coming kingdom of heaven.

With Rev. Moon's coming, these life spirits were able to leave paradise and return to earth to help others believe and become divine spirits eligible for the kingdom of heaven. By this back-to-earth mission, these paradise-dwelling life spirits are also able to become divine spirits and gain entrance into the kingdom of heaven.

Sacred Texts

> Unificationists believe the Divine Principle offers never-before-known revelation for those living in the age of Moon, who is embraced as Messiah and who has come to establish the kingdom of God on earth.

In the same way that Mormons read the Bible but boast of having a newer and more "final" scripture (*The Book of Mormon*), Unification Church adherents have their own revelation. The holy book for Unificationists is called the Divine Principle. It was written by Sun Myung Moon and was published in 1957.

A blend of Christian beliefs and Eastern thought, The Divine Principle is presented by the Unification Church as "the Completed Testament." They see the Old Testament as descriptive of life from creation to the coming of Christ, and the New Testament as written for the age from Christ's first advent to the coming of the Lord of the second advent.

Worship Services

Unificationists observe a pledge service at 5:00 a.m. each Sunday, usually at home. They may dress in white robes, and standing before a table that bears a picture of Rev. Moon and his wife, they devote themselves afresh to God and to the "true parents." They also renew their commitment at this time to helping establish the kingdom of God on earth.

Corporate services are similar in liturgy to evangelical Christian churches: prayers, singing, readings (from the Bible and from *The Divine Principle*), and a sermon.

Weddings are always a high and holy occasion in the Unification Church tradition, since they feature a divine blessing that makes couples participants in the building of God's "true family."

Important Dates

Unificationists follow a complicated lunar *and* solar calendar, which means that dates vary from year to year. The Unification Church calendar includes the assorted birthdays of members of the extended Moon family, the many anniversaries of mass weddings and "blessings" of Unification Church couples performed by Rev. Moon, and commemorations of the founding of various UC organizations.

Major holidays are:

True God's Day (January 1)—the most important of all holidays, "a day for God"

True Parents' Birthday (January 6 by the lunar calendar)—
an honoring of Rev. and Mrs. Moon

True Parents' Day (March 1)—a day for remembering God's restoration of fallen humanity via the marriage of Rev. Moon and Hak Ja Han

True Day of All Things (May 1)—a day for celebrating the restoration of the environment

True Children's Day (October 1)—a commemoration of the birth of Rev. and Mrs. Moon's first children, symbolizing the birth of the true family

"Unitarian Universalists search for truth along many paths. Instead of centering our religion on specific beliefs, we gather around shared moral values that include the inherent worth and dignity of every person."
—Web site description

Number of Followers

Formed officially in 1961, the "Unitarian Universalist Association" (sometimes referred to as "UUs" or "UUism") boasts some eight hundred thousand worldwide adherents (mostly in the United States). There are currently more than one thousand Unitarian Universalist congregations in the United States.

Major Figures/Prophets

- **Michael Servetus** (1511–1553)—a Spanish writer who rejected Trinitarian theology, thus becoming the "founder" of the modern Unitarian movement

- **John Biddle** (1615–1662)—the earliest successful advocate for Unitarian ideals in Great Britain, sometimes called the "Father of English Unitarianism"

- **Joseph Priestly** (1733–1804)—credited with establishing and organizing the first Unitarian church in America

- **James Relly** (1722–1778)—a Welsh minister who rejected the doctrine of hell and advocated salvation for all, thus becoming the modern originator of Universalism.

- **John Murray** (1741–1815)—an Anglican preacher who converted to the doctrines of Universalism and is credited with bringing the "all will be saved" theology to America

Benjamin Franklin was one of many Founding Fathers involved with early Unitarian Universalism

Other famous Unitarian Universalists in history include John Adams, Benjamin Franklin, Thomas Paine, Susan B. Anthony, Ray Bradbury, Rod Sterling, Christopher Reeve, and Charles Darwin.

Short History

Disagreement with the Christian doctrine of hell has occurred since the time of the early church. However, Universalism did not become an official group or movement in the United States until 1793, with the creation of the Universalist Church of America.

In a similar way, various opponents of the teaching of Trinitarianism have surfaced throughout church history. But not until 1825 in America, did Unitarians unite to form the American Unitarian Association.

For more than 150 years, these two liberal denominations existed side by side, often mirroring one another's beliefs and practices. In 1961, the groups merged in Boston, Massachusetts.

Basic Beliefs and Values

In the strictest terms, a Unitarian opposes the theological teaching of the Trinity (one God existing eternally as three persons—Father, Son, and Holy Spirit). A Universalist believes that God will ultimately save everyone—that is, no one will suffer eternal condemnation. In the words of Thomas Starr King, a Unitarian minister in the 1860s: "Universalists believe that God is too good to damn people, and the Unitarians believe that people are too good to be damned by God."

Membership in the Unitarian Universalist church is not defined by these two issues alone. Modern Unitarian Universalism is a true "whatever" faith. Adherents are allowed to believe in anything, everything, or nothing. There is no creed. There are no dogmatic articles of faith. Some adherents come from religious backgrounds and hold to some kind of belief in God. Others are thoroughly irreligious, perhaps even agnostic or atheistic.

Belief	Unitarian Universalism
Sacred Text(s)	Members find inspiration in many "holy books." Ultimate truth is found by looking within one's own heart, soul, and mind, relying on reason, and following one's conscience
Nature of God	If there is a God, this deity may be nothing more than the spirit of life, or the name given to impersonal forces in the universe—like evolution or love
Jesus Christ	If he existed, a wise moral and ethical teacher, but not born of a virgin, a doer of miracles, or resurrected from the dead; not the only way to God
Human nature	Basically good; able to choose to live compassionate lives of integrity and honesty
About human need	To live free of dogma, to choose to improve oneself and the world
Salvation	Not really an issue; do not believe in the concept of sin or predestination; all will be saved
Afterlife	Few believe in a continuing existence after this life or a real place called heaven; immortality means leaving a legacy

Major Differences from Christianity

In a survey done in 2001 by researchers from Ohio University, Unitarian Universalist adherents were asked to pick labels that best described their theological views (more than one designation was allowed). The results were as follows: 54 percent described themselves as humanist; 33 percent as agnostic; 18 percent as atheist; 16.5 percent as Buddhist; 13.1 percent as pagan; and another 13.1 percent as Christian.

Here is a scattershot of broad observations about Unitarian Universalism:

- Truth is relative not absolute, personal not universal, and subjective not objective. Beliefs may be borrowed from any religious tradition (truth is found in all religions) or none.

- The individual—not a holy book, a religious institution, a historic tradition or creed—is the ultimate authority. Each person is encouraged to develop a personal philosophy of life.

- Individuals should strive to be people of integrity, truth, and compassion.

- In joining the Unitarian Universalist church, no conversion is expected; no baptism is required; no renouncing of one's previous faith is mandated; no creedal confessions must be made; youth within the church develop their own personal belief (or credo) statements, and then, in a special Coming of Age ceremony, read these statements to the congregation.

- Adherents should engage in the individual and collective pursuit of social justice, environmental protection, human rights and peace.

- Unitarian Universalists champion individuality, inclusivism, pluralism, tolerance, and diversity.

View of God

Among Unitarian Universalists, there is no specified doctrine of God. Members are free to develop personal and even contradictory concepts of God, or to reject the notion of deity completely.

Some embrace atheism and see the world as the result of natural, evolutionary processes. Others are pantheistic, believing in a vague, impersonal, but universal life force that permeates all things. Still others are deistic, believing in a Creator who is transcendent and uninvolved in the workings of the natural world or in one's daily life.

Worldview

At the heart of the Unitarian Universalist faith is the idea that people should live moral and compassionate lives, not in order to be saved, but in order to better the world. According to the official Unitarian Universalist website: "We believe it is our deeds, not our creeds, that are most important." Most Unitarian Universalists are actively engaged in community affairs and attempt to work for the betterment of society. They see these efforts, not as tangential to the faith but as the natural overflow of a spiritual life. Good faith produces good works.

View of the Afterlife

Most Unitarian Universalists focus on the here and now and do not believe in any kind of individual continuing existence after this life. One would be hard pressed to find adherents who believe in a literal place called heaven. Immortality is achieved by living memorably and unselfishly here—in short, by leaving a legacy of compassionate service to others, pursuing love and justice.

Sacred Texts

The official Unitarian Universalism Web site explains that its congregants find wisdom, inspiration, and guidance, not from any one holy book, but from multiple sources:

- "Direct experience of that transcending mystery and wonder, affirmed in all cultures, which moves us to a renewal of the spirit and an openness to the forces which create and uphold life;

- "Words and deeds of prophetic women and men which challenge us to confront powers and structures of evil with justice, compassion, and the transforming power of love;

- "Wisdom from the world's religions which inspires us in our ethical and spiritual life;

- "Jewish and Christian teachings which call us to respond to God's love by loving our neighbors as ourselves;

- "Humanist teachings which counsel us to heed the guidance of reason and the results of science, and warn us against idolatries of the mind and spirit;

- "Spiritual teachings of earth-centered traditions which celebrate the sacred circle of life and instruct us to live in harmony with the rhythms of nature."

Worship Services

Most Unitarian Universalist congregations gather on Sunday, and their regular meetings are usually structured in much the same way as the worship services at conservative Christian churches. Religious education classes are commonly held for children and youth.

Congregants sing and may also listen to religious music performed by a choir. As the Unitarian Universalist Web site describes it, "The type of music featured in each congregation can vary wildly from one congregation and one service to the next. Everything from Christian hymns to Pagan chants to rock songs might be included in any service, if they relate to the topic of the sermon."

Ordained ministers can be men or women of any sexual orientation. They preside over services, offer pastoral care and counseling, and officiate at weddings and funerals. Groups without a minister are known as fellowships.

Important Dates

With its open acceptance of all religious traditions, Unitarian Universalist celebrate just about every holiday one can imagine—everything from Christmas and Easter to the Pagan Winter Solstice and the Jewish Yom Kippur. Many Unitarian Universalist congregations also observe secular holidays like Earth Day and Labor Day, and even have special events on Martin Luther King, Jr. Sunday.

Two holidays unique to Unitarian Universalism are:

The Water Communion (held at the beginning of the new church year in September)—each member brings a small amount of water from a place that is special to him or her. During the water ceremony, one by one, all pour their water into a large bowl, explaining why the water is special. Some congregations boil the water and save it to use for the congregation's "holy water" in upcoming religious ceremonies

The Flower Communion (held in the spring around Easter)—each worshipper brings a flower to the sanctuary and puts it on the altar or in a common vase. The minister blesses these flowers, and then members take a different flower home

"I don't know anything about God or ultimate reality. Neither do you. So let's get together and share our not-knowingness."
—Brian Hines

Number of Followers

Universism, a short-lived philosophical experiment for those who believe that no universal religious truth exists, and that meaning and truth must be discovered by each individual, probably had around ten thousand adherents (mostly freethinking deists, atheists, and agnostics) during its heyday in late 2005.

Major Figures/Prophets

- **Ford Vox**—a medical student doctor and self-taught philosopher, founder of Universism

- **John Armstrong**—deist author (*God Versus the Bible*), former spokesman for Universism

Short History

In 1999, a group of freethinkers initiated the Deus Project to try to develop a safe, rational religion for the future. These skeptics were weary of people of faith dictating to them what to believe, and hoped to neutralize the increasing (and what they regarded as both dangerous and unconstitutional) influence of religious groups in American culture. In 2003, as the Deus Project was concluding, Ford Vox, a Presbyterian-turned-infidel and an Alabama-born medical student, launched a new initiative called the "Universist Movement." Its goal was to oppose faith (specifically active fundamentalism).

An official Web site gave like-minded unbelievers the opportunity to formally join the group. As large numbers did join, a basic

Belief	Universism
Sacred Text(s)	None. There is no objective, ultimate, absolute truth
Nature of God	If there is a God (a notion not held by many Universists), it is impossible to say what that being or force is like
Jesus Christ	Not revered or worshipped; if He existed at all, He was an itinerant ethical teacher
Human nature	Noble, rational creatures with the capacity to question and search, and the power to achieve a better day for self and others
About human need	Freedom from the chains of religious dogma, freedom to question and reason
Salvation	No spiritual salvation required
Afterlife	Who knows?

Major Differences from Christianity

infrastructure began to develop around Universism, such as member blogs, online and regional discussion groups, and so forth. The group garnered a good bit of press attention, but as more effort went into attempting to organize the movement, the new unreligion began to encounter some of the very same problems inherent in the organized religion it decried. Concluded one follower, "I've become a believer in a Religion of One. I've got mine; you've got yours; everyone else has theirs. No problem. Each to his or her own. Problems begin with a Religion of Two, and escalate from there. . . . Dogmatic religious belief can't be countered by dogmatic non-religious belief."

Vox pulled the plug on the group in the spring of 2006. In a thread entitled *Universism Officially Dead* at the "Internet Infidels Discussion Board," a posting bearing the signature "Ford" attributed the group's demise to a shortage of resources "to establish an active, growing membership organization."

Disillusioned Universists blamed Vox himself. In tendering his resignation, group spokesman John Armstrong claimed that the movement fizzled not because of its ideas, but because Vox tried to maintain strict control of the group—an ironic and frustrating dynamic in a group supposedly devoted to free thought.

In an e-mail dialogue in early 2008, Vox said: "Naturally I would dispute Armstrong's claim that I was trying to maintain 'strict' control, but he did indeed assert that, and there was a group that agreed with him.

"I think an inevitable human psychology comes into play with any religio-philosophical movement: a strong interest in the founder even when that is not the founder's intention. I became uncomfortable with the focus on myself and the type of leadership I was being pulled into. I was becoming the go-to guru, articulating the 'Universist' position for any given issue, idea or problem, as mind-bendingly incongruous with the philosophy as that is! This is the primary predicament for any 'religion,' whether as watered-down as Universism or as robust as Wahhabism: melding static thought with a dynamic world requires making the world static (as the Amish have attempted), or releasing the thought from stasis, editing as the need arises (demonstrated by the evolution of Christianity). Universism, starting with so little, and embracing the dynamic world, only required three years to wash out into the cacophony of individual thought. I think every religion is at some point on this path. Ultimately, all religions will hold single followers as

Ford Vox, the "founder" of Universism

each successive individual, through each successive generation, applies his unique edits. Universism took three years; Christianity may take three thousand, but it will also end up indistinguishable from where it began."

Though the Universism experiment is officially over, many who share the movement's beliefs continue to blog and gather, continuing their freethinking search.

Basic Beliefs and Values

The abrupt rise and fall of Universism left many scratching their heads. Was it all the tongue-in-cheek joke of a mischievous young skeptic and his followers? Was it an earnest philosophical disaster? No one really knows. But here are a few beliefs and values that characterizes Universism:

- There is no revelation, no faith, no dogma or doctrine.

- Anti-faith rather than blind faith; blind faith is dangerous because it involves letting others think for you; religion gives you a list of truths and you're supposed to just mindlessly trust in it and follow it; it also divides people and groups, leading to hatred.

- No absolute truth, no discovering universal answers to any of life's big questions; no one person has the ability to know what applies to everyone.

- The goal is the continual search for truth; questions and endless uncertainty. The key principle is uncertainty. A 2006 report on CNN called Universism "a religion about nothing."

- No uniform belief system; personal beliefs are just that—personal; only science can establish truths that belong to everyone.

- Differs from Unitarian Universalism, which allows belief in anything and everything; Universism discourages belief in anything.

Critics contended that Universism was, from the very beginning, a self-defeating philosophy in that it was essentially a dogmatic non-religion criticizing the dogmatism of religion.

In the above-mentioned post, announcing the end of this anti-faith, the writer claiming to be "Ford" Vox concluded: "What is Universism? It's just a word. Live your life, that's all that matters."

Worship Services

In Universism there were no "worship" services, since Universists maintained there is no objectively identifiable God to worship. Skeptics gathered to discuss and debate theological and philosophical ideas. A vigorous online community also gathered around the group's short-lived Web site: www.universist.org.

Important Dates

None are cited.

"Vodoun is the heritage of the ancient African nations that were exiled in the new world. Its ways have been born throughout the darkest times by our forefathers in order to teach us how to live today and tomorrow. . . .

"Vodoun is more than one thing; it is medicine, justice, police; it is art, dance, music as well as religious ritual. It is the common ground upon which we, the children of the African New World diaspora, stand together. . . .

"It is perfectly ordinary to be Vodoun without being religious, as one can be Jewish and agnostic. So much so that in Haiti, the use of the word 'vodoun' (or voodoo, vaudou, vodu, and so on) is a sign of alienation."

—Online sources

Belief	**Vodou**
Sacred Text(s)	Oral traditions passed down through the centuries
Nature of God	The great Creator God is distant; contact with the divine comes through lesser spirits called *loas*
Jesus Christ	Not emphasized in traditional, ancient African Vodou; is a peripheral aspect of Caribbean Vodou because of its syncretism with Catholicism
Human nature	The human soul is comprised of both a big and a little guardian angel (The little one leaves the body at times, for example, during sleep and Vodou rituals)
About human need	To get on and stay on the good side of the spirits
Salvation	Faithfully participating in the prescribed rituals of Vodou
Afterlife	The dead live in an ill-defined spiritual realm and are capable of influencing the living

Major Differences from Christianity

Number of Followers

In West Africa, some thirty million people are thought to be practitioners of Vodou. In the country of Benin, Vodou became the official religion in 1996. Worldwide, Vodou may have as many as sixty million practitioners. It is the dominant religion in Haiti, though many residents there also say they are Catholic.

Major Figures/Prophets

Vodou is a religion resulting from the merging of ancient African traditional beliefs with Euro-American-Caribbean religious culture over many centuries. Vodou has no single founder, nor does it boast any prominent leaders, prophets, theologians, or organizers.

Short History

Most people hear the word "voodoo" and think of Hollywood zombies or wild-eyed witch doctors sticking pins in dolls. True voodoo is a far cry from these depictions. The word *voodoo* is a corruption of the word *vodun,* which means "god" or "spirit" in the West African Fon language (spoken in Benin).

Known and spelled variously as Vodun, Vudun, Vodon, Vodoun, Vudu, and Voodoo, *Vodou* is the label ascribed to a group of distinct, but related African spiritualities practiced among tribal groups in the countries of Benin, Togo, Ghana, Ivory Coast, Burkina Faso, and Senegal. The essential tenets of Vodou spread from West Africa to the Caribbean, especially Haiti and the Dominican Republic, and the Americas during the African diaspora.

Because Vodou's hard-to-understand folk beliefs and exotic magical practices were forbidden by wary slave owners, the transplanted Africans in Haiti gradually merged their ancient customs and beliefs with the prevailing religion—Roman Catholicism. For example, they disguised their pantheon of ancestral spirits as Catholic saints. Haitian Vodou also included other ingredients, such as the native Indian culture of what was then called Hispaniola, with all its rituals and the unique history of the Caribbean.

A Vodun practitioner

In 1791, during a Vodou ceremony, the Haitian Revolution was born. By 1804, French colonial rule had ended and Haiti became the first independent republic of blacks in world history.

The practice of Haitian Vodou in the United States grew in the late 1960s and 1970s, when large numbers of Haitians fled their homeland during the corrupt and violent Duvalier regime. In 2003, the Haitian government of President Jean-Betrand Aristide officially sanctioned the practice of Vodou.

Basic Beliefs and Values

Vodou seeks to understand the forces of the universe, to control or at least influence those forces, and to influence other people.

Vodou involves:

- *Much superstition* —Belief in good luck and bad luck.
- *Magic*—Used for both good ("white" magic) and ill ("black" magic); consulting of sorcerers, healers, or witch doctors known as *bokors.*
- *Access to and help from spirits* (called *loas*)—each individual is believed to have a special kinship with one spirit, a *met tet,* who is said to "own one's head."

- *Elements of Roman Catholicism*—Many Haitians do not see any incompatibility between their practice of Vodou and their Catholic beliefs. They serve the "spirits" even as they attend Mass and pray the rosary.

View of God

The origins of the well-known practice of sticking pins in voodoo dolls is not known; this is not a common feature in Haitian Vodou. It is more prevalent in the Hoodoo version of Vodou found in New Orleans. Reports of zombie activity are also exaggerated. While some rare instances are claimed in rural areas, this is not a normal facet of Vodou.

From culture to culture there are variations, but Haitian Vodou generally proposes a complicated, multi-tiered pantheon of divine beings. At the top is the true creator deity named *Bondye,* (from the French phrase "bon dieu," which means "Good God"). Bondye is regarded as the boundless one who presides over the spirit world (but has little to do with human affairs). Bondye is sometimes known as *Gran Met* (the "grand master").

The loas are second-level, lesser divinities—actually the living spirits of great and powerful ancestors. These so-called saints or angels or mysteries are the active divine spirits in Vodou religion. They "do the work," and it is they whom followers of Vodou serve and with whom they interact. Adherents divide these loas into families and give them surnames. For example, the spirits of the Ogou family are regarded as the military spirits; the Ezili loas govern the feminine aspects of life; the Ghede family of spirits have influence over fertility and death; and the Azaka family specializes in agriculture. Other Vodou practitioners organize these countless spirits according to basic personality—whether they are cool spirits (warm and congenial) or hot spirits (combative, unpredictable, prone to anger).

At the bottom level are the dead. These are the collective spirits of the departed.

View of the Afterlife

The dead are revered, as indicated by elaborate funeral rites and ornate burial tombs. They can appear via dreams or speak through ceremonies. They can bless and help or bring misfortune. Heaven and hell are not emphasized.

Sacred Texts

Vodou is an oral tradition, passed down through families, most often through rituals and songs. One online source says: "Vodoun songs are the walls, carrels, and books of the great Vodoun public library in that we don't just let them be stored and retrieved occasionally; rather, we live in them and we live through them. Ask any question of one of the Vodoun people, and he or she is liable to answer with a song. Snippets of songs are in ordinary conversations."

Worship Services

Vodou clergy oversee all rituals. They have the responsibility to mediate between the spirits and the community as a whole. Priests are called *houngans*; priestesses are referred to as *mambos*. Assistants are called *hounsis*.

A typical Haitian Vodou service can take place in either a Vodou temple or a private home, though it is a true community affair. It can take days to prepare (cooking special foods for a preceremonial feast, setting up altars, and so forth). The actual ceremony includes animal sacrifice, Catholic prayers, African prayers, singing, drumming, and rituals that include naming and greeting the spirits by families.

Worldview

Life is permeated and surrounded by the spiritual realm. One must be careful not to anger the spirits, and one must work diligently to appease them. This involves carrying out elaborate Vodou rituals. But mostly it includes showing respect and remembering to honor God, the spirits, one's family, community, and one's self.

The most common practice in Vodou worship is possession by one of the loas. These lesser divinities are not truly gods, but the spirits of great ancestors, male and female. Worshippers summon them and entice these powerful spirits to control them, using their bodies and voices to speak to others—giving readings (using tarot cards or similar objects) and spiritual advice to all who approach. These services are energetic, ecstatic, and exhausting, as they often last for hours.

On a personal level, devotees of Vodou erect and maintain small altars in their homes. These typically include statues of saints, pictures of ancestors, candles, and various gifts favored by certain loas. Individuals in the home, on certain days, light candles and say prayers (often Catholic prayers).

Important Dates

Many Haitians "double up" on their religious celebrations—utilizing a wide assortment of Catholic holidays to also honor the spirits of Vodou. One example is the week-long Saut d'Eau pilgrimage in July. Legend says that in the mid-1800s, the Virgin Mary appeared near the waterfalls in Saut d'Eau, Haiti. Thus, each summer, pilgrims come from all over to this remote mountain location. There at the one hundred-foot falls, they honor Erzulie, Vodou's equivalent to the Virgin Mary, by stripping and bathing, praying, and, in some instances, becoming possessed by Vodou spirits. Leaving their old clothes in the water, they then return home.

"We should educate people that 'Witch' is not evil but ancient and positive. The first time I called myself a 'Witch' was the most magical moment of my life."
—Margot Adler

Major Differences from Christianity

Belief	Wicca
Sacred Text(s)	No single, official holy text (though many modern writings are widely read and respected)
Nature of God	Belief varies person to person—adherents may be polytheistic, animistic, pantheistic, and agnostic. Typically, God is impersonal, a creative force—both female and male—that permeates the world
Jesus Christ	Not regarded or respected by Wiccans as God incarnate nor as the Savior of the world
Human nature	Humans are spiritual beings connected to and part of every other spirit
About human need	To respect others, revere the earth, and reach out and within for the god/goddess
Salvation	Not a rescue from sin and spiritual death, but deliverance into a magical life through practicing Wiccan beliefs and rituals
Afterlife	Some believe in a place called Summerland; others embrace a positive form of reincarnation, eventually leading to a higher form of existence

Number of Followers

The number of Wicca followers is difficult to determine. Wiccans do not have a centralized, organizational hierarchy. Craig Hawkins, author of *Goddess Worship, Witchcraft, and Neopaganism*, estimates some 400,000 practitioners of Wicca worldwide. The 2001 American Religion Identification Survey estimates 134,000 Wiccans in the United States, contrasted with another online source that claims there are 500,000 Wiccans just in the United States. While firm numbers are hard to come by, evidence suggests Wicca is one of the fastest growing religions today—especially among teenagers and young adults.

Major Figures/Prophets

- **Margaret Murray** (1863–1963) —British scholar and author of *The Witch-Cult in Western Europe* (published in 1921), which is credited for reviving modern interest in witchcraft and ancient pagan beliefs.

- **Gerald Gardner** (1884–1964) —amateur British archaeologist, who reportedly read Murray's work, and then wrote *Witchcraft Today* (1954) and *The Meaning of Witchcraft* (1959), popular texts for modern Wiccans. He is regarded by many as the founder of modern Wicca.

- **Doreen Valiente** (1922–1999)—a high priestess/disciple of Gardner, who is considered by many as the "mother of modern witchcraft." The author of *An ABC of Witchcraft Past and Present* and *Natural Magic* (1975), Valiente continually stressed the differences between Wicca and Satanism.

- **Silver Ravenwolf** (1956–present)—leader of the Black Forest Circle and Seminary, an organization of almost forty clans (each consisting of several covens), and the author of eighteen books, including the controversial but popular *Teen Witch: Wicca for a New Generation*.

Short History

The term *Wicca* (also known as witchcraft, Magick, the Craft, the Old Religion) derives from the Anglo Saxon term *wicce*, which means "female sorceress, or witch." Originally it was used to refer to pagan practitioners of magic, who experimented with herbal medicines.

Wicca has roots in the ancient, popular pre-Christian European nature and mystery religions, such as the Celts, Egyptians, Greeks, and Sumerians. During

A Pentacle

the Inquisition of the twelfth and thirteenth centuries, witches were brought before theological tribunals of the Catholic Church and condemned as heretics and blasphemers. Such witch hunts continued into the Early Modern period (1400s to 1700s), and include the famous Salem witch trials in Massachusetts in 1692.

Over the last century, as Western society has become more eclectic and more tolerant, Wicca has experienced a revival. The Pagan Federation was established in 1971 to advocate for the rights of witches and other neopagans, and to engage in altering public opinion about pagan beliefs and practices. A spate of popular television shows (such as *Bewitched, Sabrina the Teenage Witch, Charmed*) and movies (*The Witches of Eastwick, Practical Magic, The Craft*) have helped make Wiccan practices more mainstream and accessible, especially to younger audiences.

Today, Wicca is recognized by the United States government as a legitimate, tax-exempt religious entity. Even Army chaplains are given instruction in how to interact with soldiers who are adherents to Wicca.

Basic Beliefs and Values

Wicca is part of a group of similar modern religions often lumped together under the umbrella terms of paganism or neopaganism. These groups include Asatru (page 5), Druidry (page 59), Shamanism, and Heathenism. The common goal of

Wiccans and other neopagans is to encounter the deities of the ancient mystery cults and nature religions.

Wiccans hold five primary beliefs:

- *The Wiccan Rede*—The most important rule, this essentially states, "If it harms none, do what you will."

- *Law of Attraction*—The idea that whatever one does to or for other living creatures, one draws back upon oneself.

- *Harmony and Serenity*—Living in conjunction with the balanced rhythms of nature.

- *Power through knowledge*—Learning how to tap into and control the power or energy that resides in and flows through all things.

- *Progressive reincarnation*—Learning and improving through a series of life experiences.

Most Wiccans are eager to distinguish themselves from Satanists. They insist they do not worship or believe in the Devil as depicted in the Bible. They see Satan as a symbol of rebellion against the Christian and Jewish religions and not relevant to their Wiccan belief system.

The five points of the Wiccan pentagram or pentacle represent five natural elements in descending density: earth, water, air, fire, spirit/ether.

Various Wiccan implements

View of God

It is difficult to summarize Wiccan views of God (sometimes called "the All" or "the One"). Wiccan beliefs are so varied; thus there is no theological consensus. Some are animistic, believing that "all things are imbued with the life force of vitality" (Margot Adler, *Drawing Down the Moon*). To these adherents, God is a form of transcendent consciousness—the energy of the universe. Others are polytheistic, worshipping and seeking connection with multiple, assorted pagan deities of the past. Pantheism—the idea that God is in everything and everything is within God—is held by some.

Wiccans typically view the earth as a living organism called Mother Earth, the

Goddess, or Gaia. Since spirits or gods inhabit places, this makes the world itself a sacred place. Some Wiccans point out that they technically do not worship nature, but rather the divine within nature. In any case, God is viewed as impersonal, both male and female, immanent (living within us) and transcendent (existing outside and around us).

Worldview

- The manifestation of the divine in the natural world and its laws
- Equality: Since the divine being is present in all of us, women are given an equal status to men
- Cosmic system of justice—a kind of Wiccan adaptation of the Eastern law of karma. This simple idea of eventual penalty/reward is sometimes called the "Law of Threefold Return" or the "Law of Attraction"
- Personal responsibility; we must accept the consequences of our choices
- Anti-authoritarian and antidogma; truth is relative (do what works for you)
- Tolerance—respectful of other beliefs, not given to proselytizing, open to and accepting of any sexual behavior between consenting adults
- Eclectic—a mix-and-match of personal experience, modern ideas, and ancient beliefs and rituals

Wiccans believe in the following:

View of the Afterlife

There is no clearly developed, universally agreed upon doctrine of the afterlife among Wiccans. A few believe this life is all there is. Others believe their souls will go to a peaceful place called Summerland. Still others embrace a positive form of reincarnation (unlike the Hindu version, which sees rebirth as a punishment for bad karma). These Wiccans believe successive lives represent an upward evolution toward an unclear, unknown higher form of existence.

Sacred Texts

There is no official text for Wiccans. Most covens maintain a handwritten collection of beliefs and rituals, typically referred to as a Book of Shadows. Access to this collection is usually restricted to formal initiates of Wicca. Part of the indoctrination or catechism of new Wiccans involves each new initiate copying this book by hand.

Over time, covens add new material, rituals, and spells to this group document.

Highly regarded "textbooks" for Wiccans include Gerald Gardner's *Witchcraft Today* and *The Meaning of Witchcraft*, and Doreen Valiente's *An ABC of Witchcraft Past and Present* and *Natural Magic*.

Worship Services

Because Wicca is an earth-based religion, the preference is for conducting services outdoors. Often these rituals are practiced by groups of witches (covens) at night. Many Wiccans opt to worship in the nude (called "skyclad"), feeling this is a more natural state and as such brings them closer to the god or goddess.

These regular gatherings, called *esbats*, typically occur at the time of a new or full moon. They include the casting of a circle—a Wiccan practice of consecrating a place and making it sacred. Participants then invoke spirits and deities by chanting and reading invocations (spiritual poems). Magic (sometimes spelled *magick,* to distinguish it from the sleight-of-hand practiced by illusionists) is practiced, both natural and high magic. Spells are cast. There may be singing, dancing, and readings. Some covens will partake of a meal together. Before dispersing, a coven will banish the circle, restoring the area to common use.

Important Dates

Wiccans observe eight festivals called *Sabbats.* These celebrations, linked to the

Samhain/All Hallows Eve (October 31)—the festival of the dead
Winter Solstice/Yule (December 19–21)—the coming of winter
Imbolc (February 1–2)—the heralding of spring
Vernal/Spring Equinox (March 19–22)—a celebration of fertility
Beltane (April 30)—the maypole representing the sacred marriage of the god and goddess
Summer Solstice/Litha (June 21–23)—a celebration of light
Lammas/Ludhnasadh (August 1)—a celebration of the first harvest of wheat
Fall Equinox/Mabon (September 21–23)—the feast of the ingathering

"Our former old covenant approach fostered attitudes of exclusivism and superiority rather than the new covenant teaching of brotherhood and unity. We overemphasized predictive prophecy and prophetic speculation, minimizing the true gospel of salvation through Jesus Christ. "These teachings and practices are a source of supreme regret. We are painfully mindful of the heartache and suffering that has resulted from them. We've been wrong."
—Joseph Tkach Jr., third president of the Worldwide Church of God

Number of Followers

The Worldwide Church of God reached a peak of some 150,000 international members in the 1980s. Following the death of Herbert Armstrong in 1986, the church lost at least half its followers. The Worldwide Church of God now claims 64,000 members in 860 congregations in 90 nations. About half of these adherents are in the United States.

Major Figures/Prophets

Garner Ted Armstrong

- **Herbert W. Armstrong** (1892–1986)—the founder of the Worldwide Church of God

- **Garner Ted Armstrong** (1930–2003)—the telegenic son of founder Herbert Armstrong, who became the face of the church's television productions in 1957 that eventually enjoyed an audience of an estimated twenty million viewers weekly

- **Joseph Tkach Sr.** (1927–1995)—the bold, controversial successor to Herbert Armstrong, who guided the Worldwide Church of God from its unorthodox theological roots to acceptance of mainstream Christian beliefs

- **Joseph Tkach Jr.** (1951–present)—the third president and pastor general of the Worldwide Church of God

Short History

The story of the Worldwide Church of God is a rare and fascinating account of an entire religious movement changing its essential doctrinal beliefs. The group that many had long labeled a cult suddenly converted into an orthodox Christian church embraced by its most vocal evangelical critics.

Major Differences from Christianity

Belief	Worldwide Church of God
Sacred Text(s)	*Old*: The Bible (especially the Old Testament); *New*: same as historic Christianity
Nature of God	*Old*: God as a family—the Father and Jesus as separate beings, and resurrected humans as eventual members; *New*: holds same beliefs as historic Christianity
Jesus Christ	*Old*: Lord and Savior, but not resurrected physically; *New*: same as historic Christianity
Human nature	*Old*: People spiritually born of God's will, after the resurrection, become God; *New*: same as historic Christianity
About human need	*Old*: to believe in Christ and follow the teaching of the church; *New*: same as historic Christianity
Salvation	*Old*: by faith plus strict adherence to God's law; *New*: by grace through faith in Christ
Afterlife	*Old*: annihilation of the unrepentant; *New*: accepting of historic Christian doctrines

Herbert W. Armstrong was born in Des Moines, Iowa in 1892 to Quaker parents. In 1924 he moved to Oregon with dreams of a career in advertising. His wife's encounter with a Seventh-Day Adventist prompted Armstrong to begin a diligent study of the Bible. This search led to his conversion and baptism in 1927. He attended various churches and was even ordained in the Church of God.

Disagreeing with certain Church of God beliefs and Old Testament interpretations, he left in 1933 and began his own group in Eugene, Oregon, called the "Radio Church of God." In 1934, Armstrong published the first edition of *The Plain Truth*, a magazine that would eventually reach a circulation of eight million. In 1947, the church established Ambassador College in Pasadena, California. (Before ceasing operations in 1997, the college had two other campuses.)

In 1957, Herbert's son, Garner Ted Armstrong, took over as the official media spokesman for the church. The group changed its name from the "Radio Church of God" to the "Worldwide Church of God" in 1968.

Handsome and dynamic, Garner Ted slowly acquired a huge television and radio audience. He was excommunicated briefly in the early 1970s for alleged sexual impropriety. He was "dis-fellowshipped" for good in 1978 for "liberal" beliefs. He promptly launched several new ministries that never attracted more than a few thousand followers. He died in 2003.

In the late 1970s, the group experienced a number of financial and theological difficulties. Allegations of fiscal mismanagement resulted in lawsuits, which ended up with the church going into receivership in 1979.

In 1986, the elder Armstrong died, but not before arranging for Joseph W. Tkach Sr. (pronounced TA-KOTCH) to succeed him as Pastor General of the Worldwide Church of God. A couple of years later, Tkach shocked religious experts and angered many church members when he began to institute major changes in the church's official doctrine (see below). Upon Tkach's death in 1995, Joseph W. Tkach Jr.

Radio Church of God radio broadcast

became leader of the church, continuing the unprecedented doctrinal reforms of his father. So thorough was the church's theological transformation that, in 1997, the group applied for and was accepted for membership in the National Association of Evangelicals.

These landmark changes, however, prompted a severe backlash among the faithful. Membership plummeted and church revenues dropped 75 percent.

Basic Beliefs and Values

Some former beliefs of the Worldwide Church of God under Herbert W. Armstrong include:

- *Anglo-Israelism*—The claim that the British peoples (and their American, Canadian, and Australian descendants) are the lost tribes of Israel.

- *Rejection of the Trinity*—The Holy Spirit is not a distinct Person, but is the power of God.

- *Old Testament law*—Modern-day church members are obligated to follow the commands and practices set out in the Old Testament.

- *Salvation*—Achieved by faith and works.

- *Saturday*—Considered by adherents to be the true "Lord's Day."

- *Strict requirements*—Members required to follow practices such as tithing.

- *Emphasis*—on end-times prophetic speculation.

- *Rejection of the traditional Christian belief in hell*—Those who neither believe nor follow Jesus will be given a second chance after death. If they still reject the truth, they will be cast into the lake of fire (annihilation).
- *The Worldwide Church of God*—The only true church.

The *reformed* beliefs of the Worldwide Church of God since the presidency of Joseph Tkach Sr. include:

- A repudiation of Anglo-Israelism.
- Acceptance of the historic orthodox Christian teaching on the Trinity.
- Viewing the Worldwide Church of God as a New Covenant church, not bound by the laws and practices of the Old Testament. This giant theological shift was announced in the famous "Christmas Eve Sermon of 1994."
- Salvation by grace through faith (*not* works).
- Worship on Sundays.
- Voluntary, freewill giving.
- An emphasis on Christ's substitutionary sacrifice to save sinners.
- An acceptance of the biblical teaching of hell.
- Belief that the family of faith includes many denominations.

Worldview

Under the leadership of Joseph Tkach Sr. and the continued guidance of his son, the Worldwide Church of God has made a difficult doctrinal journey. The result is a much smaller church, but a more accepting church that teaches and models grace. The Worldwide Church of God sees a world in need of deep transformation and offers Christ as the One who alone is able to effect that change. It offers itself as a prime example of the Lord's powerful ability to rescue and remake that which was lost.

View of God

Under the old Worldwide Church of God, the doctrine of the Trinity was denied. A theological duality was taught—God the Father and God the Son, separate divine beings. Also, Herbert Armstrong introduced the novel concept of God as "family": redeemed humans have the opportunity to join the family of the Father and the Son and literally achieve divine status at the resurrection.

Under the new Worldwide Church of God, He is believed to be One divine Being in three eternal, co-essential, distinct Persons; Father, Son, and Holy Spirit. God is holy, loving, all-powerful, and gracious.

View of the Afterlife

The teaching of the "old" Worldwide Church of God was that at the resurrection believers will be raised to live on the new earth, while unbelievers will be given a second chance to believe and live forever, or face annihilation in the lake of fire.

The "new" Worldwide Church of God, more in line with historic Christianity, teaches the reality of heaven and hell. Allowance is also made for those who believe in either a conscious or unconscious intermediate state. At the resurrection of the dead, the saved will be raised to life and enjoy the everlasting presence of God.

Worship Services

The Worldwide Church of God (under the leadership of Herbert Armstrong) worshipped on Saturday. They also celebrated three ordinances: baptism (by total immersion), the Lord's Supper, and foot-washing.

Under the reformed Worldwide Church of God, services are held on Sunday. The goal is "discipleship and teaching in an environment of praise and worship." The liturgy typically involves congregational singing, prayer, a message by the pastor, and a closing hymn. Bible classes are also offered for children. Small groups meet during the week for prayer, Bible discussions, and encouragement.

Sacred Texts

The Worldwide Church of God has always claimed the Bible as its holy book. However, under Herbert Armstrong, the emphasis was on the Old Testament and on prophecies about the end times. In the reformed Worldwide Church of God, the emphasis upon the New Testament (the New Covenant in Christ) has been greatly increased.

Important Dates

The Worldwide Church of God (under the leadership of Herbert Armstrong) celebrated all the Jewish Festivals—Pentecost, Day of Atonement, Feast of Tabernacles, and so forth. They did not celebrate Christmas and Easter (viewing them as stemming from pagan traditions).	The Worldwide Church of God (under the new leadership of Joseph Tkach Sr. and Tkach Jr.) no longer observes traditional Jewish holidays. It allows and encourages church members to celebrate traditional Christian holidays.

"I profess myself a Mazda-worshipper, a Zoroastrian, having vowed it and professed it. I pledge myself to the well-thought thought, I pledge myself to the well-spoken word, I pledge myself to the well-done action."
—from *The Zoroastrianism Creed*, translated by J. H. Peterson, 1997

Number of Followers

Zoroastrianism has 130,000 to 200,000 members worldwide. Most adherents are found in India, Pakistan, and Iran, and are known as *Parsees*.

Major Figures/Prophets:

* **Zoroaster,** also known as **Zarathustra** in ancient Persian—founder of Zoroastrianism was a Persian prophet and priest. He was born near the Oxus River in Persia (modern-day Iran). Some historians/sources believe he lived between 1500 and 1000 BC. Others put his birth much later (about 650 BC).

Zoroaster

Short History

Depending on which source one trusts, Zarathustra was born sometime between 1400 and 650 BC. Tradition says he was the son of a camel merchant and a restless seeker of truth.

While fetching water at about thirty years of age, Zarathustra claimed an experience of enlightenment. Specifically, he told of a vision in which he was ushered by a being named Vohu Manah ("good mind" or "good thought") into the presence of Ahura Mazda, who revealed that he was the one true God. When Zarathustra's own people rejected this testimony of monotheism, he found and joined a new tribe led by a powerful prince Vishtaspa. Vishtaspa not only accepted the preaching of Zoroaster, but defended this new religion and its converts.

The faith flourished from the sixth century BC through the seventh century AD. This would include the years during which the Jewish Old Testament prophet Daniel was in exile, when the Persians conquered the Babylonians. Some scholars speculate that Darius the Mede, whom Daniel served, may have been an adherent to Zoroastrian beliefs.

From AD 220–651 the various Zoroastrian sacred texts were compiled and written down.

Belief	Zoroastrianism
Sacred Text(s)	The *Avesta*
Nature of God	One God, who is a holy, radiant creator, but not personal; Ahura Mazda is co-equal and co-eternal with his arch rival Angra Mainyu
Jesus Christ	Discussions of Christ are absent from Zoroastrian documents both ancient and recent
Human nature	All possess the divine essence and must learn to choose the right and work according to God's plan
About human need	Does not emphasize or provide for the removal of personal sin
Salvation	Teaches eternal life by means of doing good
Afterlife	The righteous will be rewarded, the unrighteous punished

Beginning about AD 650, Muslims invaded Persia. This advance into Persia (and the Islamic policy of forced conversions and persecution) resulted in a sharp decline in Zoroastrianism's popularity. Later, AD 910–950 witnessed a mass migration of Zoroastrians to western India to escape the powerful, intolerant Islamic majority.

Most Zoroastrians live now either in the western Iranian desert (though many fled Iran after the Iranian Revolution in 1979), in and near Bombay, India (they are called the Parsees or "Persians" there), and in many major cities in Britain, Canada, the United States, and elsewhere.

Basic Beliefs and Values

Ahura Mazda (also known as Ohrmazd) is the "Supreme Creator" or "Wise Lord" who is responsible for all the good in life. Angra Mainyu (also known as Ohriman) is the "Destructive Spirit" who is the embodiment of evil. He is responsible for all evil and suffering in the world. Like Mazda, he is eternal.

Ahura Mazda and Angra Mainyu are the two great opposing forces in the cosmos. It is the duty of all mankind to choose the good—depending on Ahura Mazda, and striving to have good thoughts, say good words, and do good deeds. Those who live in such a way will find happiness. Those who oppose what is good and live an evil life end in sorrow. Ultimately, good will triumph over evil.

> In Zoarastrian belief, the Bounteous Immortals (also known as *Amesha Spentas*) are archangels/coworkers with Ahura Mazda. They serve as guardians of the seven good creations: sky, water, earth, plants, cattle, humanity, and fire.

The Bounteous Immortals (also known as *Amesha Spentas*) are archangels/coworkers with Ahura Mazda. They serve as guardians of the seven good creations: sky, water, earth, plants, cattle, humanity, and fire.

Fravashi is the term for the guardian spirit or angel that watches over each person throughout life. It is also the ideal god essence that a person seeks to emulate and becomes one with after death. This spirit will help and guide if summoned. Fravashis work for good and order in the world.

Mazda established "Primal Principles of Life" in order to create and sustain the universe. The primary principles are *Asha*, the law of precision; *Vohu Manah*, good thinking; *Vohu Khshathra*, good dominion or good order; *Spenta Aramaiti*, progressive peace; *Seraosha*, divine communion. Faithfully practiced, these lead to *Haurvatât*, a term that signifies wholeness, supreme excellence, and *Ameretât*, or immortality.

Within Zoroastrianism, "good thoughts, good words, good deeds" are practiced specifically through hygiene and cleanliness, cultivating self-reliance, pursuing justice, and exhibiting civic virtue, charity, compassion and service to others. Ascetic tendencies (celibacy, fasting, and so forth) are not promoted. Marriage is regarded as a great blessing and virtue.

View of God	Worldview
Zoroastrians believe in one god, Ahura Mazda. He is symbolized by fire. He is described in grand and holy, though impersonal, terms.	Life as we experience it is a great cosmic battle between good and evil (dualism). Good will triumph in the end.

View of the Afterlife

Though Zoroastrianism teaches the existence of hell, it describes it only as a temporary place of suffering for sinners. When the evil Angra Mainyu is vanquished, the souls of sinners will be released, purified, and allowed to join the congregation of the righteous. Thus, this ancient faith of Zarathurstra advocates resurrection, not reincarnation.

Frashegird, which means "making wonderful," is the term used to describe the final judgment and defeat of evil and the renovation of the universe. Individuals will be judged according to how they fought for good—thinking good thoughts, saying good words, doing good deeds

Sacred Texts

The Avesta is the holy book of Zoroastrianism. Transmitted orally up until about the ninth century AD, this collection of revered writings includes several sections:

- Yasna (including Zoroastrian sacred liturgy and the Gathas, five hymns written by Zarathustra to Ahura Mazda)
- Visperad (liturgical instructions)
- Vendidad (myths, purity laws, and medical texts)
- The Khorda Avesta ("Small Avesta") contains prayers, other hymns, poetry, assorted ceremonial instructions, and excerpts from the Avesta

Worship Services

Padyab and Nirang-I Kusti are short handwashing and prayer rituals performed several times a day during which Zoroastrians retie their *kusti* (a cord which is worn around the waist and is regarded as a sacred garment).

Yasna is the name of a prayer ceremony in which consecrated liquor made from the haoma plant (believed to possess both spiritual and medicinal properties) is both consumed and offered to the sacred fire. This act is believed to confer immortality on the worshipper.

Jashan is a common ceremony of thanksgiving conducted by a priest (called a *zaotar*) and an assistant priest (known as a *raspi*). The goal of this ritual is to extend thanks and to request favor from the spiritual world. Worshippers invite the "Bounteous Immortals" and the souls of the virtuous departed to the ceremony of Jashan.

Gahambars are six major seasonal communal festivals attended by the faithful.

Navjote is the term for a ceremony (similar to Catholic catechism or the Jewish bar-mitzvah/bat-mitzvah) in which young Zoroastrians (between the ages of seven and twelve) are formally initiated into the faith, agreeing to embrace and live out the teachings of Zoroastrianism

Animal sacrifice was once a feature of Zoroastrianism; it is no longer practiced.

Worship takes place inside a "fire temple." Fire is a common element in Zoroastrian worship. Fire is thought to be the Holy Spirit of Ahura Mazda, the original light of God. Adherents do not worship fire, but seek to worship Ahura Mazda by means of the fire. Only barefooted Zoroastrians are allowed inside the fire temples.

A Zoroastrian priest is a *magus* (plural is *magi*).

Important Dates

In addition to the Gahambars (see above) the Zoroastrian calendar includes other feasts including:

Sadeh (January 24)—a mid-winter celebration in which the community gathers wood and builds bonfires
Tiragan (July 1)—a rain festival
Mihragen (October 1)—a festival celebration that includes prayers of thanksgiving and gratitude

Views on other Religions

Zoroastrianism does not accept the Hindu teaching of reincarnation. A debate is ongoing within Zoroastrian circles about the subject of conversion. Traditionalists do not believe in or advocate the conversion of non-Zoroastrians. Reformers emphasize the importance of encouraging those of other faiths to join the Zoroastrian religion.

SOURCES

Introduction- C. S. Lewis quote cited in *What's So Amazing About Grace?* (Grand Rapids: Zondervan, 1997), p. 45.
African Traditional- www.adherents.com, http://afgen.com/religion.html, http://www.africaworld.net/afrel, http://www.bbc.co.uk/worldservice/africa/features/storyofafrica/index_section6.shtml, http://www.geocities.com/Athens/Forum/1699/African.html, http://www.mamiwata.com/OATH.html, http://nalane.net/xhosa/english/atr.htm. **Asatru**- http://www.asatru.org, http://www.friggasweb.org, http://www.irminsul.org, http://www.ravenkindred.com, http://www.religionfacts.com/neopaganism/paths/asatru.htm, http://www.runestone.org/flash/home.html, http://www.thetroth.org. **Bahai**- www.bahai.com, www.bahaifaith.net, www.bahai-faith.org, www.bahaindex.com, www.us.bahai.org, http://www.bahai.us/, www.bcca.org/bahaivision, http://info.bahai.org, www.religioustolerance.org/bahai.htm, http://info.bahai.org/article-1-3-2-20.html. **Buddhism**- http://www.bbc.co.uk/religion/religions/buddhism/, http://www.buddhanet.net/, http://buddhism.about.com, http://www.ciolek.com/WWWVL Buddhism.html, http://www.religionfacts.com/buddhism/index.htm, http://www.worldbookonline.com/wb/Article ?id=ar081080. **Cao Dai**- http://altreligion.about.com/gi/dynamic/offsite.htm?site=http://www%2Dpersonal.usyd.edu.au/%257Ecdao/tanluat.htm, www.About.com, http://caodai.org, http://www.caodai.net/, www.religioustolerance.org/caodaism.htm. **Chinese Traditional**- Arthur Yaopo Chiang, A Brief Look at Chinese Folk Religion (www.fccj.edu/library/chi-reli/chi-reli.htm), http://www.csupomona.edu/~plin/folkreligion/chinesefolkrel.html, http://www.fccj.edu/library/chi-reli/chi-reli.htm, http://hirr.hartsem.edu/ency/Asian.htm, http://www.religiousbeliefs.com/chinese-religion.htm, http://www.religionfacts.com/chinese_religion/beliefs/afterlife.htm, http://www.religionfacts.com/chinese_religion/index.htm. **Christian Science**- http://www.religionfacts.com/a-z-religion-index/christian_science.htm, http://religiousmovements.lib.virginia.edu/nrms/chrissci.html, www.spirituality.com, http://www.tfccs.com/index.jhtml, http://thebookmark.com. **Church of Satan**- Anton LaVey, interview in the *Washington Post Magazine* (February 23, 1986), http://altreligion.about.com/library/weekly/aa052003a.htm, http://www.churchofsatan.com/home.html, http://www.churchofsatan.com/Pages/cosinfopack.pdf, http://www.churchofsatan.org/faq.html, http://www.religioustolerance.org/satanism.htm, http://www.satanosphere.com/story/2001/9/7/121041/3661. **Dadaji**- http://www.dadaji.info/, http://www.religioustolerance.org/dadaji.htm. **Damanhur**- http://www.damanhur.info/en/html/ArcMagazineDet.asp?IDArt=1), http://www.damanhur.info/en/html/home.asp, http://www.damanhur.org, http://www.damanhur.org/temple/, http://damanhur.tribe.net/thread/95f1ec56-58c4-47a4-a7b8-f1863139c37d, http://members.aol.com/RPeyser/damanhur.htm, http://www.olamidamanhur.com, http://www.religioustolerance.org/damanhur.htm. **Deism**- http://www.deism.com, http://www.deism.com/deism_vs.htm, http://www.dynamicdeism.org, http://www.positivedeism.com, http://www.religioustolerance.org/deism.htm, http://www.sullivan-county.com/deism.htm. **Druidism**- http://www.adf.org/core/, http://druidry.org, http://www.keltria.org, http://www.themystica.com/mystica/articles/d/druidism.html, http://www.religioustolerance.org/druid.htm, http://www.wildideas.net/cathbad/pagan/dr-guide1.html. **Druze**- www.altreligion.about.com/library/faqs/bl_druze.htm, http://atheism.about.com/library/FAQs/islam/blfaq_islam_druze.htm, http://www.bbc.co.uk/dna/h2g2/A3694809, http://www.druze.com, http://lexicorient.com/e.o/druze.htm, http://www.muslimhope.com/Druze.htm, www.religionfacts.com, http://www.religioustolerance.org/druse.htm. **Eckankar**- Sri Harold Klemp, *The Art of Spiritual Dreaming* (Eckankar: 1999)., http://altreligion.about.com/gi/dynamic/offsite.htm?zi=1/XJ/Ya&sdn=altreligion&cdn=religion&tm=12&f=22&tt=14&bt=1&bts=0&zu=http%3A//www.geocities.com/eckcult/http://www.britannica.com/eb/article-9125806/ECKANKAR, http://www.darwingrosstruthfile.homestead.com/dgtf.html. http://www.eckankar.org/?source=google_home1&gclid=CJmh_KyexI4CFQQjPAodUwGZxA, http://www.religion-encyclopedia.com/E/eckankar.htm, http://www.religionfacts.com/a-z-religion-index/eckankar.htm, http://en.wikipedia.org/wiki/Eckankar. **Falun Dafa/Falun Gong**- http://altreligion.about.com/library/faqs/bl_falundafa.htm, http://dawn.thot.net/fofg/whatis.html, http://www.falundafa.org, http://www.falundafa.org/book/eng/zflus.html (an English version of Li Hongzhi's writings and lectures), http://news.bbc.co.uk/2/hi/asia-pacific/1223317.stm, http://www.religion-encyclopedia.com/F/falun_gong.htm, http://www.religioustolerance.org/falungong1.htm. **Gnosticism**- Dan Brown, *The Da Vinci Code* (New York: Doubleday, 2003), Elaine Pagels, *The Gnostic Gospels* (London: Phoenix, Orion, 2006), and *Beyond Belief: The Secret Gospel of Thomas* (London: Pan Books, 2005), http://altreligion.about.com/od/gnosticimages/Gnostic_Images.htm, http://www.gnosis.org, http://www.gnostic-church.org., http://www.johannite.org/johannite.html (featuring the Apostolic Johannite Church, an esoteric Gnostic Christian community), http://www.lumen.org/ (the Web site of *Gnosis* magazine), http://www.religion-encyclopedia.com/G/gnosticism.htm, http://www.religionfacts.com/christianity/texts/gnostic.htm, http://www.religioustolerance.org/gnostic.htm, http://www.webcom.com/~gnosis/library.html. **Goddess Worship**- Al Gore, *Earth in the Balance* (New York: Rodale, 1992), Elinor Gadon, *The Once and Future Goddess* (San Francisco: Harper One, 1989), Margot Adler, *Drawing Down the Moon* (New York: Penguin, 2006), Merlin Stone, *When God Was a Woman* (Harvest/Harcourt Brace: Orlando, FL: 1976), Interview with the Reverend Ava of the Goddess Temple of Orange County, California, by Matt Coker in *OC Weekly*, July 6, 2006; http://www.ocweekly.com/news/news/god-shes-hot/25434)Starhawk, *The Spiral Dance* (San Francisco: Harper One, 1999), Susy Flory, "The Goddess Unmasked," at www.christianitytoday.com/ tcw/ 2007/mayjun/5.30.html, http://www.goddessgift.com, http://www.goddesstemple.org/Vision/index.htm, http://www.goddesstempleoforangecounty.com, http://www.goddessworshipblog.typepad.com, http://www.leaderu.com/org/probe/docs/goddess.html, http://www.religioustolerance.

org/goddess.htm, http://www-unix.oit.umass.edu/~clit387/Worship.html (this deals with Greek/Roman mythology; contains some history as well as stories). **Gypsies-** The World Wide Web Virtual Library: "Roma /Gypsies: An Introduction", http://www.geocities.com/Paris/5121/beliefs.htm#Religion, http://www.geocities.com/Paris/5121/vlib/introduction.htm, http://www.geocities.com/~patrin/beliefs.htm, http://www.religioustolerance.org/roma2.htm, http://www.romani.org. **Hare Krishna-** http://www.harekrishna.com, http://www.iskcon.com, www.iskcon.com/about/index.html, http://www.krishna.org. **Hinduism-** John R. Hinnells, ed., *The Penguin Dictionary of Religions*, 2nd ed., (New York, Penguin: 1997), http://hinduism.about.com, http://www.hinduism.co.za, http://www.hinduismtoday.com, http://www.hinduweb.org, http://www.religionfacts.com/hinduism, http://www.religioustolerance.org/hinduism.htm. **Islam-** Yahiya Emerick, *The Complete Idiot's Guide to Understanding Islam* (New York: Alpha Books, 2002), http://www.al-islam.org, http://www.islam.com, http://www.islamicity.com, http://www.islamworld.net/, http://www.islam101.com. **Jainism-** Anita Ganeri. *The Atlas of World Religions* (New York: McGraw-Hill Children's Publishing, 2002), http://www.cs.colostate.edu/~malaiya/jainlinks.html, http://www.jainnet.com, http://www.jainworld.com, http://www.jainworld.com/scriptures/index.asp, http://www.religionfacts.com, http://religiousmovements.lib.virginia.edu/nrms/jainism.html, http://www.umich.edu/~umjains. **Jehovah's Witnesses-** http://jehovah.to/, http://www.jw-media.org, http://www.religionfacts.com/jehovahs_witnesses/, http://www.watchtower.org, http://www.watchtower.org/e/rq/index.htm?article=article_11.htm. **Juche-** Kim Il Sung, New Year's message, January 1, 1992, http://www.adherents.com/largecom/Juche.html, http://www.adherents.com/Religions_By_Adherents.html,http://www.cnet-ta.ne.jp/juche/DEFAULTE.htm,http://www.itf-information.com/sounds/ps15.wav, http://www.korea-dpr.com. **Judaism-** http://www.bbc.co.uk/religion/religions/judaism/, http://www.jewfaq.org/toc.htm, http://www.jewsforjudaism.org, http://judaism.about.com, http://www.leaderu.com/wri-table2/judaism.html, http://www.religionfacts.com/judaism/index.htm. **Kabbalah-** Kim Zetter, *Simple Kabbalah* (Berkeley, Calif.: Conari Press, 1999), http://www.kabbalah.com/kabbalah/?cid=quigo, http://www.kabbalah.info. **Mormonism-** Joseph Smith and Orson Pratt, *The Doctrine and Covenants of the Church of Jesus Christ of Latter-day Saints Doctrine and Covenants* (Salt Lake City: The Church of Jesus Christ of Latter Day Saints, 1948), Joseph Smith, *Gospel Doctrine* (Salt Lake City: Deseret Book Company, 1986), "Sharing the Gospel with Others," comp. by Preston Nibley (Salt Lake City: *Deseret News Press*, 1948), James Talmadge, quoted in *A Study of the Articles of Faith* (Salt Lake City: The Church of Jesus Christ of Latter Day Saints, 1952), p. 430, www.adherents.com, http://www.bbc.co.uk/religion/religions/mormon/, http://www.mormon.org, http://www.mormon.org/mormonorg/eng/basic-beliefs/the-restoration-of-truth/the-great-apostasy, http://www.religionfacts.com/mormonism/index.htm. **Nation of Islam-** Elijah Muhammad, "Message to the Black Man in America," 1965, *Elijah Muhammad, Our Savior Has Arrived.* (online copy: http://www.seventhfam.com/temple/books/our_saviour/saviour.htm), http://www.noi.org/ (the official Web site), http://religiousmovements.lib.virginia.edu/nrms/Nofislam.html, http://www.seventhfam.com/mgt/ (training for girls in the Nation of Islam), http://www.stanford.edu/group/Thinker/v2/v2n3/NOIBackground.html, http://www.worldbookonline.com, ("What the Muslims Believe," http://www.noi.org/muslim_program.htm) [from page 147]. **Native American Spirituality-** Charles Alexander Eastman, *The Soul of the Indian*, first published in 1911. (Later New York, New York: Courier Dover Publications, 2003), Earnest Thompson Seton, *The Gospel of the Redman*, (Bloomington, IN: World Wisdom, Inc., 2005), Mariah Jones, "Spiritual Commodification and Misappropriation," www.sonomacountyfreepress.com/features/native.html, *The Sacred Text Archive* cited on the Internet offers an array of information about Native American religious folklore. Many oral traditions and legends have now been collected and made available at: http://altreligion.about.com/gi/dynamic/offsite.htm?zi=1/XJ/Ya&sdn=altreligion&cdn=religion&tm=6&f=22&tt=14&bt=1&bts=0&zu=http%3A//www.sacred-texts.com/nam/, www.adherents.com, http://altreligion.about.com/od/nativeamerican/Native_American_Spirituality.htm?terms=Native+American%20Spirituality, http://www.hanksville.com/NAresources/, http://www.joyofsects.com/world/indians.shtml, http://www.nativeculturelinks.com/indians.html, http://www.native-languages.org/religion.htm, http://www.nativeweb.org/resources/religion_spirituality/, http://religiousmovements.lib.virginia.edu/nrms/naspirit.html, http://www.religioustolerance.org/nataspir.htm, http://www.sonomacountyfreepress.com/features/native.html, http://web.archive.org/web/20050330085408/http://college.hmco.com/history/readerscomp/naind/html/na_032600_religion.htm. **New Age Spirituality-** http://healing.about.com/od/newage/New_Age_Topics.htm, http://religiousmovements.lib.virginia.edu/nrms/newage.html, http://www.religioustolerance.org/newage.htm. **Osho-** http://www.meditate-celebrate.com, http://www.Osho(r).com, http://www.oshoworld.com, http://www.otoons.com, http://www.otoons.com/osho/askosho_religion1.htm, http://www.rebelliousspirit.com, www.sannyas.net. **Rastafarianism-** Leonard E. Barrett, *The Rastafarians* (Boston: Beacon Press, 1997), http://altreligion.about.com/library/faqs/bl_rastafarianism.htm, http://www.jamaicans.com/culture/rasta/interview_popup.shtml), http://www.nomadfx.com/old/rasta1.html, http://www.religionfacts.com/a-z-religion-index/rastafarianism.htm, http://religiousmovements.lib.virginia.edu/nrms/rast.html#Babylon, http://www.sacred-texts.com/afr/piby/piby01.htm, http://www.watchman.org/profile/rastapro.htm. **Sai Baba-** http://www.eaisai.com/baba, http://www.saibaba.org, http://www.saibabaofshirdi.net, http://www.saibaba.ws, http://www.sathyasai.org. **Scientology-** http://www.lronhubbard.org,http://www.religion-encyclopedia.com/S/scientology.htm,http://www.religionfacts.com/scientology/,http://religiousmovements.lib.virginia.edu/nrms/scientology.html,http://www.religioustolerance.org/scientol.htm, http://www.scientology.org, http://www.scientologytoday.org/Common/question/pg33.htm. **Secular Humanism-** Paul Kurtz, "A Secular Humanist Declaration," Paul Kurtz, editor, *Humanist Manifesto I and II* (New

York: Prometheus, 1973), Larry Reyka, "Taking a Stand for Humanism" (cited at: http://www.americanhumanist.org/humanism/on_humanism.php), http://www.americanhumanist.org/index.html, http://religiousmovements.lib.virginia.edu/nrms/secular_humanism, http://www.secularhumanism.org. **Shinto**- Alan L. Miller. "Shinto," *World Book Online Reference Center*, 2007, Norman Anderson, ed. *The World's Religions* (Grand Rapids: Eerdmans, 1976), http://www.asahi-net.or.jp/~QM9T-KNDU/shintoism.htm, http://www.religion-encyclopedia.com/S/shinto.htm, http://www.religionfacts.com/shinto/index.htm, http://religiousmovements.lib.virginia.edu/nrms/shinto.html, http://www.religioustolerance.org/shinto.htm, http://www.shinto.org, http://www.trincoll.edu/zines/tj/tj4.4.96/articles/cover.html **Sikhism**- M.A. McAuliffe, *Sikh Religion: Its Gurus, Sacred Writings, and Authors* (London: Oxford University Press, 1909), pp. 33-35, Internet Encyclopedia of Religion, *Time Almanac*, 2000, http://www.bbc.co.uk/religion/religions/sikhism/, http://www.infoaboutsikhs.com/faqs.htm, http://www.religionfacts.com/sikhism/, http://www.sikhnet.com, http://www.sikhs.org, http://www.srigurugranthsahib.org. **Spiritism**- http://www.fst.org, http://www.geae.inf.br/en/, http://www.nsac.org/spiritualism.htm, http://www.seedoflight.org.au/english_html/spiritism.html, http://www.seedoflight.org.au/index-2.html, http://www.spiritistdoctrine.com, http://www.spiritist.org/english/Get%20To%20Know%20Spiritism.htm **Taoism**- http://www.chebucto.ns.ca/Philosophy/Taichi/lao.html, http://www.crystalinks.com/taoism.html, http://www.daoiststudies.org, http://www.edepot.com/taoism.shtml, http://www.religionfacts.com/taoism/beliefs/tao.htm_, http://www.religiousworlds.com/taoism/intros.html, http://www.siutao.com, http://www.symynet.com/tao_te_ching/core_beliefs.htm, http://www.tao.org, http://www.taoism.net/, http://www.taopage.org. **Tenrikyo**- http://www.adherents.com/Religions_By_Adherents.html#Tenrikyo, http://religiousmovements.lib.virginia.edu/nrms/tenrikyo.html, http://www.tenrikyo.com, http://www.tenrikyo.or.jp/, http://www.tenrikyo.or.jp/en/teaching/teachings/besseki.html, http://www.tenrikyo.or.jp/en/teaching/teachings/dust.html, http://www.tenrikyo.or.jp/en/teaching/teachings/service.html. **The Aetherius Society**- http://www.aetherius.org, http://www.aetherius.org/index.cfm?app=content&SectionID=40&PageID=41, http://www.aetherius.org/index.cfm?app=content&SectionID=45&PageID=66, http://altreligion.about.com/cs/cults/bl_ufocults.htm, http://www.heavensgate.com, http://www.rael.org, http://religiousmovements.lib.virginia.edu/nrms/aetherius.html, ("Mars Sector 6," The Nine Freedoms, February 19, 1961). **The Creativity Movement**- http://www.adl.org/learn/extremism_in_america_updates/groups/creativity_movement/Creativity_Update_3_14_05.htmhttp://creativitymovement.net/, http://www.rickross.com/groups/hale.html, http://www.religioustolerance.org/wcotc1.htm, http://en.wikipedia.org/wiki/Creativity_Movement. **The Way International**- *The Way Magazine*, September/October 1974, http://www.ex-way.com, http://www.theway.org, http://religiousmovements.lib.virginia.edu/nrms/wayintl.html#sunday, http://www.religioustolerance.org/the_way.htm. **Unification Church**- Sun Myung Moon, "The Necessity of Prayer" (message on June 2, 1980, Tarrytown, New York), http://www.geocities.com/unificationism/, http://kathryncoman.home.att.net/2008.txt, http://www.religionfacts.com/unification_church/index.htm, http://www.religioustolerance.org/unificat.htm, http://www.reverendsunmyungmoon.org/index.html, http://www.unification.net/, http://www.unification.net/dp96/, http://www.unification.org. **Unitarian Universalism**- www.religionfacts.com, http://www.religionfacts.com a-z-religion-index/unitarian_universalism.htm, www.religiousmovements.lib.virgina.edu/nrms/uua.html), http://www.uua.org, http://www.uua.org/visitors/index.shtml, http://www.uufaq.com. **Universism**- Brian Hines, from his blog, "Church of the Churchless" (February 16, 2006), http://drvox.com/, http://www.geocities.com/cathcongphil/what.html, http://hinessight.blogs.com/church_of_the_churchless/2006/04/death_of_a_reli.html, http://www.iidb.org/vbb/showthread.php?t=160851, http://www.johnhorgan.org/work15.htm, http://open-site.org/p/Society/Religion/Universism, http://www.signonsandiego.com/uniontrib/20050602/news_lz1c02vox.html **Vodou/Voodoo**- http://countrystudies.us/haiti/33.htm, http://geocities.com/Athens/Delphi/5319/, http://www.hartford-hwp.com/archives/43a/index-faa.html, http://www.religioustolerance.org/voodoo.htm. **Wicca**- Margot Adler, *Drawing Down the Moon* (New York: Penguin Group, 2006), Craig Hawkins, *Goddess Worship, Witchcraft, and Neo-Paganism* (Grand Rapids: Zondervan, 1998), http://www.geocities.com/Area51/Shadowlands/9142/Wicca.html, http://www.neopagan.net/, http://paganwiccan.about.com/od/wiccaandpaganismbasics/p/Wiccan_Basics.htm, http://www.religioustolerance.org/witchcra.htm, http://www.wicca.org, http://www.wicca.com/celtic/wicca/military.htm, http://www.witchvox.com. **Worldwide Church of God**- Joseph Tkach Jr., sermon entitled "Forgive Us Our Trespasses," http://www.religioustolerance.org/wwcog.htm, http://www.wcg.org, http://www.wcg.org/lit/aboutus/media/fringe.htm. **Zoroastrianism**- Myrtle Langley, *Religion*. (New York: Dorling Kindersley Eyewitness Books), http://www.avesta.org/avesta.html (features the sacred Scriptures of Zoroastrianism), http://religiousmovements.lib.virginia.edu/nrms/Zoro1.html, http://shiraz.freeservers.com, http://www.worldbookonline.com/wb/Article?id=ar617540&st=zoroastrianism, http://www.zarathushtra.com/z/article/overview.htm, http://www.zoroastrian.org/

PHOTO CREDITS